SACRED VIOLENCE

Law, Meaning, and Violence

The scope of Law, Meaning, and Violence is defined by the wide-ranging scholarly debates signaled by each of the words in the title. Those debates have taken place among and between lawyers, anthropologists, political theorists, sociologists, and historians, as well as literary and cultural critics. This series is intended to recognize the importance of such ongoing conversations about law, meaning, and violence as well as to encourage and further them.

Series Editors: Martha Minow, Harvard Law School
                    Austin Sarat, Amherst College

RECENT TITLES IN THE SERIES

SACRED VIOLENCE

TORTURE, TERROR, AND SOVEREIGNTY

Paul W. Kahn

The University of Michigan Press :: Ann Arbor

2011   2010   2009   2008   4   3   2   1

A CIP catalog record for this book is available from the British Library.

Library of Congress Cataloging-in-Publication Data

Kahn, Paul W., 1952–
      Sacred violence : torture, terror, and sovereignty / Paul W. Kahn.
         p.   cm. — (Law, meaning, and violence)
      Includes bibliographical references and index.
      ISBN-13: 978-0-472-07047-3 (cloth : alk. paper)
      ISBN-10: 0-472-07047-9 (cloth : alk. paper)
      ISBN-13: 978-0-472-05047-5 (pbk. : alk. paper)
      ISBN-10: 0-472-05047-8 (pbk. : alk. paper)
      1. Torture.   2. Sovereignty.   3. Political violence.   4. War on
Terrorism, 2001– —Law and legislation.   I. Title.

   K5304.K34   2008
   341.6—dc22   2008011488

In memory of my mother,
ELIZABETH KAHN
1926–2007

ACKNOWLEDGMENTS

MANY COLLEAGUES, FRIENDS, AND STUDENTS generously helped me with this manuscript. I especially appreciate their efforts because in many instances they did not agree with my arguments. I hope that I have adequately responded to at least some of their criticisms. On some points, however, we will simply continue to disagree and argue. These are the disagreements that make a scholarly career rewarding.

I am sure I owe the most to those who most disagreed with me. Here I want especially to thank David Luban, Bruce Ackerman, Robert Post, Samuel Moyn, and Jonathan Schell. I also owe special thanks to the participants in an SIAS summer workshop on the concept of the political, which I led with my friend and colleague Ulrich Haltern in New Haven and Berlin. Tico Taussig and Benjamin Berger, members of that workshop, continued to contribute their time and effort to correcting my errors. Others I would like to recognize for their help, knowing or unknowing, are Chibli Mallat, Harry Frankfurt, Owen Fiss, Michael Doyle, and Douglas MacLean and Susan Wolf, at whose home I furiously wrote some of the most difficult parts of the manuscript.

I also benefited greatly from research assistance provided by a number of students at Yale Law School, including Kate Desormeau, Robert Hemm, Adam Romero, and Samuel Clark. To Barbara Mianzo I owe thanks for the efficient organization of the production of this work, just as she has helped me with all of my other books. Finally, I must thank my family, who continue to teach me about the meaning of love, commitment, and sacrifice.

CONTENTS

INTRODUCTION:

THE PUZZLE OF TORTURE

IF WE ARE QUITE WILLING TO KILL, why not torture? In the midst of a "war on terror," we find ourselves engaged with this question again. Much seems to be at stake in the debate: legally, historically, and morally.

The elimination of torture from penal and investigatory practices was a central element in the development of modern law. The American Constitution prohibited "cruel and unusual punishment"; the French Declaration of the Rights of Man prohibited "all harshness not essential to the securing of the prisoner's person." Two hundred years later, the prohibition on torture is at the center of modern international law, both human rights law and humanitarian law. The prohibition on torture appeared immediately after World War II in the Universal Declaration of Human Rights and then in Common Article 3 of the 1949 Geneva Conventions; it reappeared in the International Covenant on Civil and Political Rights in 1976; and finally it was entrenched in the separate Convention against Torture that came into force in 1987.

In both the earlier moment of constitutionalism and the later moment of internationalism, the prohibition on torture symbolized the idea of a government of law.[1] Political power without law is the practice of tyranny, and out of this comes torture. That, at least, is the fear. Is our present debate, then, about the limits of our commitment to this ideal of the rule of law in both its constitutional and international forms? The contemporary arguments over torture open up the most difficult questions about the nature of political life. Are the borders of law adequate to the necessities of the political community? Is there a space of sovereignty beyond law? Does a "war on terror" occupy that space?[2] Today's torture debate has the virtue of transforming these matters of theory into questions that are concrete and compelling to a wide audience. All of us need to take a position on the deployment of violence in our name. Before we take a position, it may be helpful to understand what is at stake.

Just as the reach and character of law are at stake in the torture debate, so is our relationship to our own history. Torture has a distinctly premodern feel to it. In the movie *Pulp Fiction*, a character threatening torture says he is going "to get medieval." Modern criminal law has been a story of the progressive elimination of torture. Modern penology begins with a reconsideration of the functions and forms of punishment.[3] The spectacle of torture was replaced with the modern penitentiary, and the deployment of bodily pain with the ambition to reform the criminal personality.[4] Modern criminal procedure is similarly skeptical of the epistemic value of torture, believing it not to be a reliable method of finding the truth. The law of torture has been displaced by the law of procedure: the suspect is told of his rights rather than tortured for whatever information he might have.[5] Facing the threat of terrorism, however, we are not sure whether we are confronting a postmodern problem or a premodern form of violence. Either way many have no confidence that modern criminal procedure will allow us to obtain the information we seek or that the ordinary tools of criminal punishment will have much relevance as either deterrence or retribution. The symbol of both lines of frustration is Guantánamo, and, of course, it has allegedly been a site of torture.[6]

Cutting across the investigative and penal practice of premodern torture was the act of confession. The object of torture was confession, which had the dual purpose of providing information and acknowledging sin—whether against God or the sovereign. The first function collapses once torture is seen as an ineffective investigatory technique. Information obtained under torture might be false. The second function collapses once legitimate political order is understood to be founded on consent, not force. When acknowledgment of sovereign authority is brought on by torture, it might not be sincere. Does our current interest in torture represent a turn away from a practice of consent toward one of confession? While the torture debate is usually framed in terms of a need for information, undeniably the war on terror has a strong element of conflict between confessional faiths—if not directly Muslim versus Christian, then Islamic fundamentalist versus a Judeo-Christian tradition carried forward in modern Western culture. Many of the reported instances of torture also involve desecration of religious symbols. Moreover, just as terror is associated with Islamic fundamentalism, the American administration associated with torture has deep connections to Christian fundamentalism.[7]

To the legal, political, and moral narratives of progress away from the practice of torture, we need to add yet another dimension: a concern not just for the victim but also for the torturer. We cannot have torture without torturers.[8] Where in our contemporary moral economy is there room for the torturer? Is it possible for us to imagine the virtuous torturer? Can one imagine telling family and friends that one practices torture for the state? Deniability is important both to governments and to individual practitioners.[9] With the disappearance of the penal spectacle, the practice of torture became a secret practice. The torture that survives occurs in places closed to public regard, under conditions of deniability, and by agents whose own relationship to the state is likely to be "shadowy."[10] The modern phenomenon of torture has the opaque presence of the "deniable." It must be known but not seen; it must be spoken of but never speak itself. It is a political practice that cannot exist in a public space. Nevertheless, to be effective the threat of torture must taint the public space. It is always just beyond view.

For the modern state, the publicly accessible space of state action is exactly the locus of the rule of law.[11] Therefore, when torture does break into public view, it will always be denounced as illegal. There will be threats, and even occasional acts, of prosecution. Nevertheless, we have no reason to accept at face value the state's presentation of its own relationship to torture. The United States, the site of the current torture debate, not only signed the Convention against Torture, but it enacted domestic legislation that flatly prohibits all torture.[12] If torture is a political practice beyond law, those who cross that border and return to law are in a difficult position. They have seen and done too much. Perhaps we should think of these exposed agents of torture as scapegoats: having been revealed, they must now be sacrificed. Disposing of the detritus of war's violence has been a problem for the state since the middle of the last century. Consider, for example, the problems the French have confronted with respect to veterans of their war in Algeria or the Argentine efforts to prosecute those who participated in their "dirty" war.[13] We seem just recently to have "settled accounts" with Vietnam veterans. As yet, we have no idea what will be the felt needs of, and society's response to, the Iraq War veterans.[14]

The contemporary torture debate raises all of these questions about the character of the achievement of modern politics, about whether there is a political practice of violence beyond the reach of law, and about the citizen's relationship to these practices. It raises these issues as matters of fact, not just of normative design. The United States does subscribe to the legal prohibition on torture. Yet appeals to that law—as if the debate arises simply from a mistake about what the law requires—have not been sufficient to quell the debate over our current practices. If torture remains a state practice of violence, it advances understanding not at all to say that it is illegal or even that it conflicts with fundamental ideas of the rule of law. Of course, torture violates the most ordinary understanding of our legal norms and political institutions. Similarly, it violates our ordinary moral intuitions. We don't need legal scholars to tell us this. Theory's role must be to explain torture as a political phenomenon, not simply to identify it as a legal violation. That explanation can be achieved only by examining the manner in which violence creates and sustains political meaning. We will never even begin that inquiry so long as we see torture only as individual pathology or legal violation.

To most liberals, torture appears as a display of pure power: the torturer says to the victim, "I can do this to you, and there is nothing you can do about it." This asymmetry of power is anathema to liberal morality, which insists on the equal dignity of and respect for every individual.[15] From the liberal perspective, law has no place for torture and politics must be circumscribed by law. Most academic work today is little more than repeated demonstrations that torture violates the fundamental principles of liberalism. In truth, liberalism has nothing interesting to say about torture.

Despite the claim that there is no place for torture in a legitimate political practice, over and over we confront practices of torture. What is more, today we find tentative efforts to justify the practice. For the most part, these suggestions are attempts to find a space for torture within the premises of liberal political practice. Liberals, too, must be concerned about the life and well-being of citizens. Those open to the possibility of torture appeal to what they imagine as a certain political hardheadedness in the war against terror. What if the proposed victim of torture has knowledge of a ticking time bomb? What if it is a nuclear bomb? Do not such threats pose political and moral demands that excuse or even justify abandonment of the legal prohibition?[16] If so, our torturers may be in a hard spot, but they should be respected for doing what is necessary. The prohibition on torture, in this view, reflects a kind of utopianism founded on an idea of a global order of law that never really emerged. It is an aspiration out of sync with the contemporary threat.

Torture thus becomes the fulcrum of an alternative reading of modern history. Gone are the narratives of the growth of international law, of procedural justice, and of the triumph of a liberal constitutionalism of dignity and respect. Rather, we remain embedded in an older story of war. The West must defend itself against enemies who oppose its political form, its moral beliefs, its power, and its religions—who oppose, in short, its liberalism. We are in a "clash of civilizations." Our enemies, we are told, hate us "for our freedom." They are "Islamo-fascists." To these contemporary realists, none of the lessons about torture—legal, historical, or moral—amounts to a compelling reason not to be open to its use if it proves to be necessary to our own defense.

Both sides of this debate agree that fundamental questions about ourselves are at stake. Both sides also agree that we have been thrust into this debate because of the emergence of terror as a means of warfare. The terrorist acts outside of the norms of modern humanitarian law. Formally, his deployment of violence is not covered by the detailed provisions of the Geneva Conventions.[17] Substantively, he rejects the norms of discrimination and proportionality on which humanitarian law is founded. The contemporary terrorist attacks noncombatants as they go about their ordinary activities within civil society. He breaches the boundaries separating the battlefield from the rest of the political order. Terrorist violence can occur anywhere, at any time, and against anyone. It aims for a disproportionate impact—that is, for a violent spectacle. Thus, the terrorist, who never openly signals his character and intent—he wears no uniform and does not openly carry his arms—intrudes deep into the interior of the state. Violating the law, he is, of course, a criminal. Yet there is a widespread sense—at least in the United States—that he is more than a criminal and that the techniques of the domestic criminal law are not adequate to the threat. The criminal law, we are reminded, is not designed to deal with the potential use of a weapon of mass destruction. More than that, it is not designed to deal with a political enemy.

Just as terrorism is not adequately comprehended in the ordinary category of crime, it is not assimilable to other threats to public well-being. Terror may strike in unpredictable ways, but that does not make it like the outbreak of a disease. More people die from flu each year than died from the 9/11 attacks, but we hardly find that thought comforting. Such statistics do not help us to put the attack "in perspective." Terror is a political practice of the spectacle, not a matter of public health and mortality rates. It is a communicative practice, while a virus—even one more deadly than a terrorist attack—has nothing to say to us. Torture, too, is a political practice intended to communicate a message. Torture and terror are linked forms of communication; they are speaking to each other in the language of degradation and humiliation.[18]

Both torture and terror are political performances that inscribe meanings on bodies through pain and the threat of pain. Each proclaims the presence of an idea so powerful that it can determine life and death. Conflicts between political ideas that power a life-and-death competition are what we ordinarily call war. Torture and terror, accordingly, have to be assessed as practices of warfare. For the West, such an assessment often appears easy—too easy. Torture is a war crime. Similarly, if terror is a form of combat, then it, too, must be judged a war crime.[19] The war on terror is fought against an enemy that we describe as "unlawful combatants," as if this makes the enemy somehow more of an enemy.

The terrorist, however, reminds us of something that should be obvious but that we seem to have forgotten: we don't, in the end, get to write the rules of warfare. We don't get to do so regardless of how inclusive the "we" is. An enemy willing to kill and be killed may also be quite willing to violate any rule it perceives as a barrier to its ends.[20] The project of creating a humanitarian law that would mitigate the horrors of war assumes an underlying transnational community of interest. It assumes that war is an exceptional state and that the parties have a common interest in containing its damage for the sake of the peaceful relations that are to accompany the return to normalcy.[21] Humanitarian law assumes a minimal common morality and a shared ethical point of view that can be separated from the adversaries' conflicting political beliefs. For example, that noncombatants should be protected as much as possible assumes that both sides are committed to something more than, or at least other than, their mutual engagement in killing and being killed. Humanitarian law assumes, as a theoretical and practical matter, either that adversaries are willing to lose their wars rather than violate these rules or that a violation will itself increase the chances of defeat. Both of these propositions have proven false. Without one or the other being true, why would an adversary stick to the rules when hard-pressed? One way to think about the terrorist's relationship to humanitarian law is to consider him "hard-pressed" from the beginning. He has no capacity to fight a conventional war. If he is to use violence effectively, he must disregard that law. This is surely the lesson that observers of the Palestinian deployment of terror against Israel have learned over the last generation.

The modern, liberal state was to be a state in which individuals could flourish in the pursuit of life plans that they chose for themselves. This state was willing to abandon torture and instead try to respect an ideal of Kantian morality—to treat everyone with the dignity due an autonomous, rational agent. It connected a liberal morality of law to a utilitarian ideal of advancing the general welfare of the entire population. Respecting the moral dignity of each would bring us collectively to prosperity. This vision of security, respect, and mutual well-being has been at the heart of the project of the liberal nation-state.[22] The threat of terror signals a potential failure of this political ambition, for freedom from fear was the precondition of dignity and productivity.[23] It is exactly the freedom that Hobbes sought at the start of this tradition.

Many had thought that the end of the Cold War marked an end to the threat of violent political conflict in the West. At the geographic edges—for example, in the former Yugoslavia—there might be transitional problems, but these could be dealt with through politically astute interventions. Armies were no longer for defense, but for the advancement of a global project of human rights. Future wars were to be humanitarian interventions. Contemporary terror, however, brings political violence and insecurity to Manhattan—or London or Madrid. Moreover, this is not the familiar violence of domestic terrorist groups such as the Irish Republican Army or the Basque separatist group ETA. The new terrorist threat leads quickly to a fear that weapons of mass destruction will be used.[24] Many—including our political leaders—believe that if terrorists have access to such weapons they will use them. The ambition of the 9/11 attack was, after all, to kill tens of thousands. Had it occurred thirty minutes later, it might have succeeded.

The new terrorism, then, represents an existential threat to the nation. This, at least, is what many Americans imagine. They don't imagine that the United States is about to be defeated, but they do imagine the terrorist as someone who seeks to accomplish his ends by killing Americans—as many as possible. They read the terrorists' message as a statement that we are not secure within our borders and that the government cannot protect us. Ordinary individuals are forced to think that their political identity alone makes them a potential target of violence. They already see that the terrorist threat is causing profound changes to what is loosely called "our way of life." They cannot imagine a resolution of this conflict outside the defeat of the enemy, for they see no grounds for compromise. These are the conditions under which citizens can be asked to kill and be killed for the maintenance of the state. In short, the "war on terror" is indeed imagined as a war.[25]

If we are at war, the conflict is over fundamental beliefs. This, too, has shocked us. The West had assumed that after the fall of the Soviet Union we would see an increasing global convergence on a common morality. We expected the linked growth of democratic constitutionalism, international human rights, and global trade. All disagreement would be channeled into the processes of economic competition, political elections, and legal adjudication. The terrorism that threatens the West today seeks to prove the failure of this global project. We face not the triumph of a single order of trade, law, and morality but the possibility that ideological conflict may have brought us a new form of world war. Contrary to what we might have thought, there is no universal agreement on what is morally required of each person. There is no common attitude that constitutes the rule of law, and there is no convergence on a single form of political order.

If terror includes an actual threat of the use of weapons of mass destruction, then the progressive narrative—of which the disappearance of torture was a central part—has proved false. History may be a story not of the realization of security and well-being but rather of increased risk and destruction. The narrative line may be not the progressive realization of law but rather the proliferation of weapons and the generalization of the threat of mass destruction. Instead of a new global reign of liberalism, the new technology of mass destruction has been linked to the most ancient of sources of conflict—religious belief. The threat of a terror of mass destruction forces us to imagine that our entire political edifice, our civil society, and our moral order can all fall apart despite our vast achievements. That fall may not be gradual at all; we could wake up tomorrow to realize that Chicago, or perhaps Berlin, is simply gone.

Of course, one response to the threat of terrorism is to deny these implications. The Western state, and the West itself, has so far been quite secure. The actual, rather than possible, insecurities of the age come from a disturbed nature—for example, climate change or avian flu—and failed states, not from terrorists. The fears generated by the terrorist threat may be nothing more than the product of wild imaginings, perhaps manipulated for political purposes. The West survived the very real threat of nuclear holocaust during the Cold War. A few hijacked airplanes, tragic as the consequences were, do not begin to approach that level of threat. Terrorism creates a disproportionate fear because it combines a moderate physical threat to the society with the high drama of entertainment. Good policy, however, should begin by distinguishing reality from theatrics. The response to terrorism, in this view, should be a renewed commitment to the values of the liberal state. We will defeat terrorism by being true to ourselves.[26]

We hear endlessly that terrorism is encouraged by the failures of liberalism—for example, economic exploitation, support for illegitimate regimes, and neglect of law. A return to a political practice of torture, in this view, not only betrays our own values but is bound to be counterproductive. It does not defeat an enemy but creates new ones. An antiterrorism policy should begin with development aid and scrupulous adherence to law, not with military intervention and a threat of unrestrained violence. The presence of terrorism tells us that we still have far to go on the path of establishing a global order of law and wellbeing founded on universal human rights, respect for cultural diversity, and wealth redistribution. It does not tell us that we are going in the wrong direction.

There are two problems with this quite sensible response. First, we really cannot know which side of the dispute has a better grasp of the risk. This might look like a sensible appraisal right up until the moment that a dirty bomb goes off in New York or a deadly pathogen is released in Paris. We have no reason to think that terrorism follows a path of moderate, gradual development amenable to reasonable interventions. Terrorism is as dangerous as the weapons individuals can manage to obtain. History is often driven by the extremists, not the moderate majority. Look at the Middle East. To defeat all the terrorists but the one with a nuclear bomb is not to defeat terrorism at all. The scope of the threat, accordingly, is a function of the accidents of history, not generalizations about progress. About such accidents, no one is in a position to make confident predictions. The spread of the technology of weapons of mass destruction makes the possibility of a world-historical incident of destruction increasingly likely but hardly inevitable. This is not an excuse for abandoning support for the spread of liberal values. We should be clear, however, that we pursue that path because we believe in these values. We should do so even as we acknowledge that it may have little effect on the terrorist threat, however large or small we judge the threat to be.

Second, politics is an exercise not in reason but in imagination. A state that feels the threat of terror is never far from the Hobbesian state of nature. Indeed, the aim of terrorism is to undermine the sense of security that characterizes passage out of the state of nature. A polity struggling in the state of nature will reconsider the progressive narrative that casts torture as an anachronistic practice. Torture disappeared from the modern state in substantial part because terror was thought to have been eliminated from that state. If terrorism subjects us to that which we find intolerable—an imagined threat of total annihilation—then we will reconsider the limits on our own practices. If our law, history, and morality have left us open to the terrorist assault, that is ground enough for most people to question whatever lessons they thought they had learned about the use of torture. Liberal practices depend on liberal citizens. Such citizens imagine themselves as establishing relationships with others based on the idea of a social contract.[27] Citizens today cannot imagine any such contract with the terrorists who threaten them.

Wherever terrorism has reappeared, torture has never been far behind. Recall Latin America and Southeast Asia in the 1960s and 1970s and before that the wars of decolonization. More recently, think of the former Yugoslavia, Chechnya, and the Middle East. Torture and terror are reciprocal phenomena: terror is met with torture, and torture with terror. Terror and torture both work in the most primitive register of political meaning. In that register, violence aims not only to injure but to degrade, and not simply to degrade the immediate victim, but also all those who see in the victim's actions an expression of their own political beliefs. Slavery, a practice analogous to torture, was degrading not just to its immediate victims but to all blacks—free or not. An inquiry into torture and terror must therefore investigate the character of political degradation.

Until we uncover the political dynamic of violent degradation, we will continue to make arguments that are really quite beside the point. We are arguing about the definition of *torture* (When do we move from "rough interrogation" to torture?), the usefulness of torture (Does it yield important information?), the political morality of torture (Must we be utilitarians in our political judgments?), and the procedures for torture (Can we juridify torture?). This is like debating the geography of heaven—Which angel stands where in relationship to God?—instead of asking about the elementary sources of religious meaning.[28] Elsewhere, I have argued that politics is based on sacrifice, not contract.[29] Terror and torture press up against the sacrificial character of the state. Each works in a political-theological context, for each works to undermine the faith of the enemy. This is the context within which we must understand the political psychology of degradation. Torture and terror seek to break the sacrificial practices of the other. A failure of sacrifice is experienced as degradation.[30] It is experienced as the failure of one's god.

If we are to answer those who want to reconsider the prohibition on torture, we must do more than point to law, history, and morals as united in a progressive movement toward the total elimination of torture. Both sides of the debate are expressing views about torture that have their sources in deeper structures of the imagination. We must explore those deeper structures. Torture is vigorously debated today because we possess conflicting social imaginaries that establish the nature of political meaning: an imaginative structure of law, on the one hand, and of sovereignty on the other. Terror invokes torture because terror moves us beyond law to sovereignty. This is the deepest question that this work aims to explore: Does an imagined space remain for a practice of sovereignty beyond law? If there is such space, this is where we will find torture.

I pose this as a philosophical, not a normative, question. The first task of philosophy is to explain why meanings appear as they do, not to make judgments about those meanings. A judgment is always made from a situated position, but it is precisely the task of philosophy to expose the contingency of every such position—including that of the philosopher.[31] Of course, philosophers are also subjects and citizens. They are as entitled to make political judgments as anyone else, but they cannot ground those judgments in the free thought that is the first task of philosophy. This is not to say that philosophy does not have a critical role to play in exposing beliefs, assumptions, tensions, and contradictions. But with respect to first principles, philosophy knows only the free practice of thought itself. For this reason, where the genuine philosophical engagement will lead or even whether it will lead to the same point twice is unpredictable.[32] Thus, philosophy has no view on whether the sacrificial practices of fundamentalist Islam are better or worse than those of the Western nation-state. It will insist, however, on identifying both as historically contingent practices involving the construction of meaning from acts of killing and being killed.

The ambition of philosophy must be to show us those truths about ourselves that structure our world of meaning but of which we are not fully aware. Torture and terror come out of that world of meaning. To say that something is a "truth about ourselves" is not to proclaim it to be some sort of universal essence. These truths are historical, not essential. They are practices and beliefs that we are free to reject. This freedom, however, is metaphysical, not psychological. Whether we can take up our own freedom is a question each person must answer for himself. The analogy is to language: we are free to take up a new language, even though most of us may not be psychologically capable of the task should we choose to try. Philosophy can tell us about the beginning point—not the resting point—of the project of self-formation.

Much of what I have to say might be misunderstood as a defense of torture. I am most certainly against torture just as I am against terror. My point is not that torture is a justified response to terror but that terror will be met by a turn to torture. This will happen because terror and torture are reciprocal forms of creating and sustaining political meaning. Personally, I believe we can and should try to control the turn to torture, but I suspect the impulse is deeper than law's capacity to control. That doesn't mean that we should not try, but it does mean that we should not imagine torture's appearance to be the product of a few pathological individuals. I also believe we should prosecute torturers, but we should understand that such prosecutions do little more than create scapegoats for a broad practice of torture in the war on terror. We need scapegoats to expiate our own sin against the rule of law even when those sins are inevitable. To be treated as a scapegoat is cruel, but then so is warfare.

In the end, we will control torture only when we control terror. This is not because terror is so much more dangerous than conventional warfare but because terror and torture speak in the same voice: they are matched forms of behavior at the level of symbolic meanings. Terror and torture are reciprocal rituals of pain. Pain presents us with a twofold task: first, to eliminate it; but, second, to make sense of it. These tasks can be in tension—so much meaning might be invested in pain that we lose the aspiration for its elimination.[33] This can be as true in politics as in religion, which often places suffering at the core of the experience of the sacred. This is, for example, the symbolism of the Cross: the sacred enters the world through the violence of sacrifice. Politics, too, creates meaning through sacrifice. Political meaning often enters the world through the killing and being killed of war. We take our first step toward torture when we take up arms in defense of the state. This is the step from law to sovereignty.

Personally, I believe that we are better off to the degree that we can eliminate pain and find meanings elsewhere. I do not want torture in my world any more than I would want terror. But, for that matter, I do not want the state and politics as a form of meaning founded in violent sacrifice. We can dream of peace; we can imagine a global order of perfect lawfulness. But we dream of these things from a position deep within the political formation of a state that has its origins in violence, that will maintain itself through violence, and that claims a unique right to demand sacrifice of all of its citizens. Before there is terror or torture, there is a political imagination that finds ultimate meanings in acts of killing and being killed.

Out of this matrix of violence in the creation and support of political meaning come the twin phenomena of terror and torture. My personal attitude toward violence has as little to do with understanding torture and terror as with understanding any other symbolic form— for example, religion, myth, or art.[34] We inherit our political forms of meaning just as we inherit the forms of language and the structure of religious belief. Each of us can set ourselves against these structures of meaning; each of us can attempt a revolution. Even a revolution, however, can only build from the conceptual materials at hand. No one should operate with the illusion that speaking a little truth will reshape the fundamental structures of the imagination. Athens executed the first philosopher who spoke truth to power. If the state is more tolerant of philosophers today, it is only because they have become less threatening.

Torture emerges for us in the context of a war on terror. To ask how war generates meaning is not to defend war. Terror and torture are political phenomena that create and sustain a world of meaning through violence. All of history teaches us that we cannot have just a little bit of this violence, that no victory is final, and that the capacity of the state to kill others, as well as the willingness of citizens to sacrifice, is virtually endless. Two hundred years ago, Clausewitz theorized the logic of war's escalation without limit. Political practices of the twentieth century demonstrated the truth of his theory. Terrorism and torture are set squarely within this world of violence. If we ignore this fact, our debates over torture will never be more than an element of our political practice. I don't mean to condemn that debate or suggest that it may not be helpful to political decision-making. Philosophy's aim, however, is not the reform of politics but the development of understanding. Participants in the contemporary torture debate are still a long way from understanding what they are talking about.

A world of terror is a world of torture. I hope to show why that is so. The place to begin is with the development of a modern legal attitude that measures itself against torture. In both domestic and international law, torture has been conceptualized as "law's other." This is the topic of chapters 1 and 2. I then turn in chapter 3 to the contemporary debate over torture in an effort to bring to awareness the deeper structures of meaning at play there. The point of these inquiries is to explore the way in which the modern social imaginaries of law and politics have located themselves in relation to torture. These inquiries will put us in a position, in part II, to examine the character of a sovereign space beyond law and of the political imagination as it negotiates the border between law and sovereign violence.

PART I :: GENEALOGICAL INQUIRIES

TODAY, TERROR AND TORTURE appear as the moral and legal patholo-
gies characteristic of opposing sides in what is effectively, if not formally, a war. Terror is what terrorists do; torture is what governments
do. Terror evokes torture in response, and torture evokes terror.
Viewed from a distance, there is a significant overlap between these two
forms of violent behavior. The news from Iraq shows us that it is often
difficult to distinguish terrorists from torturers and vice versa. We
might say very roughly that terror is intended to silence while torture is
intended to force speech. Terror silences a potential opposition while
torture eliminates all but a scripted speech. Yet the one is a pregnant silence and the other a speech that silences. They quickly come to the
same thing. Was Saddam Hussein's regime one of torture or terror?
What about the reign of the generals in Argentina? Here we are likely
to think that the effort to draw analytic distinctions has gone one step
too far.[1]

That there is a connection between torture and terror is implicit in
the frequently heard charge that the American use of torture in the war
on terror undermines the legitimacy of that war by creating a kind of
moral equivalence between the two sides. Critics argue that to deploy
torture is to abandon those principles that justified the war on terror in

the first place. In this view, the point of the war is not just to defeat an enemy but to vindicate a set of values put at issue by the terrorist. The principles are those of a liberal democracy committed to the rule of law. Torture, with its asymmetrical application of power and its denial of personal dignity, is the antithesis of these principles. To focus on violation of these principles is to cast the war in moral terms reminiscent of earlier religious wars. One did not pray to the enemy's god for success. Rather, one lived and died with one's own faith. So should we, and our faith is in liberalism and the rule of law. The former Israeli chief justice Aaron Barak appeals to this idea when he writes that constitutional democracies must fight their wars with "one hand tied behind [their] back[s]. . . . This is the destiny of a democracy—she does not see all means as acceptable, and the ways of her enemies are not always open before her."[2]

This form of taking the moral high ground is appealing as long as the war is going even moderately well. It has, however, been quite out of place in the larger context of modern warfare. States have tended to subordinate the moral to the political. First defeat the enemy, then worry about principles. One used the tools at hand: gas in World War I, strategic bombing and nuclear weapons in World War II. That the need for military success could trump any legal rule was formally expressed in the doctrine of military necessity, or *kriegsraison,* which held that when defeat was the alternative, the limits on the means of warfare were suspended.[3] More broadly, the priority of practical judgment over principle—whether legal or moral—was seen in the shifting alliances that marked a political strategy of balancing powers. Throughout the Cold War, and now in the war on terror, the United States has found itself pursuing alliances with regimes whose principles it must simultaneously condemn. Chief Justice Barak may offer a form of moral reassurance, but the overwhelming fact has been that, under conditions of warfare, what otherwise passes for moral hypocrisy is the norm. War has been about success, warfare about tactics. When people today argue for a need to torture in the face of the terrorist threat, they are placing themselves in this tradition and expressing a readiness to use all of the available tools. The vigorous opposition this invokes reflects a contemporary effort to subordinate politics to law—and to a set of moral ideals assumed to inform a legal regime. War, like every other government act, is to be a law-based activity. To take up torture is to join the terrorist in the pursuit of violence outside of law. That is the nub of the problem.

A larger shift is at stake, then, in this claim that the use of torture delegitimates the war effort—a shift from politics to law. The Allies did not think the strategic bombing of German cities delegitimated their war effort; the United States had no second thoughts about the success of its war effort following Hiroshima and Nagasaki.[4] Victory was still victory. Of course, as the political event recedes, reconsideration of the tactics of victory becomes possible.[5] Even that, however, remains a matter of theory, which does not undermine the enduring celebration of victory.[6] Warfare has always been a matter of force and counterforce. Why, then, this emphatic reaction against torture as a reciprocal response to terror?[7] After all, of all the terrible things that happen in war, torture is not clearly the worst.

More is at stake than a practical judgment that torture is not a useful means of achieving military objectives. How did it come about that the traditional role of reprisal—torture for terror—was displaced by a legal absolutism with respect to the no-torture principle?[8] Why was the political end of success at war subordinated to this particular legal rule? Today even the traditional claim of "military necessity" takes a legal form, becoming a defense to a potential criminal prosecution brought against a torturer.[9] Of course, short of defeat and victor's justice, it is hard to imagine such a prosecution being brought in a case in which there is a reasonable claim in support of the defense. Conversely, if the conditions exist for that prosecution, it is hard to imagine the defense being successful. While the proposed necessity defense may describe an empty set, we do see here yet another indication of a displacement of politics by law. For Chief Justice Barak, the very meaning of a democracy is that there is no place for state violence beyond law.

The answer to the puzzle of the place of torture is surely not that we—meaning, in particular, Americans—have progressed so much in our moral sensibilities in the last hundred years or so that we are more reluctant today than in the past to use force in the pursuit of our political ends. Americans have effectively been in a state of war, quasi war, or preparation for international war for close to one hundred years; before that, the Revolution and the Civil War shaped the American self-conception. There was a brief respite after the collapse of the Soviet Union, but that was exactly the period in which Americans took up the use of force for humanitarian ends. The legitimate means of warfare are certainly as physically destructive as torture—more so—and they, too, can effectively terrorize civilian populations. Shock and awe remain their end, as the recent American intervention in Iraq publicly announced.[10] Perhaps the most morally significant fact about the development of modern warfare over the last hundred years has been the dramatic increase in civilian casualties—commonly estimated as an increase from 10 to 90 percent of the totals. Even with the use of "smart weapons" in Iraq, the number of noncombatant casualties has outpaced those of combatants.[11] The same was true of Israel's recent military action in southern Lebanon.[12]

Is it moral progress that we have become more tolerant of collateral damage or that we are now experts in the military application of casuistry? The incidents at Abu Ghraib may deeply offend us, but they are not the worst thing Americans have done in Iraq—if our measure is injury, death, and destruction. Of course, if one thinks that the no-torture rule is *the* fundamental moral principle, then this behavior is the worst by definition. But that just restates the puzzle, for among all this violence and destruction why settle on this as the first principle? If our concern is for protecting the well-being of Iraqi noncombatants, for example, then we might start with the thousands killed and literally millions more injured, displaced, and economically ruined. Torture occupies a special place in our political and moral imagination, and the first step of the inquiry must be to explore how it came to occupy that position.

One

TORTURE AND SOVEREIGNTY

DEBATES OVER TORTURE are often mired in questions of definition. With torture, as with pornography, agreement on paradigmatic instances does not lead to agreement on a definition. Of course, torture involves violence or the threat of violence, but so do other political practices, including punishment and combat. Not surprisingly, these are just the places at which torture is likely to occur as well. When we try to distinguish torture from these other forms of political violence, we are always in danger of being captured by our cultural sensibilities. Most Westerners will think that individuals are tortured under the punishments of sharia but not when we place criminal offenders in prison cells for decades. Americans will be offended when Europeans accuse us of torturing those we have condemned to many years on death row. Abandoned forms of punishment—for example, the stocks and the lash—will be thought of as forms of torture while modern forms will not. The same problems appear on the battlefield. Our ideas of the honorable and dishonorable reflect our customary practices. We are more likely to approve the impersonality of the mortar shell than the violence of the bayonet charge. If sorting out the methods of applying political violence is all that is at issue, then we are better off separating the "cruel" from the "unusual" than speaking of torture. All violence against the individual may be cruel, but only some is unusual.

Our reaction to torture, however, is not just a matter of moral relativism induced by culturally specific patterns of violence. Our strongly negative attitude toward torture is a product of the place of law in the modern understanding of the state. Torture signifies a state practice of violence in an entirely different symbolic dimension from that of law. At issue in today's torture debate is how violence figures in the creation of political meaning and how that violence relates to law.

Sovereignty, Torture, and Confession

Historically, torture may always have been cruel, but it was not unusual. Indeed, continental Europe produced a formal law of torture. As John Langbein has explained, the law of torture was a part of the law of evidence.[1] The end point of torture was the confession, which Langbein sees as a practical necessity when the law demanded otherwise unattainable proof. Langbein's work, however, specifically excludes from consideration violent penal sanctions against those convicted of crime. "No punishment," he writes, "no matter how gruesome, should be called torture."[2] Yet in the course of his work he demonstrates how investigatory torture could easily slip into the place of a penalty. Moreover, when the attack on torture came from the Enlightenment reformers—the significance of which Langbein discounts—the object of their attack was not limited to torture in its investigatory form. Finally, linking proof and penalty was the speech that torture aimed to produce: the confession. The very word suggests that the issue was as much contrition, obeisance, and subordination as it was meeting an evidentiary standard.

To Langbein's account of torture in the law of proof, we have to add Foucault's account of torture in the ritual of punishment—a distinction conveyed in French by the use of two words, *torture* and *supplice*.[3] *Supplice* refers to the spectacle of punishment. Foucault argues that on the scaffold a political metaphysics was as much at stake as proof of a crime. The sovereign power to take a life had to be witnessed in the double sense of being seen and acknowledged. Central to the performance of the sanction was the confession, for the public confession accomplished both ends of establishing guilt and recognizing power. Confession was a necessary aspect of the ritual of punishment. It was literally the last act of a dying man. This was not because of lingering uncertainty over guilt—whether he actually committed the crime—but because the sovereign's power over life required the moment of acknowledgment. Without acknowledgment, the sovereign might exercise violence but not power.[4]

Absent the confession, the torture victim might die a martyr to his own—not the sovereign's—beliefs. Torture, confession, and martyrdom had long been linked in the Christian tradition of the saints. Neither torturer nor victim—and surely not the audience—could fail to see this history in current practices. Elaine Scarry makes a similar point in her analysis of the use of torture in modern, authoritative regimes: the political act of torture is structured around an act of compelled speech. The issue is not information (the answer to the question), but rather the acknowledgment of power (the deconstruction of one world of meaning and the construction of another).[5] Resistance to confession is a practice of martyrdom, whether it is done in the name of Christianity, democracy, or, now, Islam.

A criminal justice system that no longer requires confession as either an element of proof or an element of punishment is one that no longer relies on torture, regardless of how offensive we may find its techniques of violent punishment. To understand the problem of torture we must keep the confession in view, not losing sight of it among the violence. The criminal justice system today, violent as it is, operates quite independently of a need for confession. Confession, if it occurs at all, is no longer an acknowledgment of the sovereign power to take a life but the showing forth of the inner state of the criminal. Modern confession is the beginning of therapy. A criminal who confesses is on his way to reform.[6] In the war on terror, on the other hand, the compelled speech of the torture victim is hardly a matter of therapy. It remains instead a sign of sovereign presence.

Before the age of democracy, torture and terror were traditional instruments of sovereignty. They had not yet broken apart into a competition over power. As a matter of course, the sovereign deployed torture to instill a kind of terror. Statecraft rested on the production of terror, not consent.[7] This was the age of the spectacle of the scaffold. On display was the power of the sovereign—a power quite literally of life and death. Power did not flow upward from subject to ruler through an expression of consent. In a fallen world, there was nothing the subject could bestow upon the sovereign. Meaning was not of this world; rather, it was a showing forth of the divine: "All earthly Lordship is a limited representation of the divine Lordship of the World. Human Lordship proceeds from, is controlled by, and issues in, divine Lordship."[8] Thus, all meaning derived from the sacred. The sovereign's power followed from his proximity to the sacred; there could be no other source. Consent of the people does not figure as a source of power, although the mob certainly figured as a potential threat of violence.

The violent act, whether of the one or the many, will call forth a violent response.[9] One strand of political theory, beginning already with the figure of Thrasymachus in *The Republic,* has argued that political power never escapes violence. Political authority is therefore nothing more than a stabilization of the will of the stronger. Plato, however, also pointed out that anybody has the capacity to perform a violent act. Hiding a knife under one's cloak will give one the ability to take a life; it hardly makes one king. Legal philosophers still worry about the difference between the criminal command obeyed because of a threat of force and the legal command backed by a threat of violent sanction—the distinction between being obliged and being obligated.[10] Violence only becomes power when it is perceived within a structure of legitimation. That structure must make sense within the available sources of meaning. Power is the production and maintenance of meaning in the world. When that meaning fails, we are left with violence alone.

The violence deployed by the traditional sovereign did not work merely as threat—although surely threat there was. Rather, it worked in the political-theological dimension of power. One sees this quite literally, for example, in the tortured executions of Catholics under Queen Elizabeth.[11] There was no distinction to be made between Elizabeth as a political sovereign and as head of the Anglican Church. The paradigmatic enemy was the secret Jesuit, whose Catholicism was equally a form of nationalism. This Catholic nationalism was treason because it entailed the belief that Elizabeth did not express the sacred. Just the opposite, in fact, for the Pope had excommunicated her. Torture was one form of mediation between the body and the well-being of the soul, but so was the sovereign "laying on of hands." Louis XVI, for example, right up to the Revolution exercised a power to heal the body through his connection to the sacred.[12]

Traditionally, the power of the state simply could not be imagined outside of questions about the well-being of the soul. Sovereign power arose at the intersection of body and soul. That intersection is the point at which violence becomes power and vice versa. One sees an inflection of the same spirit today in the Middle East when political leaders proclaim that the meaning of democracy can only be realized in Islamic law.[13] That political identity can be a source of meaning separate from Islam simply does not figure in this imagination, for to it all meaning derives from the sacred. Of course, today this position must contend with competing claims for secular political organization even in the Middle East. For a very long time, the sacral monarchs of Europe faced no such competition.

In the world of the sacral monarch, the scaffold was the site of a kind of passion play whose end was the confession of faith. This is an ancient script: the tortured body reproduces the power of the sovereign through the confession of faith. The violence done to the body is not mere negation. Rather, it is that creation through negation characteristic of sacrifice. Torture is, first of all, a form of sacrifice that inscribes on the body a sacred presence. Faith, politics, and torture were conjoined in a spectacle of sacrifice designed to produce in the audience a kind of terror—a combination of dread and awe before the sacred mystery of sovereign power.[14]

If torture was not a part of the ritual production of the sacred, it was nothing but a violent provocation. Awe—not just fear—was the end, for one can act to overcome one's fears. Political power was stabilized by the transformation of torture from mere fear of violent injury to awe before the sacred character of the sovereign.[15] The mob's access to violence was not yet access to a source of meaning that could displace the sovereign. Its members could destroy but not produce. They might kill a king, but they could not rule themselves for the simple reason that they could not save themselves. Before popular revolution could be imagined as anything other than mob violence, the people had to have access to the nation's gods. Indeed, they had to create a new god, which is the nation itself.

Torture was, accordingly, a practice of producing truth. In a premodern world, the construction of truth is not in substantial tension with the discovery of truth. When we speak of "discovery" today, we imagine an objective world that exists apart from the subject. The modern problem of truth is that of getting outside the limited perspective of the self, of seeing the object clearly. Truth seeking requires training—education—for the subject must learn to overcome his tendency to construct the objects of knowledge according to his own prior beliefs and interests. The objectivity and universality of a claim of truth depend on a subject's capacity to separate his particular perspective from the truth-seeking process. Torture is exactly not the way to accomplish this, for pain is never a good frame for objective inquiry.

There is, however, another sense of truth of which we still have some intuition. For example, the truth of character may be revealed not in moments of inquiry stripped of interest but at moments of extreme difficulty. Character is proven—as well as produced—in responding to adversity. We find out who we are when we are asked to sacrifice for an objective or person we care about. We want to know of ourselves, just as we might want to know of others, where we take a stand. The truth of the self is discovered only by constructing it. I discover the truth of myself only by being it. Some argue that the same is true of a nation.[16]

Torture, likewise, produces its own truth. Only from the perspective of third-person objectivity can we see this as an epistemic failure. Torture is embedded in that inversion of truth and faith expressed by Saint Anselm's "I have faith in order to understand." Torture was used as a test of faith. Its product was understanding for both the victim and the torturer. The outcome of this performance was a truth established in the act itself. The victim would know whether for the sake of his beliefs he would suffer self-sacrifice, that is, martyrdom. The torturer, as well as the audience, would know whether sovereign power was real. In a world in which life offers a continual test of faith, torture is a form of inquiry designed to reach truth.

Accordingly, more was at stake in torture's production of the confession than the certainty that the victim had performed an alleged criminal act. It does not take modern science or modern sensibilities to understand that under torture someone might confess to a crime he had not committed. Aristotle writes of this, as do Augustine and a whole succession of others.[17] Torture was maintained not because of a failure to understand the negative epistemic value of pain. It was pursued for reasons of faith, not fact. Today we might offer a utilitarian justification for punishment of the innocent: belief in a penal response to crime deters regardless of whether the process correctly identifies the perpetrator. In the symbolic economy of torture/confession, the same sort of displacement can occur. What matters is the display of the power of the sovereign. Of course, it would be better if power and justice ran in the same direction, but even without justice torture could be effective, for it demonstrated the power of the sovereign wholly to occupy the subject. God's presence always precedes God's justice—just read the book of Job. The same was true of the political sovereign. Justice is a debate about the deployment of sovereign power, not about its creation. It was not the law that created the community of Israel but the act of a sovereign God who gave the law.

Confession was the act by which the subject placed himself in the proper relation to the sovereign. By speaking these words, the torture victim offered a display of the sovereign's power over life and death. His last act was to make of himself a symbol: his finite being was now pure negation, while all that was positive was the sovereign power expressed in his confession. This was a literal reenactment of the power of sacred speech to create its own truth. God spoke the world into existence. The sovereign speaks the smaller world of man into existence. His voice creates and sustains the state. Before there is a theory of law, there is the belief that law is the word of the sovereign.

Torture is linked to trial because the trial is a site of sovereign power. The outcome of every trial is the sentence of the judge, who speaks in the name of the sovereign. The judgment must create its own truth: the guilty confess because the sovereign's speech creates reality. When King Lear puts on trial his daughters' love, Cordelia refuses to speak the king's words. Relying on the "objective" truth of her love, rather than a scripted royal speech, she will say "nothing." Lear's response is literally to make her nothing. Banishing her, he strips her of any claim to wealth or power. But for the dramatic needs, the king's trial would have come out only one way: tortured, she would confess her love.[18]

That torture's aim was confession signals the intersection of the ritual practices of state and church. Only to modern sensibilities does the distinction between the forced denial of the self in the ritual of torture and the voluntary denial of the self in the religious confession seem so essential as to mark a difference in kind. For us, issues of legitimacy of both church and state center on consent. Voluntarism is central to both the Protestant Reformation and the legitimacy of the modern nation-state. Coerced belief appears to us as an oxymoron because it is so antithetical to a fundamental conception of authenticity working not just in religion and politics but in art, inquiry, and social relations as well.[19] From the perspective of the premodern imagination, however, both forms of confession are practices of sacrifice. The religious confession is an element of a ritualized giving up of the finite self and a taking on of the body of a sovereign Christ. The speech of the scaffold replicated, even while it relocated, this giving up and taking on. Its grammar is the symbolic logic of sacrifice: to destroy in making present the sacred.

If man cannot save himself—if meaning always comes from without—then consent is simply not an important element in either the phenomenology of confession or its normative claim.[20] A contemporary comparison would be to the role of consent in the context of education: consent might make education easier, but it is not a necessary condition of learning. We often force the recalcitrant to learn "for their own good." When they do take up the task of learning, they often come to appreciate that which they would not otherwise have done. Indeed, if they are successful, they may come to think of themselves as a new or different person, and they are likely to try to pass on these new values to their own children—quite regardless of their consent.

For the same reason, we can never really get an answer to the question of whether sacrificial rites are consented to by those who participate. When sacrifice was of a victim, the absence of consent seems clear. But even here the victim was often made into the living presence of a god before the sacrificial act.[21] The transformation was certainly about meaning but not about consent. We cannot know what the victim thought of his own divinization. More important, in Christianity sacrifice always moves toward self-sacrifice: Christ completes the sacrifice of Isaac and leaves the West with this image of realizing the sacred. Self-sacrifice is not a voluntary act, but neither is it coerced. Voluntarism simply does not appear in this world of faith any more than it appears in the modern world of scientific truth. To locate consent in Christ's sacrifice—or that of the martyrs who follow—is to miss its sacred character. Sacrifice is compelled by the presence of the sacred: the mysterium tremendum. It does not emerge from within, as if the product of a personal decision, but neither can we say that it is forced upon us from without, as if personal identity were not at issue. At stake is not a romantic idea of an inner self but the objective truth of the world and of the self in that world.

Consent is simply the wrong category to bring to the analysis of the sacrificial imagination. Consent is not a condition of an authentic opening of the self to the sacred. It is not itself a source of power. It has no more power to create the sacred than it has to feed the hungry. In this premodern world, a failure of consent could be a tactical problem, which might require compensation by other means. Just war theory always struggled with the question of whether force could be used to overcome the ignorance—or any other vice—that prevented persons from putting themselves into the proper relationship with the sacred.[22] What, for example, did one do with the ignorant Native American who refused to recognize the divinity of Christ and the authority of the Pope?[23] Today we are more likely to force others—nonbelievers—to see the value of democracy. The form of the sacred has shifted, but the urge to force people to realize the truth of their own being has not. Whenever an ultimate truth is located outside of the self, we are inviting the same debate about the relationship between truth and freedom.

The fundamental principle of faith in the West is that the finite only gains meaning by taking on the presence of the sacred. This is the symbolic structure of sacrifice: life has positive meaning only when and to the extent that it is filled by the sacred. Isaac's life is given back to him only after his sacrifice. Christian faith begins with Paul's claim that the believer has already suffered death on the Cross with Christ. Neither of these symbolic claims works in the dimension of consent. Both, instead, work within the symbolic structure of sacrifice: destruction is a condition of consecration. There must be a "giving up" in order for there to be a "taking on." In the church, this is the practice of confession; not just the formalized ritual it comes to be but the very nature of this faith is a confessional practice. Confession is the opening of the soul to the grace of God through an emptying out of the finite self before the infinite. Confession begins in surrender and ends with sacred presence.

Torture was deployed within the practice of criminal law, but we should not read modern sensibilities into the character of that law. The law was the word of the sovereign, and crime was a kind of treason. The criminal was the enemy, for his actions effectively denied the presence of the sovereign.[24] There was no great distance between crime and sin. The torture victim was the locus of a manifestation of the mystical corpus of the sovereign. Torture demonstrated that participation in sovereign power is a literal presence unmediated by consent or representation. Whenever the sacred appears, it destroys that which stands opposed to it.

The violence of torture was the moment of destruction; confession the moment of consecration. At the moment of confession, an execution could become an act of sacrifice. Speaking, the victim gave himself to the sovereign. That this was achieved through torture, rather than consent, was no more relevant than that victory in war is achieved through violence rather than the ballot.[25] What mattered was the showing forth of sovereign power, which occurred when the victim surrendered himself fully and completely to the sovereign.

Sovereign power was this capacity to create the truth conditions of its own speech: to make law real in the body of the subject. The failure of sovereign power was not the absence of consent but the refusal of the victim to speak. A torture victim could "choose" to become a martyr and thereby defeat the sovereign claim. He could, in other words, refuse to surrender, maintaining faith in his own god. What was unimaginable was that he could withhold speech simply because he did not consent. Those without faith confess easily. In a sacred world, only one faith can displace another. For this reason, torture is associated with the struggle between faiths. Christianity retains a cult of martyrs— those who would confess only the "true" faith. The nation-states that emerged with the transfer of sovereign power from the sacral king to the people celebrated their own cults of martyrdom.[26]

Torture was deployed in a contest over the character of the sacred. That contest leads to the confession because we cannot know the meaning of the body as signifier until that final act of speech in which the victim names his god. Every act of torture is a competition between the power of the torturer to demand confession and the power of the victim to refuse and die as a martyr to his own sovereign. It may be preordained that the torturer will win the battle over the body—he can torture to the point of murder. It is not, however, preordained who will win the competition over the significance of the body's death. The tortured act of execution always represents a risk to the sovereign, for at play in the act of violence is a competition of ideas.[27] Sovereign power is the power to take a life but not to murder. When political sacrifice is seen as murder, faith in the sovereign has already failed.

When we see torture reappearing in our own world, the question we must ask is whether it continues to perform the same truth function. To answer that question, we have to take up a specifically political-theological perspective. We have to see that political truth, just like the truth of religious faith, does not arise out of a division between subject and object. Rather, political truth is constructed at the intersection of body and word. It, too, is a meaning performed on the basis of faith and tested through suffering. Of course, not every political practice occurs at that intersection. That was never the case. But the terrorist, who threatens random destruction, reminds us that political identity is embedded in a sovereign practice of life and death. The war on terror shows us yet again that sovereign authority claims the power to demand a life.

James Whitman, in *Harsh Justice,* describes premodern practices of torture as demeaning, as working through an exhibition of the shameful status of the victim.[28] That is no doubt in part true, but it cannot be enough—at least not in the deeply Christianized West. Whitman would displace the Christian perspective with an aristocratic sensibility in which honor, not faith, is the paramount value. There is, however, no point in the Western normative order at which honor escapes the reach of faith. Aristocratic values are always challenged by Christianity's privileging of the dishonored. Honor is always in danger of being too much of this world. Indeed, Christianity always threatens to invert the order of privilege. It is a religion that begins with those Whitman describes as the demeaned: "the last shall be first."

A Western practice of shaming that is not, in some part, a replication of the Christian practice of demeaning the self before the grace of God is inconceivable. Shame is not dishonor in and for itself but an element of a ritual of redemption. Neither pain nor shame is the fundamental unit of sovereign power. Both ignore the political-theological space of ultimate meanings. Sovereign power is measured by presence. *Presence* is the closest term we have for expressing the ineffable phenomenon of the sacred. It exists wholly in the present without narrative representation of the past or claims of future destiny; it singles out a particular space—or object—as no longer attached to an ordinary geography and therefore beyond cause and effect. It is the time and space of the miraculous. Thus, the sovereign is timeless (it never dies) and omnipresent (it fully occupies the territory). The sovereign is also omniscient, producing by being the only truth that it must know. The sovereign power will be represented in narrative form, establishing both a national history and a destiny tied to a specific land. Before the narrative, however, is the experience of the thing itself as pure presence.

An effective politics of sovereignty must move from the finite to the infinite, from the fallen to the sacred. It moves through shame, just as it moves through pain. They are one and the same in the economy of the sacred, for the condition from which the sacred redeems us is experienced as that absence of meaning that is the Fall. In the biblical narrative, Adam's shame is expressed in the fact of his pain. Recovery is not a recent addition to penal theory in the form of "rehabilitation." Rather, rehabilitation steps into the political-theological place of confession as the locus of sovereignty moves from a sacral monarch to a people ruling themselves through law.

Western political practices have always touched on the sacred. The power of the sovereign is the power of the infinite to appear in the finite. Coronation and torture represented the two sides of the sacred as majesty and terror—that combination constitutive of awe.[29] Both were rituals of sacrifice combining destruction and creation. The lesson of both to an awestruck population was that before the sacred the finite body is nothing at all; it remains nothing until and unless it becomes the vehicle for the showing forth of the sacred. Faith begins in an act of surrender, for all meaning comes from the sacred.

The politics of sovereignty was a set of practices by which the finite body surrendered to the sacred presence. Between torture and investiture was the performance of the oath—again, a practice that easily elides the political and the religious. It, too, was a form of speech that aligned the finite body with the infinite claim of the sacred. It was a kind of imaginative miming of the sacrificial act. The oath was given with the expectation that it might be tested by torture just as today the oath might be tested in battle.[30] Indeed, one could be confident of the oath only when it had withstood the test of torture, for men's words could be deceptive. The oath was a kind of open-ended commitment to sacrifice when called upon by the sovereign. Like Isaac, one held one's life as a gift of the sovereign. Isaac, we might say, was the first victim of the sovereign act that combines torture and terror. But, then, was he a victim at all?

The victims of sovereign torture always face the choice of whether to be martyrs for their own faith; they can deny the political sovereign the triumph of confession. Of course, "choice" here hardly means free choice. This is a test of faith, not a matter of consent. The triumph of the early Christian martyr was not to escape torture but to overcome terror. Torture remained the site for the showing forth of the sacred, but the martyr took possession of the act by contesting the direction of the sacred. Tortured, he sacrificed himself to his own God. He would confess only his own faith. Torture remains a competitive site of sacrifice: the self-sacrifice of the martyr versus the power of the sovereign to sacrifice a victim.

The Sovereign Withdrawal from Torture

The great transformation of political modernity was not the abandonment of the political-theological. Of course, there was some of this as Enlightenment values of doubt, reason, and objective investigation spread from the domains of science and production into the fields of political, economic, and social organization. Every practice and belief can be subject to the scrutiny of reason, and politics was no exception. For this reason, the modern state has a legislative/regulatory agenda of endless reform: every practice can, at every moment, be reevaluated. Justice Oliver Wendell Holmes captured this sense of the modern politics of reform under the guidance of reason when he wrote, "It is revolting to have no better reason for a rule of law than that so it was laid down in the time of Henry IV."[31] But surely it is a mistake to view political modernity solely through this lens of bureaucratic/administrative rationality. That view fails to capture the presence of nationalism, which has arguably been a far stronger political force than reason in the modern age.

The revolutionary change of modernity was in the relocation of the sovereign presence from a sacral monarch to the people as a collective, transtemporal subject. The popular sovereign remains as mystical and sacred an entity as the king ever was. It, too, inspires awe and demands sacrifice. Indeed, sovereign destruction of the finite became wider and deeper, reaching out not in the occasional display of the scaffold but as a systematic demand. In the modern nation-state, everyone has lived under the power of the oath: all have held their lives by the grace of the sovereign act. The political space has not been desacralized. The state has remained embedded in the awe of the sacred, and sovereignty has remained linked to sacrifice.

After the death of kings, citizen participation in the sovereign no longer depends on a ritual of sacral power. This sovereign god is no longer at a distance; mediation is no longer necessary. The structural change in the relationship of citizen to sovereign is exactly what the popular political revolutions of the modern period owe to the earlier revolution in faith that was the rise of Protestantism. The rejection of the priestly role of ritual mediation between parishioner and God was not a rejection of the symbolism of the body of Christ as the community of the Church. Participation in that body, however, was now immediate. Christ was an immediate presence requiring no external ritual but only an inward turning. So it is with popular sovereignty. The scaffold loses its purpose when sovereignty already dwells within the individual citizen. The ritual of torture no longer conveys the sovereign presence in a political theology of immediacy. The disappearance of the scaffold, however, hardly marks a disappearance of sacrifice or of sovereign violence as the destruction of finite limits in the presence of the infinite. The modern nation-state is, if anything, far more violent than its political predecessors.

The gap between sovereign and subject—a gap bridged by the ritual sacrifice of torture—has been permanently overcome at the moment revolution is imagined as action by the popular sovereign. The citizen still owes the sovereign his life. The king may have died, but the sacred quality of the sovereign remains, and it remains a hungry god. Since sovereignty no longer stands apart from the subject, its presence no longer terrorizes—although the awe remains. With that, the site of sacrifice fundamentally shifts from the spectacle of torture to the confrontation of national armies on the battlefield. Even the battlefield turns out to be too limited a space for sovereign violence, which continually overflows any territorial limits until it suffuses the entire domain of the state. The combatant now stands for the citizen as everyman. Anyone can be conscripted. Indeed, everyone is already vulnerable before the formal act of conscription even begins. The contemporary terrorist, in failing to respect the distinction of combatants from noncombatants, enacts the deepest meaning of citizenship in the nation-state: political identity itself, not any additional act, is a matter of life and death.

Modernity does not end the link of sovereignty to sacrifice. Rather, it generalizes sacrificial violence to an ordinary condition of life. We enter the age of citizen armies, mass mobilization, universal conscription—or at least the ever present possibility of such conscription—and pervasive vulnerability. The violence of the modern state continually lays claim to all of the resources—material and personnel—of the state. Today war can involve everyone and everything. There is no longer a distinction drawn between state and subject: all citizens exist under the sign of the oath, that is, they are always on call for the sacrificial act. Popular sovereignty is an intersubjective, transtemporal project of the creation of meaning. It is not, however, just any such project of meaning creation: political meaning is not art, and it is not just talk. Political meaning in the modern state has sustained a practice of sacrifice, of killing and being killed. This is not a necessary aspect of the political per se, but any explanation of the Western experience of the modern state as a manifestation of popular sovereignty must confront this fact.

The naturalization oath of allegiance in the United States makes explicit the sovereign demand on citizenship as an open-ended willingness to sacrifice: "I will support and defend the Constitution and laws of the United States against all enemies. . . . I will bear arms on behalf of the United States when required by law." This oath is demanded of all who would become citizens, not just that small number of them who enter the formal ranks of combatants. The oath reflects almost exactly Jefferson's statement in his first inaugural address that in this country "every man at the call of law, would fly to the standard of the law, and would meet the invasions of the public order as his own personal concern." Early in the nation's history, there was a debate over the relative merits of militias and a standing army, but no one questioned the ideal of the universal citizen-soldier. Today, that debate has been resolved by the technological need for professional training. Nevertheless, the generalization of the locus of sacrifice remains. The call to sacrifice can now appear as if from nowhere on a clear fall day in a large office building in New York. One is never released from a political identity that can demand a life.[32] We live within the imagination of the oath.

In the modern world, violence outgrew torture because sovereignty shifted from king to people. The tomb of the unknown soldier displaced the scaffold as the monument to sovereignty. The unknown soldier is not just a soldier; he is quite literally everyman. Political violence has become a practice of democratic participation. The revelatory power of the sovereign continues to occupy the body; it continues to lead to violent destruction. But the sovereign made present in the sacrificial act is the popular sovereign. The citizen reveals that which he already is. His truth lies within, not without. This does not mean that every time the state has recourse to violence the citizen-soldier steps forward to sacrifice. When the citizen fails to see the demand for violence as an expression of self-sacrifice for sovereign existence, he will see it only as an abuse of power; he will see it as killing and being killed for "no reason" at all.[33] Our deepest internal conflicts emerge when there are contrasting perceptions of the violent act: sacrifice or senseless death?

Torture is the primitive religion of the state. It signifies the presence of a sacred sovereign who has not yet fully and completely penetrated the body of the state. But in the modern state, every man already stands equally in the mystical corpus of the sovereign. This is most certainly not a shift from the mystical to the secular. Rather, at issue is the relationship of the one to the many in an experience of instantiation of an infinite meaning in a finite form. As long as the sovereign was located in the sacral monarch, there was a potential division between the mystical corpus and the citizenry, just as fallen man stands apart from his God. Torture was a ritual of mediation between sovereign and state. When it succeeded, one saw only the sovereign presence; when it failed, torture was only a brutal form of violence. The same phenomenon is visible in war today: either it increases faith in the popular sovereign or it is rejected as nothing but violence for partisan interests. About sacred presence, all one can say is that it either appears or it does not. There are no excuses, no normative claims that it "should be seen," no representations of what might have been. The death of a god is as final and complete as its presence. The sovereign king died such a death when he lost his sacred aura.

Once the body of the citizen becomes the immediate locus of the sovereign, the distance between the finite and the sacred has been overcome. What is required now is not the violent sacrificial act from without but the realization of the truth of the self from within—an inward turning. This change in the character of the political-theological subject is the symbolic condition of revolution. Revolution is direct action by the popular sovereign; acting, citizens realize the truth of their being. That revolutionary act always involves sacrifice. Giving up themselves, they become that which they already are: "We the people." For this reason, revolution has the same character as every appearance of the sacred: being and meaning coincide. The meaning of revolution is not separate from its performance. The act is the announcement of the presence of the popular sovereign, which is not striving to be something other than it already is. Revolution is never a means to some other end. It is the first act of sacrificial violence that brings forth the popular sovereign. Every sacrificial act thereafter reestablishes contact with that same sacred presence.

Once the locus of the sovereign presence shifts, the power of the king—though not necessarily his potential for violence—has already been broken. His deployment of torture is no longer a showing forth of the divine but an abuse of power. He no longer has the power to generate awe but only the power to create fear. Once the king no longer possesses the power to sacrifice, the revolution demands that he be sacrificed to the new sovereign. He has become an idol. The proof that an idol lacks divinity is found in its destruction. Thus, the king's death is the last spectacular execution, for it marks the migration of the sovereign from the one to the many.[34] This has nothing to do with secularization or the rule of law but rather with the changing locus of the sacred.

Torture falls away as an element of penal practice because it is no longer an effective symbolic practice. It now appears as mere violence, not sacrifice. It is as if Abraham continued to sacrifice Isaac when neither any longer heard the voice of God demanding the act. We pass from the sacred to the abusive, from ritual to pathology. In an age of democracy, the sovereign no longer occupies the scaffold, not because the sovereign has disappeared, but because it is already present everywhere. This hardly means that the state can no longer demand a life. It does so all the time. Nevertheless, the idea of the scaffold as a site of competition between torture and martyrdom no longer makes sense, for the criminal is no longer a challenge to the sovereign. The new site of the competition between faiths is the battlefield: one dies as a martyr for the state or one confesses a new faith. To perform the latter act is to speak the words of surrender.

We have not abandoned violence in our penal practices. In many ways, the United States has become increasingly violent in its attitude toward prisoners. The criminal, however, has been reconceived. He is no longer a point of opposition to the sovereign; he is not the traitor who must be destroyed through a display of power. He cannot be the enemy, for he has been radically depoliticized. He is nothing more than a privative expression of political life precisely because the victory of the popular sovereign has been so complete. The criminal exists in a pathological condition. He has fallen away from what he already is: a member of the sovereign body. His presence is an absence, which is literally enacted in the penitentiary. Because law is seen as the product of the popular sovereign, crime is a sin against one's own nature. His act is a product of personal failure, not treason. The criminal is no longer banished, and he is not denationalized. To contemporary sensibilities, such actions amount to violations of his human rights, for to be human is to be a part of the popular sovereign.[35] In the United States, the idea of a political prisoner verges on being an oxymoron, which is one of the reasons why there has been so much uncertainty and debate about a turn to criminal law as the response to terrorism.

Modern criminology studies the sociological, economic, and psychological causes of crime but not the political. Crime no longer takes place in a contestable political space for there is no place in which the popular sovereign is not already fully present. For this reason as well, the first reaction of the state to the threat of civil war will be to treat the opposition as criminals—just the opposite of the state's reaction to foreign enemies.[36] When elements of the black community and the Left threatened to link crime to politics in the 1960s, they were quite brutally suppressed. The power of the sovereign is at stake in this capacity to use criminal law to deny a political space to the formation of a radical opposition.

In this new world of popular sovereignty, the question is not whether the criminal has a political identity as such but whether he can be "rehabilitated" to the point at which he can bear the single truth of his political identity. One of the archetypal stories of criminal redemption in the democratic state is that of the prisoner who volunteers for military service, redeeming himself by taking on the burdens of sacrificial violence.[37] Sacrificing himself, he realizes the truth of his being. The criminal who becomes the hero is paradigmatic of the movement from sin to grace. If the scaffold produced truth by sacrificing the victim, the battlefield produces truth in an act of self-sacrifice. In the West, we are never far from the idea that through death is life. Progress, we think, is marked in this turn from being sacrificed to self-sacrifice, from the scaffold to the battlefield.

If the criminal cannot bear this political identity, he appears as less than human. He has become so because the human is now defined as the capacity to be a part of the popular sovereign. Those who cannot bear the material presence of the popular sovereign can literally be institutionalized. The criminal shares this character of removal from public appearance with the insane, the ill, and the dying. All of them have already died to sovereign presence. Any group that was thought to be "naturally" unable to bear the sovereign presence could find itself in deep trouble in the modern state: blacks, Jews, ethnic minorities.[38] There is, of course, a history of gender relations at issue here as well. These groups appeared as less than human not because they lacked a capacity for reason but because they lacked a capacity to show forth the sacred in its political-theological form. Reason, no less than physical infirmity, can be an obstruction to the sovereign presence.[39] Today we often focus less on the state's dedication to sovereignty and more on its dedication to social welfare. Indeed, we extend special care and protection to those who cannot fully participate in political life: children, the elderly, the sick, or the insane. None of this need be denied, but it hardly explains the American treatment of the criminal, the peculiar history of our racial politics, our commitment of billions of dollars to warfare, or our celebration of a narrative of sacrifice. To understand these, we have to look at other aspects of the political imagination.

Life in the penitentiary is violent and dehumanizing, but it is not a practice of torture. Torture is a political practice of making present the sovereign in the body of the victim. The criminal, in modern America, is denied any political space. Even his execution is not a positive, political act, for he cannot be sacrificed to the state. There is nothing in him over which the sovereign can triumph. He has become Agamben's *homo sacer:* someone who can be killed but cannot be sacrificed.[40] Following the logic of popular sovereignty, he may as well not exist for he cannot bear that transcendent value that comes from the sovereign. Until and unless he shows himself capable of redemption, his life is literally without meaning. Because he is seen as an absence, however, the possibility of making such a showing is likely to be denied. Without the constraints that come from outside the political—from moral and aesthetic values—he would be disposed of as fit only for labor. He is no longer a subject. Arguably, he appears as even less than a slave, for the slave always posed the threat of rebellion.

The immorality of the American prison regime—a space of violence but not awe—is a constant reminder that the sacred space of sovereignty has no necessary relationship to the morality of justice and the sensibilities of compassion. This should come as no surprise to anyone who looks to the history of the great wars of the twentieth century, on the one hand, and to the camps for those excluded from the sovereign on the other. Indeed, it is the European withdrawal from the sacred space of sovereignty that has allowed a greater place for moral judgment with respect to penal practices, including the death penalty. Of course, American penal practices are worse than European ones, for we still live in a world in which the universal morality of individual dignity must compete with the aura of the sovereign presence.

Conclusion: Torture and Sovereignty

The disavowal of torture was not a step toward a general disavowal of political violence. It is a gross misreading of the genealogy of our political practices to believe that the no-torture principle rests on a turn away from state violence or even on a general desacralization of state practices. The prohibition was rather a step on a path toward the generalization of political sacrifice that characterized Western states throughout the nineteenth and twentieth centuries—and is likely to remain true of the United States in the twenty-first. Torture has no place in the modern nation-state because it is a form of sacrifice that fails to correspond to the locus of popular sovereignty. We condemn the violence of torture, but that condemnation must sound hollow to others when they see a nation that maintains, in the name of the people, a nuclear arsenal and a million-person army—and expresses a willingness to use both. The problem is not our condemnation of torture but our failure to understand why torture offends us. To focus on the violence, the injury, or the asymmetry of torturer and tortured is to mischaracterize the offence felt in the presence of torture. Torture offends our sense of the political-theological.

With the passing of kings, the age of torture came to an end. Torture is no longer capable of embodying the relationship of sovereign to subject, for there are no more subjects—only citizens. Citizens relate to each other as equal members of the popular sovereign bound to each other through mutual participation in sacrifice, on the one hand, and following the rule of law on the other. Wherever torture appears as an expression of sovereign power, there is an anachronistic claim to the localization of sacred violence. The worry that an American administration may practice torture on its own citizens is a worry that there has been a fundamental failure in the politics of popular sovereignty. This is not primarily a failure of law or morality—although it is both—but rather a failure in the politics of the sacred. That the threat of torture should appear alongside renewed claims for exceptional presidential power—that is, claims for an "imperial president"—is no surprise. Torture is the practice of power by the sacral monarch. It makes no difference whether he is elected or born to office.[41]

The displacement of torture by self-sacrifice in a regime of popular sovereignty colors the perception of torture wherever it is pursued by the state. We do not think of ourselves as a people who practice torture. Still, the torture of the enemy alien is not the same sort of metaphysical mistake as the torture of the citizen. A regime that prohibits torture domestically could theoretically be reconciled with the pursuit of torture abroad. Why is torture not just another form of warfare even if it is no longer an acceptable form of punishment? To answer that question, we must trace the shifting attitude toward torture in the violent world of international relations.

Two

TORURE AND
INTERNATIONAL LAW

IN THE FIRST CHAPTER, I argued that political modernity was characterized by a shift from torture to war, from victims to conscripts. The
disappearance of torture as a domestic practice of power, however, does
not in itself suggest a similar disappearance of torture from the practice
of international violence. Torture was traditionally applied against enemies—domestic and foreign—of the sovereign. Treason, in English law,
was a broad category that, prior to nineteenth-century legal reform, included not just direct threats to the life of the sovereign but "any degree of violence in expressing opposition to parliamentary enact-
ments."[1] The transformation that I traced in the last chapter included
reimagining the criminal: he is no longer an enemy of the sovereign
but only a fallen citizen. Nevertheless, there remains a large category of
actual and potential enemies. If torture is the performance of sovereign violence against enemies, then in the modern era torture can be
expected to migrate from an internal ritual of sacrifice to an external
means of displaying and deploying the power of the state. The end is
the same: the victim must speak the name of the sovereign. At war, we
call that point of confession "surrender."[2]

In broad scope, I don't think the point can be denied: the destruction of bodies in modern warfare moves toward a generalized practice of torture. We have not so much abandoned the practice of torture as shifted the locus of an act of violent sacrifice—the genus within which torture is a specific cultural form.[3] The battlefield is strewn with the disemboweled and beheaded, with severed limbs and broken bodies. All have died a terrible death in a display of sovereign power. To view the battlefield is to witness the awesome power of the sovereign to occupy and destroy the finite body. It is to stand before the modern, democratic equivalent of the spectacle of the scaffold. Viewing the battlefield from a certain distance, it is not even clear who is the object of sacrifice: the enemy and the conscript suffer the same threat and burden of physical destruction for the sake of making present sovereign power. Killing and being killed are bound together just as the sacral monarch's power to take a life was always linked to his own sacrificial character. Coronation was a ceremony of rebirth, of life through death.[4] The emergence of the royal "we" follows upon the death of the personal "I." The power to take a life is always linked to the willingness to give up one's own life, for self-sacrifice marks the presence of the sovereign.

Abraham Lincoln described the democratic battlefield as "consecrated ground." It is the space within which the sacrificial character of modern politics shows itself. It is a field of reciprocal acts of self-sacrifice in which enemies offer each other the occasion for displaying sovereign power. Arguably, the battlefield only makes sense as a space within which citizens might realize the possibility of transcending the finite conditions of their individual lives. There they become more than themselves, which is why war figures in the modern imagination as such a powerful source of meaning.[5] Embedded in the practice of sacred violence, the battlefield exists in the same imaginative framework as the spectacle of the scaffold—a space for the showing forth of the creative-destructive power of the sovereign. Accordingly, it has the same vulnerability as the scaffold: when faith fails, when the sacred character of the sovereign is not seen, it presents just the awful—not awesome—sight of death and destruction. To modern, humane sensibilities, it appears thoroughly inhuman, which is only another way of noting that the sacred has always been tightly tied to the polluted.

In this chapter, I take up a particular form of this failure of faith—

not that which characterizes the existential angst of the soldier who finds himself in the trenches of World War I, the rice paddies of Vietnam or the cities of Iraq with no understanding of why he is there. For him, the sacrificial claims of the sovereign may sound more like rhetorical fraud than sacred speech. My topic here is not that individual crisis of faith but a general shift in the representation of violence in the culture of modern international law. At issue is the failure of the possibility of faith—the death of sovereignty, not of a particular sovereign. If the wars of the first half of the twentieth century show us the power of the sovereign to demand sacrifice, the developments in international law that follow those wars resolutely turn away from any recognition of a connection between violence and the sacred.

This turn to international law and away from the violence of combat was, in many respects, a replay of a "humanization" of criminal law that occurred almost two hundred years earlier in the wake of the French Revolution. Then the object of reform was the use of torture and corporal punishment within domestic penal practice.[6] I argued in the last chapter that it was not merely sympathy and Enlightenment ideals of reason that drove that earlier reform movement. Rather, it was a shift in the relationship of the subject to the sovereign—not a rejection of pain but a relocation of the locus of sacrifice. The twentieth-century "reform" movement is, in this sense, more revolutionary, for it rejects the very idea of sacrificial violence. That, however, cannot be done without rejecting the faith that supports the practice of political violence by grounding its sacred character in the idea of the sovereign. This modern revolution appears to itself as the fulfillment of the Enlightenment ideal of a politics of reason, the end of which is individual well-being.[7] The radicalness of this claim is both its strength and its weakness, for reason can no more prove the death of the sovereign than it could the death of God.

Whether and to what extent faith in sovereign power—sacred violence—continues are questions that cannot be answered in the abstract. We can only say that whenever the connection between violence and the sacred is broken the continued existence of sovereignty will be in doubt. Without that connection, a regime of sovereign states will be viewed as increasingly anachronistic. It will appear as an obstacle to the emergence of a global order of law under the guidance of reason. Conversely, wherever sovereignty remains a vital presence, the connection of violence and meaning will be maintained and the claims of international law will be in doubt.

Torture and Warfare

Modern warfare has been the generalization of the practice of violent sacrifice that was at work in premodern displays of torture. Both work at the intersection of body and idea, and both work through the political psychology of degradation.[8] Torture is a kind of laboratory of degradation, while warfare is its generalized practice. Torture fell out of place within the regulative ideals of European combat in the nineteenth and twentieth centuries. Of what use is the rack once we have seen the trenches of World War I or the strategic bombing of World War II? The executioner is an anachronism when political death has been thoroughly democratized. As a practical matter, torture lost much of its usefulness under modern conditions of warfare: enemy combatants are unlikely to have useful information when armies are organized in a strictly hierarchical manner. Nor is there is any point in trying to shift the allegiance of particular victims when the outcome of the war turns on the performance of mass armies in the field or entire populations working to support the war effort. Such practical concerns, however, are really only incidental to the broad shift in the character and locus of sovereign violence. The form of the appearance of the sacred is never a matter of efficiency. Otherwise, religion would have had a very short life in the history of civilization.

Just as efficiency is not at stake, neither is moral progress. The move from torture to strategic bombing is not a moral advance. If we rank the different forms of sovereign violence on any normative scale other than that of physical destruction and death, we become complicit in that violence. Our own practices will always look more sensible to us than those of other cultures—including our own past. Westerners cannot help but feel a moral superiority to Muslims when, for example, they see that sharia contemplates amputation and stoning as forms of punishment. But there is no universal moral calculus by which we can measure a lifetime in an American prison against an amputation.

Some theorists attempt to distinguish torture from combat by noting the asymmetry of power in the former. They focus on the helplessness of the torture victim before a torturer who acts in total disregard of his or her will.[9] But the question is "compared to what?" Does one compare torture to law or to war? In both combat and torture, action is taken in disregard of the well-being of the other. The Western history of chivalry suggests that inflicting violent injury and maintaining dignity are not necessarily incompatible. We are, however, a long way from the age of chivalry. If combat preserves dignity today, it does so by denying any room for individual subjectivity. Killing and being killed occur on a field of anonymity.

Torture begins where an interaction between subjects with unique wills begins. In its combination of recognition and denial, torture is the paradigm of an illiberal act. Still, it is difficult to understand how combat is any more liberal a practice. Combat so deeply denies recognition of the dignity of the other that torture never begins because dignity is never glimpsed.[10] It is simply wrong to suggest that combat differs from torture because combatants must take account of the initiative of their opponents.[11] This is an effort to cast combat in the form of the moral economy of consent. The logic of warfare, however, is not that of a "fair" competition between consenting, sui juris subjects. That may have been the logic of the duel, but it is hardly that of national armies at war. Rather, the logic of combat seeks as its ideal a total asymmetry in the application of force.[12] Its end is to obtain a position from which no harm can result to one's own side while all the injury is suffered by the enemy. This is just the logic of total control obtained in the microcosm of torture. In both cases, one may hope to make this asymmetry so visible and certain that the threat alone is sufficient to achieve one's ends, whether confession or surrender. Combat, like torture, is more successful the less it actually has to be deployed—in part because action generates far more contingencies than threat. But again, like torture, combat cannot simply disappear entirely from the practice of violence. For the threat to remain, the belief that the act will be accomplished if necessary must be sustained.[13]

Nor is it the case that combatants, unlike torture victims, can simply take themselves out of the violence by laying down their arms—a right formally given them under the Geneva Conventions.[14] Under conditions of modern warfare, the capacity to communicate that choice is simply not available. Laying down one's arms before a missile attack makes no sense. Proof of this was seen in the first Gulf War on the "highway of death" as the Iraqi army fled Kuwait City. Again, the point is not just practical. Conceptually, soldiers are not free agents. They can be literally threatened by deadly force from their own officers; they can certainly be prosecuted, and punished by execution, if they make the choice to concede defeat on the basis of nothing more than their own free will.[15] In between the moment when combatants take up the task of self-sacrifice and that in which they effectively surrender, their situation is one of "being sacrificed." In this in-between period, they are very close—politically and phenomenologically—to the classic victim of torture: each is made to bear the presence of the sovereign in and through the destruction of his or her body.

Warfare is simply not a practice founded on consent. Like torture, it is founded on sacrifice. Indeed, it is not too much to say that warfare wants to become torture: its logic moves toward the same asymmetry of power. When the battle situation appears as asymmetrical as the use of force in torture—when one side appears as pure victim—defeat becomes possible. So, too, does martyrdom, for one can choose death over life. This is just the position at which the analysis of torture in chapter 1 left us.[16]

Even were warfare conducted within the rules of humanitarian law, that would no more eliminate its underlying sacrificial quality than did the fact that the practice of torture in some European countries was subject to legal regulation. International humanitarian law may specify the class of potential victims and limit the means of their destruction, but it does not change the underlying logic of conflict: killing and being killed for the sovereign. Nevertheless, many people today have a sense that the war on terror is upending the progress of international human rights law and humanitarian law by returning to a prohibited practice of torture. They distinguish between lawful combat and unlawful torture. They argue that this distinction is morally compelling. But is it? Is it moral advance or simply historical difference that creates the possibility of condemning torture while pursuing warfare?

International Law

Classic international law of the nineteenth and early twentieth centuries was the law of interstate relations. Individuals were not rights-bearing subjects within this system. An injury to an individual was cognizable as a matter of international law only insofar as it was an injury to the state of which he or she was a citizen.[17] Whether to pursue redress for such a legal injury was wholly a matter for decision by the state or states involved. Just as there were no subjects apart from states, there was no regulation of states apart from rules to which they had freely subjected themselves.[18] Since all international law was derived from state consent, all law had the same normative character. There was no hierarchy of norms—no *jus cogens* claims—except for the principle of sovereignty itself, which was the source of all other norms.[19] If one went so far as to think that a sovereign state must be free to withdraw its consent at every moment, international law risked dissolving into the tautology that state consent reaches no farther than present state action. The response to this dilemma was to claim that the very idea of international law rests on the principle of *pacta sunta servanda*—treaties must be observed. Even here, however, a state that declined to follow its treaty obligations was not so much violating a superior norm as providing a ground for reciprocal action, and even war, on the part of an injured state. In a world in which the first principle is unconstrained sovereignty, every other norm is contingent. The world of international law was binding just as long as states remained committed to it.

Concretely, this focus on consent had a specific, practical meaning: a state retained absolute authority over the decision whether or not to go to war against any other state. That decision, as a matter of law, could be neither right nor wrong. This was the meaning of sovereignty from an international perspective. International law did not regulate the decision for war or peace but only offered a legal regime—the law of war or the law of peace—once that decision had been made.[20] The decision for war was a sovereign prerogative beyond any conceivable regime of law.[21] War was limited by politics—alliances and threats—not by legal rules. This fact, that at the heart of international relations lay a sovereign right to have recourse to violence, sustained the question that was inseparable from every assertion of international law: Is it really law?

International law in the second half of the twentieth century moved through two dramatic paradigm shifts. The first occurred with the founding of the United Nations. The charter regime is based on the principle that unilateral state recourse to force is now illegal apart from the single exception for self-defense. International law thereby entered the forbidden domain of sovereign recourse to war.[22] More than that, the charter imagined an enforcement regime under the authority of the Security Council. Member states formally delegated this central feature of sovereign power to the council. The link of sovereignty to interstate violence was thereby broken.

Of course, neither practically nor theoretically was there a clean break with the old paradigm. The major powers retained a veto. They had not delegated to the council their own decision-making authority over violence, even if they had formally accepted the new legal rule. Practically, other states also continued to threaten and use force against each other. More than ever, the shape of international relations in the second half of the twentieth century was characterized by violence and the threat of violence. Had the new paradigm actually taken hold, it would have raised critical questions: What is sovereignty stripped of a capacity to demand sacrifice? Can we even speak of sovereignty in a postsacrificial politics? That question was hardly even glimpsed in a world threatened by nuclear destruction, on the one hand, and countless smaller wars, on the other.

The second paradigm shift struggled for recognition throughout the Cold War but was not achieved, even as a theoretical matter, until the 1990s. This was to extend the international legal regulation of sovereign recourse to violence from state-to-state relationships to the relationship between governments and individuals, including a state's own citizens. Just as the earlier shift expanded the range of international legal subjects—those with legal rights and obligations—beyond states to transnational institutions such as the Security Council, this new shift expanded that range to include individuals. Indeed, the moral foundation of international law shifted from the protection of states against the use of force to the protection of individuals: it shifted from peace to human rights. At the start of the new century, international law, at least for many theorists and practitioners, has been reconceived. No longer the law of nations, it is the law of human rights.[23]

The first shift conceived of the United Nations as exercising certain delegated powers over states for the sake of their own well-being. This second move is more radical, conceiving of states themselves as exercising power delegated to them by a global regime of law, the constituent members of which are individuals.[24] Earlier, individuals had been thought of as instruments of state power; now states are thought to exercise their powers for the sake of individuals. The institutional expressions of this new paradigm are, first, a willingness to engage in humanitarian intervention and, second, the creation of international criminal courts. War and law continue as the twin forms of politics, but now both are turned toward a new cosmopolitanism at the center of which is the rights-bearing individual. Although neither institutional innovation has been very effective practically, both are symbolic of a profound challenge to the classic idea of sovereignty.

Under the first paradigm shift, war represented the antithesis of law; under the second, torture took the place of law's antithesis. Thus, torture in human rights law mimics the earlier place of war in the law of the UN Charter. Indeed, torture is cast as a sort of internal war—a war by a regime against members of its own national community. To prohibit both war and torture is to place the sovereign power of life and death under the rule of law.[25] The sovereign is to be stripped of its capacity for violence outside of law, whether applied externally or internally. This can happen only with the abandonment of faith in the sacred character of the sovereign and in the rituals of sacrifice that accompany that faith. The international legal project of the latter part of the twentieth century is deliberately set against the claim that one confronts the sacred through sovereign violence.

The deeply felt, but little understood, link of sovereignty to violence easily led international law theorists at the end of the twentieth century to think that the emerging global order would be a postsovereignty world. By that, they meant that there would be no space in the international order beyond legal regulation and thus no space for the appearance of sacred violence. Law would go global, and with that the sacrificial force of sovereign violence—whether directed outwardly or inwardly—would end. If state violence is the problem to which law is addressed, then the elimination of sovereignty is the answer. Henceforth, state violence would be limited to law enforcement. As such, it would be a matter of substantial indifference who exactly exercised that violence. Effective law enforcement could as easily be provided by external as by internal forces, and by private as by public forces. The questions are all practical. What matters is the security of individual rights. Everything else is a means to that end.

Of course, one cannot simply declare the end of the sovereign state any more than one can eliminate torture by declaring it illegal. Instead, theorists spoke of institutional trends, emerging regimes, normative ideals, and long-term goals. The postsovereignty world was that toward which we were heading. Networks, markets, and jurists—not politicians—would take us there, or perhaps we had already arrived while no one was quite looking.[26] If the threat of violence continued to inform state practices, one could turn to the courts for support in this new age of law. Torturers such as Augusto Pinochet would be criminally prosecuted wherever they went, while states that continued to deploy the threat of sovereign violence—for example, in the shape of nuclear weapons—would be brought before the International Court of Justice. Only on closer inspection would anyone notice that Pinochet went home and the ICJ failed to declare nuclear weapons illegal.[27] The trends, after all, were in the right direction.

One could always point to the European Union as a postsovereignty political arrangement. It was a regime wholly defined by law. As a consequence, it had eliminated war among its members and torture of its citizens. The human rights of its citizens were protected by transnational courts. It was structurally incapable of making a claim to occupy a sovereign space of violence beyond law. That the EU was not particularly democratic was an issue to be addressed in the long term. In the meantime, its law would derive its legitimacy from expertise and process. Indeed, progress in the project of the EU was measured by increasing restrictions on the sovereign right of members to veto proposed actions.[28] Only the unconverted could have imagined that in 2005 voters would reject a European Constitution on grounds such as nationalism, religion, economic interests, and fear of the Islamic other.

Given the historical centrality of violence to the self-conception of the sovereign nation-state, this turn to law as a force in opposition to violence is somewhat surprising. International law, after all, had long operated as an adjunct to that system of violence—protecting, not eliminating, the state's right to take up arms. To understand what happened to international law, we must see it as a part of the much larger modernist project of liberal reform under the guidance of reason.

By the late twentieth century, international law had effectively become a political "counter-religion." Jan Assmann describes a counter-
religion as one that is constructed through an inversion of the values of
the dominant religion.[29] By inverting the inversion, we can read the
norms of the dominant religion out of the beliefs and rituals of the
counter-religion. Thus, the first principle of the UN Charter is the prohibition on state recourse to force, which is to be enforced by the Security Council—a collective agent operating on a global scale. This is a
perfectly inverted picture of the modern nation-state as it existed from
the age of revolution until the end of World War II. Essential to that
state was its capacity to use or threaten force. Sovereignty was the capacity to call on citizens to kill and be killed—to sacrifice—in defense
of the national interest. The state might form strategic alliances, but
they were always subject to the state's own judgment concerning political necessity. There was no independent transnational, institutional
power that could control state violence.

The second principle of the counter-religion is the proposition that
all individuals have human rights that they can assert as a matter of law
against all governments, including their own. Those rights express the
normative priority of the individual over the state, which exists for the
sake of individual well-being. Again, reality had been the inverse: the
state was a structure of collective meaning quite independent of the interests of any particular individual. That meaning was inaccessible to
the view of the outsider. To assess and regulate the meaning maintained between citizen and state from the outside would be rather like
a Jew telling a Christian what the truth of his religion must be. What
could be said, however, was that the state's meaning had proved
sufficient to create and maintain the sovereign's claim of an ultimate
power of life and death over citizens.

The religion and the counter-religion fought each other throughout the second half of the twentieth century. Many thought the
counter-religion was winning this battle after the collapse of the Soviet
Union in 1989. They thought that politics could now cease to exist as a
practice of sacrifice. Killing and being killed for the state seemed an an-
tiquated vision in a global order of law defined by human rights and
trade. Since September 11, 2001, there has been a strong resurgence
of the religion over the counter-religion—at least in the United States.

Some were shocked by the reappearance of sovereign violence and, with it, the sacrificial imagination. The behavior of the United States after 9/11 was the reappearance of the classic expression of sovereignty as sacred violence: a demand to kill and be killed. In truth, in the United States, the religion has always dominated the counter-religion—at least outside the academy. How long this conflict between the religion and counter-religion of sovereignty will continue, and which will win—if either—are completely unpredictable, but surely it is a mistake to read history as if it could move in only one direction.

Human Rights

Of the two targets of contemporary international law, war and torture, the latter appears to have been more difficult to reach and more important to prohibit. The prohibition on torture was not clearly stated as a formal matter of human rights law until twenty years after the UN Charter's birth. Nevertheless, when the prohibition does appear, it appears as an absolute. This is just the opposite of the earlier prohibition on the use of force, which was an integral part of the charter itself but was linked to an exception for self-defense.[30] There is no equivalent regime of the exception for torture. None of the conventions specifying the prohibition on torture allows for derogation under any circumstances. The Convention against Torture puts this plainly: "No exceptional circumstances whatsoever, whether a state of war or a threat of war, internal political instability or any other public emergency, may be invoked as justification for torture."[31] Here, then, we have a human rights convention placed above all sovereign authority. It purports to regulate the practice of warfare, the scope of emergency powers, and the ordinary forms of legality. How is it that the torture prohibition became the point at which the ends of politics and the expression of sovereign power break down before the claimed majesty of the law?

The torture prohibition appears for the first time in the Universal Declaration of Human Rights, approved by the UN General Assembly in 1948. Article 5 of the declaration states, "No one shall be subjected to torture or to cruel, inhuman or degrading treatment or punishment." While the UN Charter came into being as a treaty with the status of law, the declaration has no such legal status. Retrospectively, we can see that it became a rich source for claims of customary international law. Nevertheless, this evolution could not have been known in advance. Indeed, the legal significance of all General Assembly resolutions had to await the development of a practice. The very concept of "soft law" would not appear for some time.[32]

Formally, the declaration gains legal significance—although hardly legal status—through Article 1 of the charter, which speaks of "promoting and encouraging respect for human rights." The declaration provides a first content to the category of human rights, to which the new institution is formally committed. The charter's preamble, too, lists among the new organization's sources and ambitions "to reaffirm faith in fundamental human rights, in the dignity and worth of the human person, in the equal rights of men and women." Faith and encouragement, however, are hardly a rule of law. Practically, we are still in the realm of aspiration. Theoretically, there was not yet any real understanding of how international law could directly regulate the relationship between government and citizens within a sovereign state.

Alongside human rights promotion, the charter declares a commitment to respecting state sovereignty. Indeed, its fundamental strategy is not to prevent war by enforcing a regime of human rights but rather to prevent armed conflict by securing the borders within which a sovereign state is free to govern itself without outside interference. The idea of an international law of human rights stood in significant tension with this understanding. The primacy of sovereignty is seen clearly in Article 51's reservation of a right to use force in self-defense. Nothing suggests that this right to defend against armed attack is conditioned on the human rights record of a government. It is not so much that the drafters perceived the tension between self-government and human rights and then chose the former. Rather, there was an assumption that human rights abuses had their origin in illegitimate power structures. Newly decolonized nations would have no reason to abuse their citizens. On this, the theory of socialism and the theory of liberalism agreed.[33]

A similar uncertainty over the capacity of international law to exercise authority over the relationship of a government to its own citizens was simultaneously displayed at the Nuremberg trials. Something more than prosecution for traditional war crimes seemed required with respect to the leaders of the Nazi regime. The Nuremberg defendants were, accordingly, indicted both for the pursuit of an aggressive war and for violations of the human rights of their own citizens. Together these represented the primary goals of the new UN system: an end to the "scourge of war" and respect for human rights. But what was an institutional aspiration for the UN was presented as an existing legal order at Nuremberg. That claim seemed so incongruous that leading Western scholars accused the prosecution of pursuing "victor's justice."[34]

In the end, the Nuremberg judges were moved by only one half of the legal innovations offered to them. They were willing to hold that aggressive war had been made illegal by the Kellogg-Briand Pact of 1928—an argument that required turning a blind eye to the realities of interwar politics. With respect to the second innovation of the indictment, however, the judges balked. They could find no human rights equivalent of that pact. Avoiding the question of whether a free-floating human rights law was consistent with state sovereignty, they linked the alleged human rights violations to the act of launching an illegal war.

At Nuremberg, then, human rights played a supporting role to a new legal regime founded on protecting state sovereignty through the prohibition on the use of force. This is just the position reflected in the Universal Declaration of Human Rights, which is linked through the preamble and Article I to the legal prohibition on the use of force in the charter. This paradigm endures in the jurisprudence of Chapter VII of the charter, which allows the Security Council to adopt coercive measures in response to threats to, and breaches of, the peace: human rights violations become a subject of sufficient international concern to merit intervention when the effects of those violations "spill over" into third countries, raising a threat to the peace.[35]

This ambiguous postwar regime of human rights reflects less Cold War frustrations and more the difficulties of decolonization. World War II had been a war of liberation, but the business of liberation was not yet complete in much of the world. The European Allies' record of colonial invasion, occupation, and subordination was one that looked disturbingly similar to the recent German war effort. The differences were geographical and temporal—their colonial empires were located elsewhere and had developed over centuries. A colonial regime is not compatible with claims for human rights, for such a regime is fundamentally based on inequality.[36] Thus, the end of the wars of decolonization was a necessary condition for the moral aspirations of the declaration to be framed as a set of legal requirements. This new era is announced with the opening for signature of the two human rights covenants in the mid-1960s.[37]

Just as we can read the end of the era of colonization out of the transition from the declaration to the covenants, we can read the politics of the Cold War out of the odd combination of the success and failure of the covenants—formal success and practical failure. Despite the success of decolonization, the geopolitical division fundamentally undermined the political and the legal aspirations of the United Nations, which had included protection of state sovereignty, international control over the authority to use force, and the progressive development of a legal order based on human rights. The latter part of the twentieth century was among the most violent in history. If one considers the stakes in the nuclear confrontation, the entire period lay at the edge of world-destroying violence. Despite decolonization, this period of international relations looked surprisingly like a continuation of the hundred years of Great Powers politics that had preceded it. Formally independent states became client states of the powerful through consent, force, or corruption. Spheres of influence were maintained, mass armies were created, wars were threatened, and proxy wars broke out.

Not only was the war prevention function of the Security Council a dead letter, but there was no follow-up to the Nuremberg trials.[38] The latter part of the century was characterized by repeated abuses of human rights, including torture and genocide. There was no legal accountability. Ironically, in this situation of institutional failure, national conflict, moral atrocity, and individual impunity, the articulation of the law of human rights achieved a kind of formal autonomy. Human rights now appeared in the form of law, not just moral aspiration.[39] This was not law as distinct from politics let alone law as a limit on political practice. It was law that, apart from its formal announcement, could find no space to operate free of the politics that it was intended to regulate. The clearest expression of this subordination was the UN's Commission on Human Rights, on which sat regimes that were themselves gross violators of the fundamental human rights conventions.[40]

That the legal prohibition on the state use of force—Article 2(4)—died at birth did not serve as a warning against moving farther down the path of formal, but ineffective, legalization. Instead, just the opposite happened. Human rights law now advanced quite independent of any relationship to enforcement or even compliance by states that formally signed the various conventions. Entrepreneurs of the law emerged—academics, international lawyers, and nongovernmental organizations (NGOs). Because law had little practical effect, states had little interest in opposing the rhetoric of rights and some interest in supporting an ineffective legal rhetoric.[41] What, after all, was human rights law when torture was freely practiced, genocide was possible, democratic politics was repressed by force, and entire nations were kept subordinated through military occupation? Politically, human rights law became a field of inauthentic expression; morally, it was an embarrassing expression of hypocrisy.

As long as human rights law had little practical effect, it was free to develop as a formally autonomous legal order. Indeed, there was not even a need to compromise among conflicting visions of the content of rights let alone resolve conflicts between a legal regime of rights and a political practice of state sovereignty. Without practical effect, any interest could become a right; any need could be met by a legal rule. Thus, there was a proliferation of the formal law of rights, much of it ratified by regimes that were actively violating the most basic of human rights. The no-torture rule appears as Article 7 of the International Covenant on Civil and Political Rights (ICCPR), which was opened for signature in 1966 and entered into force in 1976, just as regimes of torture became typical throughout large areas of the world. In 1985, a separate Convention against Torture was opened for signature. Pinochet was still in office, Nelson Mandela was still in prison, the United States was still supporting the Contras, the Chinese reforms had yet to begin, and in the Soviet Union Mikhail Gorbachev had just become general secretary of the Communist Party.

International human rights law had so little force in this period that it was possible to take the appearance of a legal rule as an indication that the international community was not serious about the underlying issue. One surely could not look to the law to understand the shape of state practice. Human rights law failed to represent the self-ordering of any community. Thus, this period of the rapid development of human rights law ends with the accomplishment of a modern genocide in Rwanda. And why not? Surely nothing in international practice suggested to the Rwandans that the expression of law offered an institutionalized practice to which they were bound. The same can be said of the practice of torture. The Convention against Torture was an implicit acknowledgment of the regularity of the practice; it was not a serious effort to change it.

In this political context, international human rights law turned away from the language of "progressive realization" and toward the language of principle. The original postwar strategy of first eliminating war and then working on the human rights practices of secure regimes flipped around. Instead of nonintervention leading to rights, rights would lead to peaceful relations among states. Kant had argued something similar in his essay "On Perpetual Peace": republican states will not generally go to war. This two-hundred-year-old essay was recovered by and for modern theorists.[42]

The best evidence that principle had been set free of a respect for practice is found in the definition of torture set forth in the torture convention itself.

> [T]he term "torture" means any act by which severe pain or suffering . . . is intentionally inflicted on a person for such purposes as obtaining from him or a third person information or a confession, punishing him for an act he or a third person has committed or is suspected of having committed, or intimidating or coercing him or a third person . . . when such pain or suffering is inflicted by or at the instigation of or with the consent or acquiescence of a public official or other person acting in an official capacity. It does not include pain or suffering arising only from, inherent in or incidental to lawful sanctions.[43]

Strikingly, this definition was written without regard to the practice of warfare. It assumes a world wholly outside the traditional political imagination of sovereignty. The use of force for political ends has simply disappeared from view. If the definition is read literally, combat qualifies as torture, for combat surely is the intentional infliction of severe pain and suffering in order to intimidate or coerce.[44] The sovereign power to demand sacrifice of its citizens and to kill the enemy simply makes no appearance.

No doubt the drafters of the prohibition did not mean to outlaw combat in their definition of torture, but that is just the point. They no longer imagined state violence outside of the practice of law enforcement. Not even violence in the pursuit of self-defense entered their minds. Article 51's recognition of self-defense had given way to a broader and deeper rejection of violence. In short, the formal autonomy of law, which was both a sign and effect of the Cold War, literally freed the legal imagination from the politics of sovereignty. Torture became the paradigm of political violence, and all violence—except for "lawful sanctions"—is the antithesis of law. This is the imagination that could place the prohibition of torture at the pinnacle of the legal order. We are as far as can be from the violence of the Schmittian Exception: "no torture, with no exceptions" translates into "no war; no Exception."[45]

The autonomy of law, including the privileging of the torture prohibition, was purchased at the cost of recognition of political reality. Instead of an international community under law, this period of dramatic formal expansion of law actually privileged the practice of state sovereignty. There was a proliferation of new states, each of which claimed the charter's legal guarantee of secure borders and objected to any intervention in its internal affairs—even in the name of law. Despite their formal assent to the new conventions, the successor states to the colonial regimes were generally no more respectful of human rights than their predecessors. By seeking to secure the conditions of pluralism, the United Nations helped secure the conditions of the continuation of a political practice of sovereignty. That practice remained one of imagining enemies—either external or internal. A state has a meaning that informs and makes a claim on the lives of its citizens. Because these meanings are distinct, pluralism will tend to create the conditions of threat. A contest over meaning need not turn violent, but it can. In an international regime in which violence is a traditional form of interac-

tion, difference can easily become threat. Against enemies one pre-
pares to use violence. War and torture flourished right alongside the
discourse of rights. It was an era of parallel universes.

After 1989, the premises of the international legal system changed
again. What had been a kind of fantasy of subordinating sovereignty to
law now looked like a program. It was as if the lawyers had been building models just waiting for this moment to arise. In the immediate
post–Cold War period, this often appeared as the only available program that could serve as an alternative to geopolitical dominance by
the sole remaining superpower. Indeed, for many, international law
meant opposition to the United States.

States that had formally agreed to human rights conventions that
they had wholly ignored in practice were now told that law was not an
abstraction but rather a code of conduct. In place of sovereign states,
a single legal order of trade, human rights, and international institutions was emphasized. No longer were NGOs minor players of uncertain legal status; together with the international lawyers, they had
brought us to a new world order.[46] The substantive lawmaking aspect
of this project had already been largely accomplished. After 1989, the
legal issues were thought to be primarily institutional: to create enforcement mechanisms commensurate with the single global order of
law. Torturers were now to be held judicially accountable—whether
before domestic or international courts made little difference.[47] Universal jurisdiction was invoked against Pinochet, Ariel Sharon, and
then a flood of others. Ad hoc international criminal courts began to
appear: first with respect to the former Yugoslavia and then for
Rwanda. Finally, the Rome Statute brought forth a permanent international court despite the vociferous objection of the United States,
the world's most powerful state and the one most committed to the traditional idea of sovereignty.

The 1990s were seen as the moment for the recovery and comple-
tion of the postwar project of international law, which had been suspended practically, though not formally, during the Cold War. The narrative of the second half of the twentieth century was rewritten to fit
within the most conventional paradigm of the development of law: first
a new legal order is imagined in principle (the declaration); then it is
drafted in detail (the human rights covenants); and, finally, enforce-

ment institutions are put in place (the International Criminal Court). The no-torture rule moves from the soft law of the declaration, to the hard law of the covenant and the convention, to a norm enforced by a global regime of courts. International human rights law matures from a set of ideals to be adopted by sovereign states to an expression of self-regulation by a single global community. There is no room for torture in a world of democracy, trade, and rights. It has gone the way of war.

Then came 9/11, and suddenly this narrative of the triumph of a global order of law looked as if it might be no more than the successor myth to the earlier fantasy of human rights as an autonomous order of law. Terror is not gone, and we have seen once again that the response to terror is torture. Political sovereignty is not an anachronism; war remains a force that gives us meaning. At least, these are claims that are in strong contention with the legal triumphalism so prevalent at the turn of the century. We are not yet done with the politics of sovereignty; we do not yet live within a global order of human rights law. The counter-religion announced its triumph too soon. We suffer terror, and, so it seems, we respond with torture.

International Humanitarian Law

Humanitarian law purports to regulate the forms of violence used in international conflict.[48] Generally, this body of law has two aims: first, to reduce the extent of suffering by limiting the targets and means of combat; and, second, to prevent injury and abuse to those who fall within the control of an enemy power. These aims are embodied in the twin principles of discrimination and proportionality that constitute the core of humanitarian law. Under these principles, force should be directed only at combatants and should be roughly proportional to the importance of the military objective at stake.

Humanitarian law is a deeply paradoxical enterprise, for it brings a structure of reciprocity to an essentially asymmetrical activity. As a set of legal rules, humanitarian law demands that each side in a conflict recognize the same rights and duties. But combat, as an activity of killing and being killed, moves according to a logic of asymmetry: each side seeks the advantage. Given this tension between the symmetry of legal reciprocity and the asymmetry of warfare, humanitarian law could pro-

ceed only by building an ideal of "the warrior's honor," which understands the battlefield as an autonomous domain with its own practices
and norms. Those practices can have only culturally specific valences.[49]
There is no abstract measure of the forms of violent destruction. The
prohibition on torture of combatants is one of these culturally specific
practices. That combatants can injure and kill but not torture each
other is a remnant of the code of chivalry maintained by the ethos of an
aristocratic class—the class that later supplied officers. This ethos was
based on a transnational identity that could support a practice of
honor, that is, of reciprocal recognition, which might at times run
counter to an ethos of patriotic identity. Modern humanitarian law—
and, indeed, the practice of modern combat—sits uneasily in the tension between norms of class and nationalism.

Aristocrats recognized each other—indeed, they were often related—and in that mutual recognition supported a practical etiquette
of consent even in their recourse to violence. This is, paradigmatically,
the duel, which is an early modern practice of violence that stands
alongside torture. These two practices of violence divided the world
into horizontal and vertical relationships: one tortured subordinates
and dueled with equals. Thus, anyone could be tortured by the sovereign, slaves were tortured by masters, and children (and wives) were
tortured by patriarchs. In these relationships, violence was used
affirmatively to express—or deny—recognition. To be tortured was to
be treated as a slave. The duel, on the other hand, operated in a field
of reciprocal recognition. The duel was the remedial response to a failure of recognition in an affront to honor. Where there could be no
honor, there could be no recourse to such a remedy. For this reason, a
duel between master and slave was unimaginable. For the same reason,
however, the violent revolt of the subordinated—whether slave,
colonist, or indigenous person—was always understood as the rejection
of an attempt to enslave and the demand for recognition of equality.

If recognition is the condition of politics, then the duel is an in-
tensely political act. At the moment that each threatens the other, there
is a pure symmetry of recognition. Each must fully and completely acknowledge the other, for each displays to the other a power to kill. Each
is "deadly serious." In this sense, the symbolic function of the duel is
over before the act is complete. The mutual and reciprocal threat, not

injury or death, is the end. Nations that exist in a balance of power demonstrate this same principle on a grand scale.

Even after the power to demand sacrifice moves from a sacral monarch to the popular sovereign, the duel remains a vibrant form of political expression. Americans need only to remember the devastating duel between Hamilton and Burr or to recall that Andrew Jackson, when not killing Indians, fought several duels, including one in which he killed his opponent and suffered a dangerous wound himself. Jackson's life shows us the double character of political violence: dueling between equals existed alongside practices of slavery and genocide directed against those considered unequal. Where equality is unimaginable, political violence becomes torture and terror.

Denied the remedial power of the duel, the slave/subaltern will turn to terror—nonreciprocal warfare. The master or the master class always experiences the threat of violence as terror, for terror includes an element of revolt. Moreover, absent the conditions of public acknowledgment, the terrorist's goal is not likely to be equal recognition. It will instead be to reverse the hierarchy of power. It is war between enemies, not dueling among equals. Its character is asymmetry not reciprocity. The master does not worry about democracy; he fears he will be subordinated to the freed slave. He cannot imagine the reciprocal recognition that is a condition of democratic equality. That very inequality supports a practice of torture. If terror and torture are both founded on a rejection of the symmetry of recognition, then there is little reason to believe that either side in these conflicts will look to international humanitarian law.

Humanitarian law's ambition has been to model combat on the duel rather than torture. The condition for that, however, is public acknowledgment of equality. Not to see the enemy as a "subordinate" (i.e., as an inferior) is immensely difficult. To maintain a mutual and reciprocal respect for equality between combatants is the warrior's honor. This is a peculiar sort of honor, for ordinarily we excuse the combatant's violence by breaking the link between his action and responsibility for the decision to use force. Accordingly, we face the puzzle of finding dignity at the same time that we deny agency. The resolution is to recover agency by placing it within the rules themselves: the honorable combatant chooses to remain within the rules. He chooses not to be a war criminal in a situation in which he is likely to have multiple opportunities.

When we turn to the Hague and the Geneva Conventions, beyond the prohibition on torture, we find a product of modern aristocrats dealing less with issues of honor than issues of class. Those who made the law imagined combat within the ethos that shaped their conception of themselves.[50] The law affirms the equality of an aristocratic class across borders: officers share more with each other than with their troops.[51] The elite provides a set of rules appropriate for the masses who now fight the nation's wars. Combatants are treated as a kind of international proletariat. They are to be cared for, but they are also a source of labor. War is work—dangerous work—but then so is most labor in the industrial age. Strict limitations are placed on the conditions under which members of the working class can engage in legitimate violence: they must be properly uniformed, be subject to the commands of an officer class, and present themselves openly as targets when they threaten violence.[52]

That the worker might have a political identity never appears. They are to do as they are told under the direction of their officers, who are engaged in a transnational project of managing the working class. Thus, the rules are concerned with specifying the kind of work the laborers can be given, the conditions for carrying out that work, and the appropriate compensation for that labor. In a democratic age, the elite manages the lower classes by means of a mix of claims: expertise, representation, and traditional deference. Torture has gone the way of slavery.[53] To torture is to treat one's subordinates as if they were slaves.

The development of twentieth-century humanitarian law was, in large part, the struggle to apply an ethos of class to control the democratic violence of the popular sovereign. The difficulty of the project was to militarize a population without politicizing it or, at least, without creating a space for a violent popular politics. That effort did not, and could not, succeed, for the massive war effort of the twentieth century required a deep popular politicalization. Citizens who believe that they embody the popular sovereign will pursue a politics of violent sacrifice quite independent of the rules of humanitarian law. This was seen in the violent popular struggles of decolonization and in the horrendous civil wars of the twentieth century. It was seen as well in the turn to weapons of mass destruction.

If citizens believe they are linked by political bonds of solidarity, if all are committed to a sacrificial struggle against the enemy, there is risk in every direction—including from those who seem to have fallen outside of combat and from those who never took on the formal markings of combatants. There is no release from the sacrificial demand of the popular sovereign: anyone can be asked to die—and to kill—for the state. Mao writes of the guerrilla fighter swimming in a sea of peasants. This is just a low-tech version of the capacity of the modern nation-state to pursue total war by drawing on its entire population and all of its productive resources. With that, the category of hors de combat collapses: everyone is politicized, and everyone is a potential threat.

The ethos of the Geneva Conventions, if not always anachronistic, certainly became so with the demise of the aristocratic values of honor and class on which they had been built.[54] The warrior's honor, with its implicit ideals of recognition, reciprocity, and equality, cannot stand up to the asymmetrical logic of warfare between mobilized national communities committed to a politics of ultimate meanings. Only the sacrificial claims of a popular sovereign could move the great mass of the population to support and suffer this violence. In retrospect, we can see that the popular, mass violence of modernity responded less to the ethos of class and more to that of race. A race is kept subordinate by a practice of degradation. The Western colonial practice of racial humiliation seeped back into the European metropole by midcentury. The object of that humiliation, in the first instance, was the Jew: the embodiment of racial difference in the Old World. Much of World War II, particularly on the Eastern front, where the Jew and the Bolshevik were molded into a single image of the enemy, was pursued in complete disregard of the ethos of class embodied in humanitarian law.

The Geneva Conventions were greatly expanded and elaborated after the war in an effort to recover the earlier ethos of class for humanitarian law. But by that time the forms of warfare had rendered European class sentiments anachronistic. Within Europe—as well as North America—the confrontation of organized mass armies on the field of battle was ending despite continued preparation for such a war. In-

stead, there was the threat of nuclear Armageddon, which would eliminate all distinctions and practices of humanitarian restraint. This is the
end point of the ethos of democratic warfare: total and complete
sacrifice for the sovereign. Torture drops from sight when combat is
imagined as universal destruction.

Outside of Europe, the shape of warfare was now defined by the
struggle for liberation against colonial powers. These wars were fought,
as one might have predicted, within the ethos of race and religion—not
class. They demonstrated no concern for the laboring class but reciprocal efforts to invert and maintain the governing group hierarchy.
They were, accordingly, wars in which torture was not at the margins—
appearing, for example, when there was a failure of command authority. Rather, torture and terror were paradigmatic of the nature of warfare on both sides. These are the instruments of degradation. We see
exactly what that means in contemporary Iraq, where the political and
the theological completely overlap.

Too often, the European contribution to Third World politics was
not a lesson in democratic power but rather a lesson in humiliation as
the practice of power. Not the dignity of the autonomous agent but the
subordination of race and the ideology of hierarchy were the messages
of colonial power. That power was perceived by its victims as a form of
slavery, and it provoked a comparable rebellion.[55] This is the polar opposite of the ethos of the duel, which begins from an ideal of honor
and equal recognition.

War today is still fought within the imaginative patterns established
in the wars of decolonization. Torture and terror, not the duel, govern
the imagination. This is true in Israel and throughout the Middle East.
It is true in Africa as well, where race and ethnicity have fueled civil wars
since the withdrawal of the Europeans. Even in the former Yugoslavia,
war was fought under the ethos of ethnos.[56] Neither the values of the
aristocracy nor even those of the middle class could control the violence. Today's warfare tends toward a competition in reciprocal degradation. What we saw in the former Yugoslavia we see now in Iraq. Perhaps this is not altogether bad. For the alternative to the ethos of
ethnos may no longer be the ethos of the warrior's honor, and it is certainly not the Victorian class morality of the Geneva Conventions.
Rather, the alternative is the ethos of nuclear annihilation.

The discourse of terror and torture today is also the discourse of nuclear weapons. This is just the point at which the twentieth century left us. Then it was nuclear Armageddon in the First World and torture in the Third. Globalization has brought together these distinct spaces with the result that the Third World now threatens nuclear destruction of the First. Terror threatens to go nuclear, and the response has been a "rediscovery" of torture. Hence the ticking time bomb hypothetical, for we all know that the bomb at issue is nuclear.

Conclusion

The standard account portrays the movement from soft to hard law, from sovereignty constrained only by the conscience of the king to a law of international human rights, as moral progress. That claim for progress, however, has certainly not been based on a new willingness actually to intervene to prevent the abuse of human rights. Humanitarian interventions were nonexistent throughout the Cold War; they remain rare today. After Afghanistan and Iraq, they are likely to be rarer still. Nor was the triumphalism of twentieth-century human rights discourse based on a new moralization of international relations. Throughout the Cold War, the practice of international relations remained committed to a brutal realism, whether we look at the Soviets in Eastern Europe or the United States in Latin America and Southeast Asia. Such realism is again on the agenda of American politics, as well as on that of the emerging powers: China, India, and Russia.

The real source of the claim for progress was a change in the imagination of a cosmopolitan elite. Its members sought to place "the global" within the modernist project, which was committed to the idea that political and social relations were malleable and could be shaped through the application of reason. Law was both the sign and the instrumentality of this process. More law meant more reform; more reform meant more reason. The way forward is always the way of reason.

The positive value of the equation of law and reason was matched by the negative value of an opposite equation of irrationality and bodily pain. The successive campaigns to subject first war and then torture to law are united in their understanding that the common enemy of reason is pain. This theme connects the "progress" of international law to the progress of modern medicine, as well to as the other sciences of human welfare. Medical analogies proliferate, beginning with war as a pathology of the body politic. Torture, too, is no longer seen as a political practice but as a behavior that expresses individual pathology. This turn away from pain also connects international law to the fundamental texts of modern political theory, which understand the state of nature as a place of pain and death. These "ideals" of modernity are so strong that, even after the disasters of the twentieth century, we continue to be shocked when we discover the ordinariness—indeed, the banality—of the torturer and the willingness of ordinary individuals to take up the burden of killing and being killed for political ideas.[57]

Postwar international institutions were to create the possibility that reason could be effective globally. Expert, functionally defined institutions were to manage not just the global commons but the needs of states in a global order: finance, commerce, communication, health, and environment. As these functional elements gained their own institutional forms, they began to drift free of the sovereign state. They developed their own ideals, norms, practices, and frames of reference. Consider not just human rights law, but the Washington Consensus or the World Trade Organization. Modern international law's home has been within these multiple functional approaches to the global.

By the end of the century, international legal theorists were wondering whether there would long remain any place for state sovereignty. Experts have more in common with each other than with their fellow citizens.[58] After 9/11, we can no longer have confidence that this vision of reason and law is a shared vision or that it extends very deeply into mobilized political communities. We can no longer be confident that we have left behind the world of colonialism and the civil wars that were the locus of terror and torture for much of the twentieth century. If we are still fighting wars over sovereignty, we have not yet arrived at that Enlightenment idea of expert management of the global that was so attractive to international lawyers, political theorists, and NGOs at the end of the century.

The torture prohibition was a statement about the relationship between sovereignty and democracy, as well as between violence and law. It was a founding principle of the counter-religion, representing the triumph of law both domestically and internationally.[59] But we should also remember that terror and torture are deeply embedded in democratic forms of violence. The democratic aspiration of popular sovereignty fueled the turn to these forms of violence in the twentieth century just as it fueled the politics of nuclear confrontation. Even today we see a resurgent Iranian nationalism taking up the cause of its own access to nuclear technology. In this, Iran is following the path of China, Pakistan, and India.

Many thought that the end of the Cold War represented the globalization of the rule of law. The premise of that position was that there is no longer to be a space of sovereignty outside of law. Terror, however, emerges from just such a political space. To respond to terror with torture is to reject the universal reach of law. The lawyer's insistence that torture is absolutely prohibited is only the rearguard action of an order of law that is in retreat before popular, democratic violence. The character of the enemy has changed, the tactics have changed, but the imaginative construction of meaning through sovereign violence has not.

Three

THE CURRENT DEBATE:

TORTURE IN THE WAR ON TERROR

THOSE WHO ARE WILLING to consider the use of torture today portray it as an investigative technique to be used in the war on terror. More narrowly still, torture's justification lies in the prevention of injury.[1] It is not to be a technique to investigate past crimes, nor is it to be a form of punishment. Rather, they claim that torture can be used to prevent terrorist acts that are about to occur: the "ticking time bomb." The debate generated by this hypothetical is really two debates—one moral and one legal. "Is torture always morally prohibited?" is not quite the same question as "Should it ever be legally permitted?" Separating the two debates is a useful starting point to see the way in which the consequentialist and nonconsequentialist arguments compete with each other. What is most interesting about the debate, however, is the way in which both arguments point to a set of practices and beliefs that is beyond the discursive capacities of the disputants. In both cases, we are left with a sense that torture resists the categories of the ordinary, whether of morality or law. We need to find a way to speak of the extraordinary domain in which torture and terror are at home. This is the domain of sovereignty beyond law.

The Moral Debate

Why not torture someone as a means to the end of preventing the explosion of a ticking time bomb that would otherwise kill many? This hypothetical scenario is a perfect test of one's torture sensibilities because it is always possible to raise the number of projected deaths. Would you torture to save ten innocents? If not ten, how about a hundred? A thousand? A hundred thousand or a million? How about the entire nation, the West, the globe? The moral absolutist will, somewhere in this endless escalation, meet his or her match.[2] The point of the hypothetical is to test the claim that we are all consequentialists in the end. It is just a matter of where one's personal sensibilities give way to the logic of numbers.

If this conflict between moral frameworks were all that is at issue, the contemporary torture debate would still have the merit of introducing into our public discourse the problem that has always been at the center of ethics classes. How do we reconcile the two great Western traditions of deontological and utilitarian ethics?[3] There is nothing special about torture from this perspective. Kant, for example, wrestled with the same problem in the context of his claim that morality requires an absolute prohibition on lying. How, he wondered, could he maintain that principle in the face of the terrible things that one can imagine following from telling a particular truth? Not many of his readers have been convinced by his Herculean efforts to stick to principle even when it means turning in one's friends to unjust authorities.[4] Does one tell the truth when the Gestapo asks about Jews hiding in the attic?

If Kant refused to take one step down the slippery slope of compromise with principle, his successors have been quick to point out how quickly we can slide down that slope once we take the first step. If lives saved is the currency of morality, why should we not be willing to cannibalize one person's body parts to save many? Are we willing to punish an innocent person in order to deter many from some harmful act? How many innocents are we willing to mistakenly torture for the sake of a possibility that there might be a ticking time bomb?[5] The ticking bomb example may seem an easy case since the terrorist does not evoke much sympathy, but how is the argument different in principle? How can we know ex ante that we even have hold of a terrorist or that there really is a bomb out there? Isn't our commitment to moral principle most tested—and most important—when it demands action contrary to our sympathies? A just legal system, for example, does not ask whether the accused is a good man; it asks whether the government can prove that he committed the offense.

Neither side in these debates has a monopoly on the language of morality. Bodily well-being—including the elimination of pain—makes a moral claim on us that can compete with that of adherence to abstract principle. The failure of universal access to quality health care in the United States is not just a problem of declining national productivity. It is a moral scandal to allow preventable suffering.

Sometimes the argument for an absolute prohibition on treating others as a means is itself supported by an appeal to consequentialist arguments—the tradition of rule utilitarianism.[6] Better overall results follow from a clear rule, it is argued, even if exceptional cases might otherwise be justified in a specific calculus of costs and benefits. We stick to the rule because we fear our capacity to identify exceptional cases correctly. In the present stem cell debate, for example, one starts with embryos, but pretty soon the worry is that one is acting on the sick or the elderly, and after that it is the Jews or their contemporary equivalent. Considering the fallible character of human judgment, this can be a powerful argument. Who exactly were the dangerous terrorists at Abu Ghraib?

If the ticking time bomb hypothetical illustrates a standard problem of the ethics class, then the lessons of such classes are also applicable. Teaching ethics is not a matter of showing students how to solve the dilemmas produced by contradictory normative demands but of showing them the richness of our multiple ethical traditions. Only ideologues believe that there is just one correct approach to moral issues. Such people become saints or authoritarians—perhaps the saints are only lucky authoritarians. As a society, we don't have a single answer to the problem of conflict among our normative first principles. We work within the conflict; we adopt our institutions, as well as our intuitions, to the tensions. We create institutional arrangements that reflect these different normative assumptions, and we assign those institutions responsibility for different problems. In the design of government benefit programs—that is, in our policy work—we are roughly consequentialist. In the adjudication of claims of individual rights to the program's benefits, we adopt procedures based on principles of equal dignity and respect. Asking whether something should be provided as a government benefit is quite a different question from asking whether I am entitled to participate in an existing program. Similarly, our tort law may target the best cost avoider, while our criminal law can rest on retributive justice.[7]

Looking more broadly, we distinguish between the morality of institutions and that of individuals. I may be willing to devote all of my resources to save a loved one, but I cannot ask the same of the state, which must make judgments of utility in the overall distribution of resources. I can ignore such judgments without a guilty conscience, but my political representative cannot do so without acting irresponsibly. Perhaps torture, like medicine, should be subject to a kind of triage by the state while prohibited to individuals. In some sense, considering the severity of punishments, as well as the possibility of military service, this may be just about where we are.

Even these broad institutional assignments become more complex in their details. Each of the two great moral perspectives contributes to an overall context within which the other makes sense as well. For example, we expect doctors to respect the autonomy of the individual patient, but we also expect public health officials, even if they are doctors, to be our consequentialists of bodily well-being. If the two practices fail to work together, the resulting asymmetries will violate our practical sense of justice. We will see too much care or too little. We ask doctors on the field of battle to treat all life equally—meaning they must treat the enemy wounded just as they treat their own casualties. But we appeal to this universal moral principle in the middle of armed conflict in which each side pursues the most consequentialist of all calculations: how many of them can we kill and at what cost in lives and resources to ourselves?[8]

This conjunction of principled and consequentialist arguments is equally evident in the criminal law. While we insist on respecting the procedural rights of the criminal defendant regardless of the consequences to the social order, we do so knowing that the rights have been established with a sense of their likely consequences. This is not so much an appeal to rule utilitarianism, although there is some of that, as it is a rough set of expectations about the limits of what is at stake. If we did not think that our criminal justice system did a "good" job of providing security, if we thought that the guilty person who goes free because of a violation of his rights is likely to commit mass murder, we would quickly reconsider our definition of the rights at stake or at least of the legal consequences of an official's mistake.[9] Something similar is going on in France, where there is rioting as I write this. The rules of the police process are being rewritten as the expectations within which the old rules "made sense" are shifting. In the United States, we are having the same debate over the appropriate procedural rights to recognize in the tribunals for the prisoners at Guantánamo.[10] In most states, this idea is formalized in the category of "martial law" or in the possibility of formal "derogation."[11]

In situations of crisis, we see a shift in our understanding of rights because there has been a shift in the background expectations. We think it morally wrong to convict the innocent, even if the conviction would serve the perfectly acceptable goal of deterrence. In exceptional situations, however, we might shift our view—for example, with respect to preventive detention. After 9/11, the Bush administration deployed virtually every tool it could find to preventively detain groups of individuals perceived to be "risky." It acted out of a worry about the possible use of weapons of mass destruction—just then anthrax had appeared in the mails. This is the ticking time bomb scenario. In such a situation, false positives may seem more acceptable. Courts are reluctant to intervene, and when they do they are likely to recognize an expanded scope for executive power. *Reluctance* need not mean never, and *expanded* does not mean unlimited.[12] Nevertheless, at moments of national security crises, courts are subject to the same pressures—symbolic and real—as everyone else.

Today's torture debate questions whether our moral intuitions of the principled limits on investigative procedures reflect a set of background conditions that no longer hold. The ticking time bomb example is meant to disturb the existing balance and set us on a search for a new point of reflective equilibrium. We are asked to juxtapose the picture of the collapse of the World Trade Center to that of the use of torture against a captured terrorist.

This juxtaposition forces recognition of a fundamental shift. The torture prohibition emerged in a context in which the normative issue was that of protecting the individual from the power of the state. The worry behind the ticking time bomb hypothetical is that the state needs protection from the individual terrorist. Has the availability of weapons of mass destruction to nonstate actors fundamentally reversed the asymmetry of power? The state appears no longer as the Leviathan but rather as a slow-moving, anachronistic target of prey. Terror has always threatened such an inversion because it renders ineffective much of the power of an organized military. But terror linked to weapons of mass destruction represents an extreme realization of that threat. The ticking time bomb hypothetical asks whether we should turn to consequentialism in order to reorient ourselves in this new set of circumstances.

The circumstances may be new, but the basic issue is that which arises whenever the unjust threaten to defeat the just.[13] If we argue that the rules of *jus in bello*, including the torture prohibition, should never yield, does not that conclusion reflect a set of contextualized judgments concerning the likely consequences of defeat? If defeat meant the killing of all the men and the selling of women and children into slavery—the premodern equivalent of nuclear destruction—would we hesitate to do whatever we thought necessary to avoid that outcome? Of course, we may fear that as soon as we make an exception every state will claim it, for every state is likely to believe that its defeat would be a disaster. While a healthy skepticism follows from this observation, it does not follow that the claim is never true. Article 51 of the UN Charter created an exception to the prohibition on the use of force for "self defense." The exception has been widely abused, but that does not mean that it should not exist. Should there be a similar exception for torture?[14] No such exception was written into the Convention against Torture, but why not? Was it only because the drafters could not imagine the sort of asymmetrical disadvantage that the modern terrorist may pose to the state?

One of the most famous examples of a change in context leading to a change of moral intuitions involved constitutional jurisprudence. To a majority of the Lochner Court in 1905, contract was the locus of freedom and dignity. The dissenters thought contractual relations could be regulated by the state in order to improve the material well-being of the society generally. It took about thirty years for the dissenters' view to triumph. By the middle of the Depression, it no longer seemed plausible to describe employment relations as a domain of freedom rather than one of power and need.

The perception of rights operates against a background understanding of the consequences of claiming such rights. There is no key by which we can determine where and when shifts of moral intuition will arise. They are a product of circumstance. One hundred years ago it was contract. Today it may be torture. The Supreme Court came to ask why defend liberty of contract if it comes to this? Just the same point is made today about torture: Why defend the prohibition on torture if it comes to this? The "this" is filled in with the ticking time bomb hypothetical. In 1937, the justices insisted that they could not "shut [their] eyes to the plainest facts of our national life."[15] Those who put forth the ticking time bomb example similarly insist that we open our eyes to what they see as the plainest facts of the contemporary threat.

Whenever we give up a principled prohibition for the sake of consequentialism, we are likely to feel some regret. We think we have dirtied our hands. Turning to consequences, we feel we are engaging the lesser morality of fallen man. Were it not for the fallen body, we think we could be true to principle. There will always be an effort to relieve that burden by denying that any principle is really at issue. Thus, the vision of contract as a domain of freedom is subject to withering critique: it never rested on anything more that "transcendental nonsense" or it was merely an ideological claim put forward to protect the class interests of the wealthy.[16] We see a similar move in the torture debate: there never was a moment when the state would not use torture as a tool in its own defense or the prohibition is really nothing more than an expression of Western aesthetic preferences regarding forms of violence. Those aesthetic norms, it is argued, are out of place when dealing with an enemy—non-Western—that practices terror.

Conversely, we often feel a kind of moral uplift when the change is in the opposite direction, that is, when we move from a framework of consequentialism to one of principled respect for the autonomous agent. We prove to ourselves and others that we can transcend the conditions of material need. We are, we think, treating every man as an image of God. We particularly feel this if we are giving up some material benefit by adhering to principle.

Many of the contemporary interventions in the torture debate take just this form. Those who argue against torture, even in the face of the ticking time bomb example, feel the moral uplift that comes with refusing to dirty one's hands. They practice a kind of moral celebration in their willingness to set themselves against a state that purports to act in the pursuit of their material interests. On the other side are those who resolve the dilemma by willingly accepting the burden of dirty hands that comes with political action. They accuse their opponents of naive idealism and claim for themselves the virtue of taking responsibility for the well-being of others. For both sides in this debate, character is at issue. Our moral resources are sufficiently rich to support both sides. We want to be both saints and sheriffs; we want to sacrifice ourselves and save others. Of course, often we end up sacrificing others and saving ourselves.

Casting the ticking time bomb scenario as a confrontation between the two great moral schemes of Western thought illuminates the character of the debate we have been having. That debate translates a problem of practice—Should we torture?—into one with which the theoretician feels comfortable: a competition between forms of respect for personhood. Pushed further, however, the same hypothetical shows us that this moral debate misses a fundamental element of our crisis over torture.

The ticking time bomb scenario ordinarily juxtaposes one person's claim to dignity against the interests of many in not suffering injury. The scenario can be changed slightly to test a different set of normative intuitions: not the general interest in well-being but the quality of very particular lives. Would you torture in response to a threat to your spouse, your children, your parents? Structurally, this is often the stuff of fiction: will the protagonist commit a wrong for the sake of love? In place of the utilitarian norm, we set the no-torture principle against a representation of what we imagine to be a different world of value. In love, we are rarely consequentialists. We do not tell our children that there are more deserving children elsewhere or our spouse that there is greater need outside the home. Neither are we Kantian moral agents.

Our preferences for those we love are beyond, or outside of, justice. We do not care—or care enough—that these preferences cannot be justified under the categorical imperative. We act for love, not because we have a moral obligation.

Wherever we find a source of value, we can tinker with the ticking time bomb hypothetical to test how powerfully we are committed to the no-torture principle. We can change the target from the intimacy of familial love to other subjects of great concern—for example, the Pope, the president, Einstein, or Mozart. Is it art you love or is it faith in the Church that claims your heart? Always the question is whether your love or faith is greater than your commitment to the prohibition on torture. How does your commitment to the value of a particular person or group place you in relation to a universal moral rule that attaches equally to every subject?

In fact, the ticking time bomb example elides a political source of value with a more general moral utilitarianism. The latter would be committed to treating equally the well-being of literally all persons regardless of their political identities. Utilitarians do not draw lines within the human community. Just the opposite, they wonder if they must extend their calculus to other sentient beings.[17] The intuition that the ticking time bomb example builds on, however, is not that the threat is to just any group of people. Rather, they are fellow citizens. They are members of our political community to whom we owe a special obligation of care. The hypothetical tests our political commitment to defend this particular community against its enemies. The person to be tortured is always imagined as an enemy. What looks like utilitarianism is not that at all. Instead, it is a judgment about the value of a particular political community and a question about our obligations to the members of that community.[18] The terrorist threatens the "homeland." The bomb is not just anywhere; it is here.

The contemporary torture debate substitutes the argument of the ethics class for the phenomenon of attachment to the state. That attachment is not about utility but about love of nation and the relationship between that nation and individual identity.[19] The threat to this community is not one set of measurable consequences. It is a threat to a self-supporting, ultimate value—full stop. Attachment to the political community involves an ethos of care.[20] Even *care* is too broad a term fully to capture what is at stake. Care can include the most trivial—I care about a sports team—to the most significant—I care about my children. Care for the polity is marked not just by the depth and breadth of the commitment but by the particular form of action that this commitment supports. The polity is a community sustained by the sacrifices of its members. That for which I am willing to sacrifice myself expresses that special form of care that is love.[21] For love, will we torture? That is the hard question and exactly the question that the ethics class never reaches.

The point is not that every political community demands a kind of xenophobic nationalism. Nor is it that every time the community demands sacrifice the citizen must go forth willingly. All of this can be rejected as crude caricature. What cannot be rejected is that circumstances are imaginable in which the polity can make a demand on my life and can demand that I take the lives of others. Killing and being killed are the two sides of political sacrifice. The source of that demand is exactly what we mean by sovereignty. Imagining that moment of action is the founding point of the social imaginary of the political.[22] For us, it connects the individual citizen to the transtemporal, collective subject that is the popular sovereign. This moment of imagined sacrifice for the nation is reflected back at us in the ticking time bomb scenario, which is the contemporary version of the founding myth of the state. It represents the point of transformation from the person as universal moral agent to the subject as citizen.

Politics, like love generally, is not a moral enterprise. That does not mean it is necessarily immoral. Rather, its principles and structures rest on a different normative foundation in just the same way that the family is not fundamentally a moral scheme. Politics begins with a set of distinctions that cannot be justified on moral terms, whether deontological or consequentialist. Neither of those moral approaches can offer a justification of the fundamental distinction between citizen and alien let alone friend and enemy. Citizens are those who participate with us in this community of sacrifice; aliens do not. Enemies are those against whom I can be called on to sacrifice.

Even those theoreticians in the current debate who support the demand for access to torture prefer to paint themselves as utilitarians rather than citizens. They would rather portray themselves as standing with mankind than with their state. There is nothing surprising in this. Theory itself has a certain universal quality. To take up an argument is ordinarily to appeal to a universal point of view. There are different ways of addressing the universal, which we see reflected in the debate between the utilitarians and the Kantians. What theory cannot do is offer an argument that justifies the particular as an ultimate value for an individual or group of individuals. What is required here is not the language of argument but that of faith. As citizens, we respond to rhetoric, not moral argument.[23] It is not that we ignore moral argument; after all, we are not only citizens but also moral agents. Nevertheless, these are incommensurate forms of speech.[24] Unlike moral argument, our political rhetoric will make no sense to those who are not members of our community. Rhetoric links citizenship to sacrifice. There is no universal citizenship, just as there is no universal love or universal faith.[25] These are matters of ultimate value that exist only in their particularity. In religious terms, this is the dimension of revelation: one faith's revelatory truths fail to speak to those outside the faith.

If torture is a political practice rooted in the rhetoric of sacrifice for a state that rests on the revelation of the sovereign, then we cannot expect much help from the theoreticians in seeking to grasp the stakes. Nevertheless, the ticking time bomb hypothetical can still point us in the right direction, for it shows us torture and terror as reciprocal acts of war. We lose our bearings with the hypothetical because it destabilizes whatever moral perspective we take. We are effectively asked to consider whether there is a point at which conflict becomes too primitive to be regulated by moral intuition or legal rule. The hypothetical thus opens the possibility of a space of sovereignty beyond morality and law.

That this is what is at stake with the ticking time bomb becomes clear if we consider enlarged visions of the scenario. What if the bomb is not the project of a small group of individuals, but of an entire community? We are then talking about something like the threat posed to the United States by a nuclear-armed Soviet Union—and vice versa. Not coincidentally, throughout the Cold War, the *Bulletin of the Atomic Scientists* published an image of a Doomsday Clock with its hands set at just a few minutes before midnight.[26] Confronting that threat, the state did not make calculations of utility, and it did not speak the language of respect for individual autonomy.[27] Rather, it responded with a threat of world-destroying potential. Absent the survival of this community, history itself was thought to lose all value. To understand how such a threat could be made and actually given life in the form of military deployment is the beginning of grasping the social imaginary of the political in the modern age.

The ticking time bomb scenario today steps into the place of mutual assured destruction, just as the war on terror steps into the place of the Cold War. It projects this structure of ultimate values into the microdynamics of the war on terror. At stake in the hypothetical is the state's survival. The scenario draws attention today because the imagined threat from weapons of mass destruction has shifted from the enemy state to the independent entrepreneur: the terrorist. This is the fundamental shift of context that has disturbed our prior moral equilibrium, which included the no-torture principle. In the Cold War confrontation of superpowers, no stress was put on this principle since torture was not an imaginable response to the perceived nuclear threat: who would be tortured and to what end?

The ticking time bomb problem returns us from the ethos of the post–Cold War period to the ethos of national survival that marked most of the twentieth century. A nation that was willing to use nuclear weapons against an enemy state is not likely to have any particular problem imagining the use of torture against an individual terrorist once it is convinced that sovereign existence is at issue. Just as it would have been wrong to try to understand the threat of nuclear destruction within the possible forms of moral argument—Is a nuclear holocaust justified on utilitarian grounds? Does it treat others as means, not ends?—it is wrong to think that torture and the threat of torture today represent the conclusion of some sort of moral argument.[28] In both cases, we have to think about the nature of the relationship of the state to violence and the way in which violence works to create meaning in the relationship between individual and state.

The Legal Controversy

Posed as a challenge to the absolutism of moral principle, the ticking time bomb hypothetical seems to offer few ways to escape the consequentialist's triumph. Legal scholars have nevertheless tried to bring some order to the spiral of destruction that the example invites. One approach is to attack the idea that the hypothetical corresponds to any real world case: a bad hypothetical will cause us to draw analogies where we should be making distinctions. David Luban follows this line, arguing that, in practice, there is never a "but for" moment, that is, a moment when we can confidently say that but for torturing this potential informant a deadly bomb will explode. We therefore have reason to believe that the hypothetical is really functioning to open a field of torture for other, less licit purposes.[29]

Alternatively, one can concede that the no-torture principle will fail under some circumstances but claim that the legal prohibition should still hold. Legal norms may be violated under some emergency conditions, but those conditions are themselves subject to juridification through the legal defense of necessity. The law may excuse the illegal behavior or a jury may refuse to convict under the circumstances even in the unlikely instance that a prosecutor were to bring such a case. In such instances, we don't really wish that the defendant had made the other choice—it was, after all, necessary. Nevertheless, we maintain the prohibition as a way of making a normative statement. We don't say that torture was the "right" thing to do, only that it had to be done.[30] This was the position taken by the Israeli Supreme Court in refusing to allow formal, legal recognition of a place for torture yet noting that the necessity defense might be available in any particular case.[31]

These responses are oddly in tension. Their relationship is like the cynical representation of the lawyer who argues that his client did not commit murder but if he did he had a good excuse. Just to the degree that the necessity defense is recognized, there is an acknowledgment that there may indeed be ticking time bomb situations that make compelling claims on those responsible for state security. Today we immediately think of the 9/11 attacks or various plots to blow up airliners. There may indeed be quite a few time bombs ticking around us if we mean by that plots that are at various stages of execution. The Israeli Supreme Court's famous torture decision leaves room for recognition of just this scenario and even asserts that ticking time bombs have been stopped in the past. It should know.

Relying on the necessity defense is likely to seem inadequate to the

agent who must act with the authority of the state under difficult circumstances. Asking him to do that which is explicitly prohibited by law,
with only the assurance that he may have a defense, is more than a bit
awkward. Can we think of another such instance of the exercise of public authority? The argument asks exactly the opposite of what we ordinarily demand of soldiers: they are told that they must resist "clearly" or
"manifestly" illegal orders.[32] If we tell them that their duty is defined
not by the clear prohibition—the no-torture rule—but by the necessity
defense, then nothing is ever clear. If the agent does what we would
have him do, indeed, what we believe he must do, why insist on a threat
of prosecution? If politics requires dirty hands, is there a reason why we
should not collectively recognize this?

Perhaps the state does sometimes need to perform acts for which it
cannot take responsibility as a political matter. If so, the burden of theory is to understand the nature of political necessity and its difficult relationship to the legal. Criminal law jurisprudence does have a long-
standing concern with a theory of excuse, but that has to do with
private acts of self-defense, not public acts of coercion.[33] To apply excuse here is rather like saying soldiers are excused from prosecution for
murder when they kill in defense of the state. At issue is the state of exception, not the possibility of individual excuse. We need instead an understanding of the scapegoat, for that is just what the unhappy torturer
has become.[34]

Ordinarily, we may tolerate some slippage between the generality of
a legal prohibition and its application to exceptional circumstances.
Law is always applied with a certain amount of discretion. But in a war
on terror—past and present—torture seems to be a regular feature, not
an occasional point of slippage. A war on terror is a regime in which
torture is practiced but, for the most part, unacknowledged. When acknowledgment is unavoidable, torture is condemned. Yet in the end
there are very few prosecutions.[35] Such a regime produces substantial
problems of indeterminacy for both the torturer and his victims. Neither knows what norms govern violence.[36]

Alan Dershowitz offers the classic lawyerly response of meeting a
substantive problem of legal uncertainty through a procedural innovation.[37] He argues that we should create a legal process to assess the
claim of threat under the particular circumstances. Relying on the in-

dividual investigator to decide between adhering to the legal rule or acting under the necessity excuse is unlikely to produce the optimal use of torture. There is no reason to think that such individual calculations will produce the socially best outcome. Our torturers may be those who are least risk adverse; they may themselves have a pathological interest in torture. In the absence of a rational regulatory scheme, we will end up with a torture practice that is arbitrary and capricious. We are, according to this set of arguments, as likely to get too little as too much torture.

Dershowitz proposes that judges issue "torture warrants": "I have no doubt that if an actual ticking-time bomb situation were to arise, our law enforcement authorities would torture. The real debate is whether such torture should take place outside of our legal system or within it."[38] He proposes to subject torture to the modernist program of reforming the institutions of state authority through the appeal to reason embodied in the ideals of judicial neutrality and objectivity. The no-torture principle is a failed legal norm that should be replaced by a new legal norm that properly assesses the costs and benefits of an alleged ticking time bomb situation. The problem of torture, in this view, is not that of violence but of lawlessness. Rather than repressing speech about torture after the event, he envisions ex ante hearings. With this, he would transform the violation of a taboo into the execution of law. A state that can rationally exercise violent penal sanctions should be able rationally to practice torture. That, at least, is the argument.

Were Dershowitz's proposal to succeed, it would resolve the legal indeterminacy of the torturer, who presently is in danger of slipping into the role of scapegoat. Scapegoats are produced where law cannot acknowledge the violence done on behalf of the sovereign. Dershowitz would end the practice of scapegoating by extending law to the far reaches of sovereign violence. The judge will relieve the torturer of his guilt not by excusing him but by taking on the burden of action. If torture is performed as the execution of a legal process, the relevant actor is now the judge. Because the judge's role is to be "no one" in particular, guilt is dissipated in the process.[39] Dershowitz's proposal looks, in the end, surprisingly like Arendt's analysis of administrative murder: we would have torture without torturers.[40] Juridification inevitably brings normalization.

American judges have played a similar role before. Enforcing the Fugitive Slave Act before the Civil War, the judge could simultaneously act against his own sense that slavery was morally wrong and celebrate the integrity of his action as a matter of law.[41] Even an abolitionist judge could practice the virtues of the rule of law.[42] The same understanding of the judicial role was recently expressed in *Planned Parenthood v. Casey*, when the Supreme Court reaffirmed its decision in *Roe v. Wade*. Whatever moral objections to abortion individual justices may have, they claimed for themselves the virtue of law's rule.[43] An act that might, on their personal views, be thought of as permitting murder of the unborn is instead celebrated as an act of personal sacrifice for the law. This act of self-sacrifice is offered up to the nation as a paradigm for all citizens: all are called on to sacrifice for the law.[44]

In all of these examples, the judge is to absorb into himself the violence of the state: slavery, abortion, torture. This is, after all, the ordinary course of the law in passing judgment on the criminal. Situated between the order of law and the violence of the state, the judge renders invisible—or at least less visible—that violence. We see the legal order, not the act of execution; we see the prison sentence, not the conditions inside the penitentiary.[45] That the judge can, in most circumstances, serve the function of shifting our gaze from violence to law, from pain to procedure, does not mean that he or she can do it in all circumstances. Would the signing of a torture warrant bring the judge—and us—too close to that violence? Congress may have thought so when it denied habeas review to foreign prisoners in the war on terror. Given the long reluctance of judges to involve themselves with considerations of sovereign violence in national defense, it is difficult to imagine the judges themselves embracing the Dershowitz proposal. Commentators have, for the most part, reacted very adversely to his idea.[46]

Judge and soldier represent the two foci of the modern sovereign— law and violence. They have, in effect, split apart two aspects of an older idea of an embodied sovereign: the king. The king, like the judge, spoke the law into being. But unlike the king, the judge does not carry the sovereign in his physical being. The death of the king could mean the death of the state. The death of a judge has no bearing on the law let alone on the existence of the sovereign state. This corporal element—the literal embodiment of the state—takes a new form in the age of popular sovereignty. The soldier's body expresses the sovereign will not as a proposition of law but as a willingness to kill and be killed. Two hundred years ago Thomas Paine wrote that "in America, law is king." He was only half right, for beyond the sovereignty of law there remains the popular sovereign pursuing a sacrificial politics of killing and being killed.

The contemporary debate over torture is so difficult and confusing because it keeps moving back and forth across these two dimensions of sovereign law and sovereign violence. Some would occupy one side or the other; some try to overcome the divide. The deepest question raised by the proposal for the torture warrants, therefore, is whether law can extend to the entire space of sovereignty. We have reason to think the effort likely to fail even apart from the hostile reception of the Dershowitz idea. The antebellum judges could not fully absorb the violence of the state, and neither has the modern Court's abortion jurisprudence quieted a violent political conflict. The decision to go to war is not subject to juridical norms; most of what occurs on the battlefield is beyond the reach of the judicial order. If law speaks at all, it is likely to refer to plenary powers, executive discretion, and political questions. Once war begins, the judge is no longer the symbol of legitimacy. He is literally displaced by the soldier, as the Constitution is displaced by the flag.[47]

An intuition that torture is not the business of the judge informs a proposal for a different kind of torture warrant. Under this proposal, the president would have to personally authorize any act of torture.[48] At issue is not so much legal regularity as political accountability: localizing authority in the president makes possible a political process in which his decisions can be debated and assessed. Torture is now seen as a political, not a legal, decision. It should accordingly be subject to a democratic, not a judicial, process of review. The proposal, however, is disturbingly close to the reconstruction of the sovereign body of the king. The king spoke the law but stood outside of the law. His violence was never murder. That the proposal could be supported by some in the Democratic leadership suggests just how confused our torture debate has become. This is what happens when the political process tries to speak that which cannot be spoken. We literally lose our bearings.

Carl Schmitt describes the political space outside of law as the state of "exception."[49] This is a thoroughly familiar idea in American political practice. The Constitution—the legal order—is understood to be the product of an act of popular sovereignty. The popular sovereign retains the power to reconsider and remake that order. Sovereignty, in our political experience, shows itself in the violence that precedes law and is never exhausted by law. Wherever the existence of the state is at issue—in the moment of creation or defense—sovereign violence exceeds the capacities of law.

To acknowledge the exceptional space of sovereignty beyond the law is not to say that we know exactly where the border is or even that any particular border is stable. The reach of law is entirely contingent. It depends not only on the strength of legal institutions but on the character and dimensions of the perceived threat. The important point is not that we know where the boundary is—theory cannot determine that—but that we recognize the idea of the boundary as an aspect of our own political and legal imagination.

In the United States, we have been arguing about that boundary for several years now. We don't know how far law can push into the domain of violence. When it does so, it extends an entirely different sort of legitimacy to the violent act, substituting the ethos of law for that of sacrifice, the metaphorical self-sacrifice of *Casey* for the thing itself. The measure of action is no longer the contest of sacrifice that is killing and being killed but the application of a legal rule. The guards at Abu Ghraib got caught on the wrong side of this border. The prisoners at Guantánamo, however, remain, as of now, on the other side. The biggest question of all is which side of the border the president occupies.[50] Can he occupy a sovereign space beyond law? Does he stand with the combatants in Iraq or does he execute the law?

The torturer claims that his actions are a necessary condition of the existence of the state. He defends the legal order from outside. But for him, the bomb will go off and then there will be no community at all within which to argue about the appropriate balance of utility and dignity or about the structure of due process. The torturer's claim is not different in kind from the traditional claim made for war: violence founds and protects the state as a domain of law. Walter Benjamin famously pointed out that the sovereign state celebrates its civilized culture of law while pursuing a practice of barbaric violence.[51] Today's war on terrorism reminds us that little has changed. The movement from culture to carnage can be as simple and swift as the transformation of love to hate.

That violence may be a necessary condition of law does not tell us that law can extend its jurisdiction to this foundational violence. The aspiration to juridify torture will remain an invitation declined. While the courts and the law can absorb much that is morally controversial, torture is, at least for now, beyond their capacity to transform sin into virtue. We cannot recognize torture without guilt. Here we are unable to separate legal judgment from moral judgment. If we must commit the sin, we need scapegoats to relieve us of the burden of acknowledgment.

Conclusion

I have made two strong claims in this exploration of the contemporary debate about torture. First, the ticking time bomb scenario masks a more "elemental" conflict. The academic debate borrows the ethics-class conflict between deontological and consequentialist thought in order to avoid looking directly at the moving forces of political life. Examined carefully, we find that the real conflict is between an ethos of love for a particular community and a moral universalism. Our attachments to the state are not justified in the language of morality. Rather, attachment to a community has a history and a destiny to which the individual finds himself bound. This attachment is tested in the ticking time bomb hypothetical.

Second, a related displacement is at stake in the legal debate. Law can be constructed on a utilitarian or deontological basis. It inevitably reaches across both, seeking some balance among multiple institutions and norms. The torture debate, however, is not really about that balance. Rather, it is about the relationship of sovereign violence to law. This is an old confrontation in the West, which reappears today in the competition between soldier/scapegoat and judge. Those who would prohibit torture agree with those who would juridify torture on a basic point: law should extend to the full reach of the state's sovereignty. There is to be no politics outside of law. As a political practice, however, torture locates itself within the embrace of a practice of sovereignty outside of law. The torture debate is not just a debate about the ethical foundation of politics but about the character of the sovereign—voice or body, law or violence?

To understand torture, we must inquire into the space of the exception. The exception is that which is politically necessary but cannot be spoken by law. This is the space of sovereignty beyond law; it is the space of killing and being killed for the state. Ultimately, we will have to understand how meaning is created and sustained in this sovereign space, which means we will have to turn to the fundamentals of political grammar: self-sacrifice through the violent act. This is the home of torture and terror.

At stake in the torture debate, then, are some very elementary ideas about law and sovereignty, morality and love, and finally violence and sacrifice. The ticking time bomb is actually defused when we turn to the traditional categories of moral and legal thought. We must turn our gaze directly to the bomb itself: its effort to kill and the torturous response it evokes. The example asks us what we would do to protect those to whom we are bound and what we would do to those who threaten to kill those whom we love. We already know the political answer: we will kill those who threaten to kill us. So we are back at the beginning: if we will kill, why not torture? The field of political violence is constructed through the logic of sacrifice. Strange as it may sound, the ethos of sacrifice is just where we must look to understand the meaning of torture.

PART II :: VIOLENCE AND THE ARCHITECTURE OF THE POLITICAL IMAGINATION

AT THE CORE OF THE ticking time bomb hypothetical is an exchange of lives: threat is met by counterthreat. What is puzzling about the hypothetical is why we would have any trouble with it at all, given that we would not hesitate to attack a person carrying the time bomb. We would likely do so even if we thought he was a morally innocent third party—for example, someone who does not know what he is doing, as when we are asked at the airport whether anyone has given us a package to carry. More commonly, moral innocence in this context takes the form of the conscript, who may not agree with or even understand the governmental ends for the sake of which he has been ordered to use deadly force. Enemy combatants are not necessarily moral wrongdoers. They are often victims of the same authoritarian or abusive regime that is the target of our own actions. From a moral point of view, we sympathize with such innocent persons, but the state does not hesitate to use force to eliminate the threat they pose. Mistakes will be made, that is, individuals will be tortured who have no information to offer. Yet similar mistakes are made in combat—noncombatants are inadvertently targeted or substantial collateral damage results. That the injury of combat does not sort itself out on moral lines is one of the reasons that "war is hell." Is torture just another aspect of this hell?

The ticking time bomb hypothetical asks us what we are willing to do to save the lives of those to whom we owe a political responsibility of care. Utility or welfare maximization is a poor theoretical substitute, I have argued, for this powerfully felt sense of responsibility. Equally poor, I explained, is the Kantian idea of morality as the "view from nowhere." The moral obligation to respect all autonomous, rational agents has little to do with the political situation in which we find ourselves. Once one is convinced that the enemy exists—that, for example, terrorism is an existential threat to one's own polity—then there is no stepping back behind the veil of ignorance. It is as strange to think it otherwise as to think that one should count equally the pains and pleasure of enemies and citizens in attempting to maximize welfare. That is a perspective available only in the ethics class. Of course, first one must be convinced that the existential threat is real. Absent that conviction, the ticking time bomb remains a parable of the need for legal vigilance, not a story of sacrifice.

Rejecting the standard forms of moral argument does not leave us confronting the ticking time bomb with simply an emotional response. We do not imagine action in the heat of the moment but rather a deliberate policy based on an ethos of political attachment. The hypothetical is a kind of mental shortcut designed to put us within the frame of reference of an entire worldview—one in which deadly threats are made, in which lives are literally put on the line and sacrifice is a regular political practice. It is also a worldview within which the order of law—the no-torture principle—is exhausted before the ethos of the political reaches its limits. To describe this social imaginary of violence beyond law is the purpose of the next two chapters.

Before we can understand torture and terror, we must confront the general phenomenon of the production of meaning through political violence. This is the aim of chapter 4. Chapter 5 then takes up the question of how exactly the modern state manages the fundamental tension between the legal and sovereign imaginations. How is it that we can maintain a double commitment to the rule of law as well as to the killing and being killed of the state of exception? Our arguments over the ticking time bomb hypothetical show us the confusion and ambiguity that emerge when the two social imaginaries come into contact. After 9/11, we lost our way. The hypothetical, more than anything else, expresses our confusion over how to move forward.

Four

A PRIMER ON

POLITICAL VIOLENCE

SINCE 9/11, a number of countries, including the United States, have made it clear that they are willing to shoot down civilian aircraft that threaten destruction to populations or important installations. Again, this looks like a utilitarian calculus—measuring lives lost against lives saved—but that is only partially correct. When the German Constitutional Court declined to accept a similar policy, it was not because there was disagreement on the calculus of utility.[1] The measures proposed are not matters of public health but of "national security." We make this judgment in this context because we think sacrifice is an appropriate demand within the ethos of political identity. The German court disagreed, finding in the German Basic Law guaranteeing human dignity a thorough disavowal of a politics of sacrifice. In the United States, we quickly made heroes of those passengers who brought down the aircraft in the fields of Pennsylvania on September 11. They are already celebrated in film. They have been effectively conscripted into a politics of life and death. They were aboard a ticking time bomb and chose sacrifice.

In one direction, the ticking time bomb hypothetical builds on its similarity to and difference from the ordinary exchange of threats and force in combat. In another direction, the hypothetical builds on an implicit contrast with what we might call the "hand grenade" hypothetical. Under it, you are asked whether you would be willing to throw yourself on a hand grenade to prevent death and injury to others. As with the ticking time bomb, there is a legal answer to the hand grenade problem. Instead of the no-torture principle, we find the principle that ordinarily no one is required to be a Good Samaritan at a substantial risk of life to oneself unless the required aid falls within one's professional role.[2] Even with respect to professionals, it is notoriously difficult to find a straightforward answer to the question of whether someone has a legal obligation to take an action that will certainly cause his death.[3] Must the policeman place himself in the line of fire to protect an innocent? Must the firefighter enter a building knowing he will not come out? Must the soldier obey an order that is certainly—not probably—suicidal? Could the U.S. military deploy suicide bombers? Could it conscript kamikaze pilots? Legally, one can save oneself from the hand grenade. Again, however, the legal rule does not match our political ethos.

The hand grenade test measures one's willingness to engage in self-sacrifice, the ticking time bomb one's willingness to sacrifice others. In both, we can raise indefinitely the number of deaths at stake in order to test the balancing point—the metric—between the ethos of the political and the regime of law. The ambiguity in the term *sacrifice* captures the issue exactly: the act of sacrifice can refer to the self or an other. Sacrifice is both transitive and intransitive. Whom do we sacrifice for the state: citizen or enemy? The very act of sacrifice suggests simultaneously identification with, and separation from, the victim—even if the victim is the self.

The imaginative linking of the two hypotheticals is the same intersection of killing and being killed, of sacrificing and being sacrificed, that is the experience of combat. Each combatant threatens the time bomb and absorbs the hand grenade. It is one and the same act that is killing and being killed. The juxtaposition of the two hypotheticals sounds as primitive as Aztec rituals. Is it the captured enemy who is sacrificed to the god or is it the member of the polity? The answer is both, for the ritual includes a symbolic exchange such that the former can substitute for the latter. One finds in archaic rituals of sacrifice a kind of "naturalization" of the enemy prior to his being sacrificed, followed by a postsacrifice identification, for example, in the wearing of his skin.[4]

A similar exchange motivates those proponents of torture who embrace the burden of guilt in violating the legal prohibition.[5] The torturer is to suffer the pains of guilt and the risk of prosecution. Torturing, he gives himself up to the law for the sake of the preservation of the community. He, not the actual victim, is the community's scapegoat. The victim's pain becomes the burden he must carry. Freud's image of the internalization of the murdered father is relevant here: the torturer is never free of the tortured.[6] So common is this experience that the unhappy torturer is a kind of trope of transitional regimes. We also find accounts of what seem to be puzzling bonds developing between torturer and victim.[7]

The link of sacrificer and sacrificed runs very deep in imagination and ritual. There is not much symbolic distance between the Aztec wearing the skin of the victim and the modern citizen bearing guilt. Each is seen and sees himself through the relationship with the victim. That relationship is simultaneously one of separation and identification. No country, other than Israel, is more identified with the history of the Jews than Germany. This moment of identification is also at work in the legal prosecution of the torturer. The very fact of a trial signals that his victim has been brought within the domain of law. Now he is embraced as a rights-bearing subject. He is not merely an enemy on the field of battle, nor is he the undifferentiated "stateless." He falls within the bordered space of law and has thus become like us.[8] The legal order reestablishes itself by embracing the victim and creating the scapegoat (the torturer)—a narrative straight out of René Girard's work on sacrificial scapegoats.[9]

Yet the juridification of the ticking time bomb hypothetical always seems to end with the doctrine of excuse. Excuse is the "gray zone" of necessary violence that remains beyond the capacity of the legal order to juridify.[10] Paradigmatically, it is the domain of self-defense where the threat to kill is the reciprocal response to the perception of a threat to be killed. The ticking time bomb hypothetical reminds us that civilization has its origins in the guilt-ridden act of violence.[11] The hand grenade example tells us that we overcome our guilt in the act of self-sacrifice. Either narrative can fail. We may come to realize there was neither a bomb nor a hand grenade, in which case we have only death and dying.

There is always an intimate connection between the two meanings of sacrifice: killing and being killed. The ancient Israelis hoped their God would smite their enemies but feared they would themselves face the demand for sacrifice. Abraham was promised he would found a great nation, but first he had to accept the demand that he sacrifice his son. He could not have one without the other. The double aspect of sacrifice—self and other—continues to this day. One can take another life only when one is willing to give up one's own. This economy of sacrifice is repeated in the intimate connection we feel between the ticking time bomb and the hand grenade hypotheticals. The torturer, if he is acting within the political ethos, must acknowledge that he will jump on the hand grenade. Conversely, a willingness to jump on the hand grenade creates the imaginative space for the torturing search for the ticking time bomb. By sacrificing themselves on United Flight 93 over the fields of Pennsylvania, the passengers symbolically licensed a practice of torture to discover ticking time bombs in the war on terror that followed. That license has nothing to do with law. Rather, it is the imagination of a politics of sovereignty in which those passengers act out the meaning of citizenship for "everyman." We see in them the self-sacrifice of the ordinary citizen.

In our normal lives, we do not expect to torture anyone and we are not expected to sacrifice ourselves for others. We do imagine situations in which we might do so, but these situations are more likely to be personal than political. We imagine situations of love: What will I do when my family is threatened? For love, we imagine ourselves doing the extraordinary: giving ourselves up completely—self-sacrifice—evokes a reciprocal willingness to take other lives—sacrificing them. There is nothing that is just about this. We do not subject such sacrificial actions to a separate moral test; we know we are beyond law. We respond to the demand and agree with King Lear's exclamation, "O reason not the need."[12] We imagine the threat to the family as one that materializes beyond the capacity of the ordinary institutions of law to save those whom we love. This is, of course, for the most part the stuff of fiction: plots of blackmail and revenge, of sacrifice and murder.[13]

When we turn from family to state, that which we imagine as fiction becomes history. What we know within the family as ordinary domestic life—an intergenerational project committed to the well-being of those to whom we are connected by love—we know within the polity as the rule of law—a similar intergenerational project of well-being. Indeed, they are mutually supportive: families flourish within law and flourishing families support the legal order. As the gay marriage movement demonstrates, legal recognition of family is an important aspect of recognition of full citizenship within the polity. The historical narrative of sacrifice for the creation and maintenance of the modern nation-state invokes the same imaginative structure as the fictional tale of enduring love.[14] We are, again, beyond law, and the question is what we will do. Do we meet threats with a willingness to sacrifice? Do we turn to killing and being killed? The rhythm of political life between peace and war reflects this movement between the ordinary, nonsacrificial pursuits of everyday life under the order of law and moments of sacrificial politics beyond law.

Institutional structure—whether of the family or the state—requires a mythical super structure. Robert Cover expressed this in writing that every nomos—formal system of law—requires a narrative.[15] The narrative explains the why; it tells us the meanings that are at stake in the life practices maintained by the legal rules. Just as the ethos of the family is situated within a fictional narrative of possibility, so is that of the polity. In both cases, the boundaries of the possible are marked by sacrifice. The narrative, accordingly, must sustain that possibility of extraordinary action beyond the pursuit of well-being that is the ordinary concern of the law and family. That narrative moves to the limits, asking what love is worth and what we will give up for love. The answer of both fiction and history is the same: everything.[16]

That the basic structures of our self-understanding—family, religion, and state—share an overlapping narrative form is hardly surprising. That insight is as old as Diotima's speech on the unity of the forms of love in Plato's *Symposium*. That narrative links the ordinary to the extraordinary, law to love, life to sacrifice. Our deepest narratives link a meaningful life to a willingness to sacrifice that life. We may try to push that sacrifice onto others—the enemy—but the myths of state, religion, and family all converge on the same point of self-sacrifice. The sacrificial demand is always the same: the parent must die for the child, Christ must die for man, and the citizen must die for the state. A life that fails to embrace the possibility of sacrifice appears to be without meaning—familial, religious, or political. Expressed so starkly, the point might be contested. Nevertheless, the sacrificial character of a meaningful life in the West is a virtual commonplace. A person unwilling to sacrifice wants "not universal love / but to be loved alone." This, W. H. Auden tells us, is the nature of evil.[17] Of course, it does not follow from the acceptance of love that we must enter into killing and being killed for the state. The forms of love often compete with each other. The only way to understand our debates over our violent political practices, however, is to begin from the recognition that they, too, sound in sacrifice.

Law and sacrifice demarcate two forms of life in a single polity. Each supports the other. Abraham must be willing to sacrifice Isaac at the sacred point of origin of the nation as a community under law. The sacrifice of the son captures in a single act the intersection of killing and being killed: Is Abraham sacrificing his son as a separate person or as a part of himself? Only the willingness to engage in self-sacrifice expresses a self-transcending faith. Only with that faith does the community embody a transcendent meaning that is then maintained through law. This is not a universal claim that wherever we find law we will find a culture of sacrifice. It is a claim about a deep cultural formation in the West, which was central to the revolutionary origins of the modern nation-state. It remains a vibrant symbolic structure of American political life. Our politics remains sacrificial in its narrative structure. Freud wrote that love and death—Eros and Thanatos—are the deepest structures of psyche and of culture.[18] What he did not see so clearly is that sacrifice is their point of intersection.

The modern nation-state has successfully linked law to violence not because government managed to monopolize the legitimate means of coercion but because it rests on the oldest form of realizing meaning in the West: sacrifice. A constitution, even if it is a perfect product of reason, has no existence until it is given material form among the citizens who will bring it into existence. A political idea for which no one will sacrifice has no place in the world; it belongs to no state. It is purely fictional. To take up a political idea as a revolutionary project does not necessarily change its content. Rather, it changes its existential status. Of all possible worlds, this one now moves across the line separating the possible from the actual; it moves from fiction to history. It remains in history as long as citizens are willing to sacrifice to support it.

Considered as ideas, we cannot separate out the dream of a constitution from the reality of a constitution, just as we cannot know from looking at the blueprint of a house whether the house exists. The house comes into existence when somebody invests himself in its material existence. The same is true of the state, only now the material investment is measured in lives offered and sacrificed for this idea. We can invest in many houses but only in one state, one family, and one religion.[19] The reason is the same: the ethos of love always makes a total claim on the self. In each of these domains, ethical practice begins from sacrifice, not contract. For this same reason, the truly threatening conflicts within a state arise from conflicting claims of love, that is, when family or religion challenges the political order. The increasingly common claim that citizenship should not be exclusive signals a radical shift in the meaning of political life, for we cannot imagine sacrifice for multiple polities.[20] This is citizenship stripped of politics as a field of love. Not so long ago dual citizenship was an oddity arising from the sometimes difficult intersection of private life and public citizenship. A woman who married outside of her nation, or the children of such marriages, produced the problem. Similarly, the problem was resolved at the point at which the young men served in the military: citizenship followed sacrifice. For many today, the link of citizenship to identity and identity to sacrifice seems a memory—a remnant—of a less cosmopolitan and more violent past.[21]

It is, of course, possible that individuals, including the new cosmopolitans, will sacrifice themselves for abstract moral ideals that are not bound to a particular time or place. These "idealists" may be willing to sacrifice themselves for whatever political formations appear as possible sites of instantiation of those ideals. Paradigmatically, there was the Lincoln Brigade in the Spanish Civil War and, more broadly still, the Communist International.[22] But this surely remains the exception—at least in the West.[23] We do not see contemporary brigades of volunteers going off to fight for human rights around the world. Just the opposite: the independent entrepreneurs of military expertise today are corporate entities, selling their skills.[24] They are motivated by profit and have no interest in sacrifice. We may loosely speak of "sacrificing oneself for others" when we mean participation in public interest projects, both here and abroad. Admirable as those projects are, the meaning of sacrifice here has nothing to do with the literal self-sacrifice of the hand grenade example. Indeed, just the opposite, for these are generally projects founded on a cosmopolitan idea of law and a universal conception of material well-being, not the killing and being killed of a sacrificial politics.[25] Many committed individuals working for NGOs around the world do put themselves in dangerous situations; they do give up a great deal to improve the lives of perfect strangers. It takes away nothing from the virtuous quality of their efforts to recognize that virtually all such organizations will withdraw when they become the targets of violence or when the danger to life passes a certain level. Like the fireman, the policeman, and the doctor, who need not sacrifice themselves, the human rights activist or aid worker performs a compelling public service that does not, and should not, pose the question of whether it is worth more than life itself.

Love binds us to particular political communities just as it binds us to particular families. We locate ourselves—really, we find ourselves—in communities that have a particular history and territory. That history is not universal history but rather the narrative of the successful overcoming of challenges by a particular community. It is a history of winners and losers, and we know which side we are on. From that particular narrative, we imagine a future. We see the whole from the perspective of the destiny of this particular. It is, for example, Christianity that is to become universal, not some abstract idea of the sacred. The same has been true of Western efforts at empire. We think of the French or British Empire, not a universal empire without a metropolitan identity. Even the most cosmopolitan of today's liberals is likely to be accused of being a neocolonialist when he tries to bring his idea of justice to communities living under sharia. There is likely to be some truth in this accusation.[26]

Socrates in Jail: Justice and Sacrifice

Ethical deliberation in the West begins with the problem of the structural relationship between what one will do to oneself and what one will do to others: the metaphorical hand grenade and the time bomb. This is the problem that Plato finds in Socrates' death. Three strands of ethical practice intersect in the figure of Socrates as he is tried and executed by Athens. First, there is Socrates the moral philosopher, who engages others in deliberation over the nature of the good and the requirements of justice. Second, there is Socrates the Athenian citizen, who participates in the legal practices of democratic Athens. Famously, we have the image of Socrates arguing with the personified Laws of Athens. Third, there is Socrates the soldier, who takes up the burden of fighting for the Athenian polity. At his trial, he tells us of his experience on the front lines fighting the Spartans. He also tells us, however, that when the Tyranny of the Thirty tried to draft him into acting against fellow Athenians—when they identified an enemy within the state rather than at the border—he simply refused to obey. Plato's dialogues on the end of Socrates' life are so compelling not because they resolve the tensions among these different strands of ethical practice but because they place them in juxtaposition without offering any resolution.

The central puzzle of these dialogues is why Socrates, who refuses to do an injustice to any other person, is nevertheless willing to do an injustice to himself. In the *Apology*, Socrates declines to do an injustice to himself by proposing an alternative penalty, short of death, for behavior that he believes to have been morally compelled and politically beneficial. Asked to name a milder penalty, Socrates declines, proposing instead that he be honored in the city's practices.[27] He will not consider exile from Athens. On its face, this is a puzzling position, not just because exile was a common practice, but more directly because it is not clear why leaving Athens to pursue philosophy elsewhere would be an injustice toward himself. It is, after all, the choice that Aristotle made when he was threatened by the city. If philosophy is the pursuit of truth through reason, then its practice is surely not dependent on political location. Philosophy is a universal practice. If Socrates can take up philosophical inquiry with anyone he meets in Athens—whether citizen or alien—why can he not pursue it equally well outside of Athens?

In the *Crito,* the problem of the philosopher's relationship to law becomes even more acute. How is Socrates' participation in his own execution not a willing participation in the performance of an unjust act? The problem is not that he will take the hemlock himself but that he remains in his cell when he has the option of leaving. When offered the choice, should he not escape and, thereby, save the city from the commission of a grave injustice? Hasn't he already told us that he will not commit an injustice even when commanded to do so by the city? Why should his attitude be any different when he is the victim of the injustice? Does an unjust act somehow become just when it is ordered by a democratic government? Would Socrates really participate in an unjust execution of another on the grounds that the decision had been reached in accordance with the processes of law? Surely, he would try to save another who had been unjustly sentenced to death. Why, then, will he not act to save himself when it would be unjust for anyone to kill him?

Socrates explains his behavior by distinguishing between suffering injustice and acting unjustly. Socrates, we can be pretty confident, would be willing to absorb the hand grenade but not to torture another. But Socrates' situation does not lend itself so easily to application of this formal distinction between suffering and acting. Indeed, this is precisely what we want to know. Is he acting unjustly by participating in his own execution, or is he merely suffering an unjust act? Once he has the choice of leaving, does omission become commission? Do we have a moral obligation not just to avoid committing injustice but to help others to avoid injustice as well?

Socrates' acceptance of the verdict against him is sometimes explained by appealing to a theory of political legitimacy, which relies on the opportunity he had to try to convince the jury to act otherwise.[28] In this view, government orders are legitimate, and thus binding, if certain procedural conditions are met. Those conditions include a fair chance to express one's own views and try to persuade the decision-maker. Politics is modeled on a debate and, after a fair exchange, one must be willing to accept the results. But did Socrates' trial meet these conditions? After all, he tells us that he lost because too many members of the jury were not open to persuasion but acted on long-standing prejudice. Socrates' pursuit of philosophy in Athens makes precisely the point that even a democratic political practice is never adequate to the conditions of a genuine, dialogic inquiry into the truth.

More broadly, debate is hardly an adequate model of the foundation of legitimacy of Athenian power. There are countless victims of Athenian political power for whom the model of debate is wholly inadequate. Most especially in this category are the victims of the wars in which Socrates tells us he participated. He speaks proudly of his military duty.

War raises the problem of a double perspective on the state's action. From the interior point of view, a contested action might satisfy the conditions of democratic legitimacy: Socrates had his chance to try to convince the Athenian polis to act justly. From the perspective of the enemy, however, there may be nothing legitimate about this decision at all. They had no chance to try to convince Athens to act in some other way. From their point of view, the fact that the decision was reached through a democratic process hardly makes it legitimate let alone just. We see an example of this asymmetry in Thucydides's Melian dialogue: a democratically reached decision may still amount to genocide. It is not simply that internal legitimacy does not guarantee justice but rather that legitimacy is itself only partial. If legitimacy is about process—not justice—it fails at the border. The ethos of war cannot, therefore, find a moral foundation in a theory of the democratic legitimacy of law. Kant and other liberal political theorists avoid this precise problem by arguing that republican states—that is, states with legitimate political institutions—will not go to war unjustly, for they are reluctant to go to war at all.[29]

Neither can Socrates the philosopher find reconciliation with Socrates the soldier in a concept of just war. It is hardly the case that every killing, even in a just war, is a just death. This is not simply an issue of collateral damage. Rather, at war states compel complete strangers—many of whom know nothing of the political circumstances that brought about the conflict, and most of whom would not otherwise pose a threat to another country's affairs—to kill and be killed.

This is just the sort of unexamined activity that Socrates believes philosophy must expose and subject to deliberate, dialogic reconsideration. It is not conceivable, however, that Socrates stopped to interrogate his enemies about the justice of their mutual engagement. On the battlefield, there could be no mutual deliberation on the question of whether their course of action was just. Socrates' moral principles and philosophical way of life seem inadequate to explain killing and being killed for the city even when he is himself at the center of that practice.

On the battlefield, Socrates is willing to kill for the polity; in prison, he is willing to die for it. He explains that he will not resist the verdict because to do so would be to wage war against the Laws. He will kill the enemy, but he will not make an enemy of his own city. From the perspective of justice, this is a distinction that cannot be defended. Democratic Athens not only murders philosophy, but in its pursuit of the Peloponnesian Wars, it is profligate—and unjust—in its attitude toward killing others and in demanding the death of its own citizens.

If philosophy is the pursuit of justice through mutual, deliberate discourse, it is a universal activity that is profoundly incompatible with the life and death of the citizen. Plato's underlying message speaks to the tension between politics and philosophy: democratic Athens executes Socrates. Socrates is both universal and particular, and, in the end, the particular destroys the universal. This may be the end of Socrates, but it is not the end of the matter, for Plato's message of incompatibility does not explain the puzzle of Socrates' own life: philosophy and justice move in one direction, but citizenship and the politics of killing and being killed move in another. Socrates' ambition as the "gadfly" of Athens is to bring about the coincidence of law and justice through philosophy. This is the enduring program of legal reform under the direction of reason that is the Socratic contribution to the Western political tradition: law should always be moving toward justice. Yet Socrates as citizen practices a politics of life and death, of killing and being killed, which seems to exist in a wholly different dimension. Try as we might, we cannot make sense of Socrates the citizen-soldier from the perspective of justice. Philosophy cannot penetrate this dimension of political life; the violent political act literally displaces philosophical talk.

Socrates paints escape from his death sentence as an "act of war" against the Laws of Athens: disobedience would threaten their existence. He refuses to go to war against his own city. His action cannot be understood as a response to a just demand. To think that would be to reject his central premise that philosophy provides the measure of law's justice. There is no doubt that the jury's judgment is unjust. Although the *Crito* does present the Athenian Laws as if they were making an argument to Socrates that their demand on him is just in light of the benefits he has received in the past, this argument of implied consent has never been found to be very convincing. The multiple benefits— "gifts"—that Athens has given Socrates over the course of his lifetime cannot establish a "right" to his life. Were he to emigrate instead of die, he would not be acting unjustly toward Athens. Hobbes offers something of the same argument for a contractual exchange between citizen and sovereign, but he acknowledges that the argument can never extend to the taking of the citizen's life.[30] Life, he recognizes, is not another item in the bargain but the very condition of there being any ongoing contractual relationship at all.

The explanation of the puzzle is simply not to be found in Socrates' ideas of justice, law, or philosophy. Fundamental, instead, is his idea that the city has a claim on his life. This belief is not founded in contract or the reciprocity of exchange. Instead, it points back to the same set of beliefs that could support Socrates' participation in the Athenian wars despite the inevitability of committing unjust acts in those engagements. Socrates in jail is the same Socrates who served at the front: he says as much. The common element is his belief that he can be sacrificed for the city. At the front, dying for the state is the reciprocal side of killing for the state, but the larger Socratic lesson is that dying has a political priority over killing.

The state can demand Socrates' death. He can argue against it; he can believe it to be an unjust demand. When the argument is over, however, and the state still demands death, the act is all that remains. This is the critical point: sacrifice is never the conclusion of a rational argument. Where the state can demand sacrifice is exactly the point at which it establishes its borders. Only within that domain can we argue about and within the law. Just for that reason, Socrates' debate with the Laws is premised on his commitment not to make war on the city. Were he to refuse to sacrifice, he would cross the border into the position of enemy. His cell is a metaphor for the polity as a bordered regime of law. Fleeing the cell, he would be crossing the border.

The state, we would say today, extends just as far as citizens are willing to die for the maintenance of sovereignty. Where the willingness to sacrifice ends, the border has been breached. The person who denies the state the right to demand his sacrifice is, for this reason, cast as the enemy of the state. He has committed an act of treason from the state's point of view. He has effectively declared war on the state—exactly what Socrates says—for without the willingness to sacrifice the state cannot survive. This proposition is literally embodied in Socrates. It is a lesson we will miss, however, if we look only at Socrates the philosopher.

Even today, while we might excuse citizens from taking up the burden of killing for the state, we do not offer any parallel excuse from the burden of dying for the state. Citizenship makes us vulnerable. This was no less true in the United States on September 11 than it was in Socrates' Athens. If the first Socratic contribution to Western politics is the effort to align law and justice, the second is to place sacrifice at the foundation of the state. The political lesson of Socrates' life is that law should reach for justice; the lesson of his death is that the citizen owes the state his life.

Plato does not have the language of sacrifice to explain what is at stake in Socrates' death. He is in Athens, not Jerusalem. Nor does he have the language of sovereignty to explain the configuration of a political imagination within which sacrifice is an act of realizing a transcendent meaning—realizing in the sense of bringing the transcendent into the finite world of space and time and thereby establishing a border. Instead of sovereignty, Plato animates and personifies the Athenian laws; instead of sacrifice, he describes a legal punishment. Yet without the language of sacrifice and sovereignty Socrates' death remains a puzzle. It has no adequate explanation from the perspective of moral philosophy and no adequate ground from within a theory of law. Socrates' agency, his giving of himself to the Laws that Plato endowed with a sovereign voice, takes us beyond punishment to sacrifice.

Standing outside of the Judeo-Christian tradition, Plato cannot say that Socrates sacrificed himself. He is, nevertheless, tantalizingly close to this language. Socrates' crime is the worship of other gods, which is to say that in his death Socrates will be made to bear the meaning of the city's gods. In his case, the other gods stand for the practice of philosophy. Philosophy does not know the distinction between citizen and alien; it is a capacity possessed by all who have the faculty of reason. As a philosopher, Socrates is a universal character; as a citizen, he has a most particular home. The city defends itself against its own dissolution in the universal. The universal Socrates is made to bear the burden of particularity. This should remind us of that other figure of sacrifice in the West: Christ. He, too, is the universal bearing the burden of political particularity. Together Christ and Socrates tell us that ours is a sacrificial culture.

Socrates, who would reform the city to bring its laws into line with reason's idea of justice, is killed. He thereby shows us that the foundation of law has little to do with justice and everything to do with violence. The original sin of politics is the violent act that creates the bounded domain of the city itself. Law may promise peace, but its birth is in violence. The domain of law is maintained at the border literally by killing and being killed. The city can maintain itself only as long as its citizens are willing to take up the burden of sacrifice in defense of this political space. Socrates chooses to die not because he believes the law to be just but because he will not go to war against his city. By acknowledging agency, the Socratic act exceeds the jurisdiction of law; it becomes the act of sacrifice that maintains the state in a political space of sovereignty. Socrates' last act is not that of the moral philosopher but that of the political martyr. Socrates does not die for philosophy but for Athens. His death is beyond justice, as is every act of sacrifice.

Sacrifice and Pledge

Ironically, in Plato's dialogues on Socrates' death, language fails. Trying to explain himself, Socrates claims only that he will not perform an unjust act. When we press the argument, however, it is no more clear that his action is just than that it is unjust. The problem arises not because we don't know the nature of justice—we are quite sure that his death sentence is unjust—but because we can't identify the behavior as action or suffering. Is Socrates the suffering object of injustice or is he a subject performing an unjust act that just happens to be his own execution? The answer to this dilemma of characterization is not to be found by deciding that he is active rather than passive or vice versa. He is inevitably both. We need, therefore, a category of behavior that is simultaneously both active and passive. The concept that we need is that of sacrifice.

Sacrifice is giving up oneself to be acted on. As is suggested by the word *passion,* it is a performance of suffering. Of course, we speak loosely of sacrifice whenever we mean giving up something of value. We see the tendency toward commodification of values in a market society when the word *sacrifice* is used to speak of an implicit exchange, for example, "I sacrificed a day off for the sake of getting a business project done." We get closer to the traditional meaning of sacrifice when we speak of sacrifice for family: "I sacrificed my dream of being an artist for the sake of my children's well-being." Here there is still carried forward an idea of actively making the self an object of destruction in the giving up of a life plan. There is the double character, active and passive, of the sacrifice. One acts for the sake of love, but what love requires is a kind of self-destruction. Sacrificing for my family can suffuse my action—the taking on of burdens—with extraordinary meaning. Sacrificing, I become a point of revelation of a larger meaning. I do so by bearing the burden of the profane. Of course, the same individual moves back and forth between these experiences, often not knowing if he is rising above himself or sinking under the weight of finitude. Jesus and Socrates both suffer doubt in the moments before death. So does the combatant. Revelation is inseparable from destruction, the sacred from the polluted, and life from death.

Part of the confusion over the character of sacrifice is semantic: *self-sacrifice* sounds as if it is only one subcategory of sacrifice. But all sacrifice drives toward self-sacrifice. I don't mean this literally, as if all sacrifice must end in the death of the sacrificer. Nevertheless, all sacrifice is about the transformation of the profane character of the self into an instantiation of the sacred. Short of that symbolic transformation of the self, sacrifice is only the exchange of one finite good for another. One must give up the self to take on the sacred; conversely, the presence of the sacred destroys the finite self. Sacrifice is this exchange of incommensurables, the object of which is to make present the sacred.[31] The first moment of sacrifice is always a dying of the self; the second is sacred presence. The third, or synthetic, moment is a showing forth of the sacred presence in and through the exercise of a power to destroy: the sacrificed becomes the sacrificer. Man becomes god, but this miracle of transformation is inseparable from destruction. The logic of the change is imaginative, not chronological. Being killed and killing can converge in the single act of combat. The sovereign wields the power of life and death, not because of a social contract, but because whoever claims sovereignty stands at the far end of this exchange.

Sacrifice involves the realization of a transcendent or ultimate meaning within the conditions of finitude. That is not an experience that can be observed from a distance; it cannot be bought or assigned to others. It is the opposite of commodification, and it is impenetrable to logic. It exists only at the intersection of being and meaning, which is the experience of sacred presence. Absent that experience, sacrifice makes no sense, for killing and dying cannot be a means to some higher, but finite, end. Absent that meaning, we never escape the conundrums of Socrates' death.

Sacrifice, like love, is of the body. Nevertheless, we must be expansive in our understanding of the boundaries of the self. Sacrifice is of the self, but it forces us to recognize that the borders of the self are not always those of the finite body. Abraham was giving up a part of himself in Isaac. The family of the conscript is sacrificing itself in the body of the child. The state is sacrificing itself in the body of the citizen. Indeed, it is not too much to say that the boundaries of the self only become clear through the imagination of sacrifice, for sacrifice circumscribes the limits of a world. Beyond these boundaries, I may have interests and concerns, but they are of measurable value and can be subordinated to other ends. The boundaries of sacrifice are those of love, which is always beyond measure.

The movement of all sacrifice toward self-sacrifice is misunderstood if we think of this as the limit of an economic equation that traces value for the individual, as if the value of the self is the end point of this function. Rather, sacrifice destroys the limits of the finite person and puts in their place an experience of the sacred. Finite experience can be interesting; it can also be entertaining. But interest and entertainment are not the sacred. No matter how intense, they are not sufficient to overcome the existential angst experienced by a subject aware of his own finitude. The finite self seeks a meaning that can overcome death itself. Every sacrifice is an exercise in the symbolic dynamics of resurrection. Through death is life. This is the violent act of sacrifice, which destroys in order to create. When sacrifice fails, we are left with only the evil of killing.[32] We may be victim or perpetrator—or both. In either case, in the absence of the sacred our actions are measured by law.

The movement of sacrifice toward self-sacrifice is clear in politics: to sacrifice for the nation is to put one's life at risk. Taxes, even high taxes, are not a sacrifice for the state. This is not because sacrifice can never be satisfied with mere property but because sacrifice is always beyond the regulatory order of law. It is beyond measure—it is "the last full measure"—while law is all about measure. As Aristotle already explained, justice is a matter of measure.[33] A tax regime should be specified by law, and it should be just. That which cannot be measured is beyond justice. The American founders pledged their wealth, but that would not have counted as a new beginning had they not also pledged their lives. Without the latter, the former is only an investment. When we speak of the "ultimate" sacrifice, we refer to an active giving of oneself to death.

The sacrifice of the self is the creative act of destruction that is the realization of the presence of the sacred. In politics, this sacred presence is the "sovereign." To understand what is at stake, we have to turn to the political rhetoric of memorialization.[34] We need Lincoln at Gettysburg, speaking of those "who gave their lives here that that nation might live." Their sacrificial act was a consecration of the battlefield, that is, they created a sacred space by making present the sovereign. Ultimately, this space expands through the presence of the sacred to include the entire nation. The boundaries of the nation literally stretch as far as the potential lines of battle at Gettysburg.

We can imagine a social contract as the source of the normative content of a legal order. Indeed, Lincoln comes close to this at Gettysburg when he speaks of the ideas that inform the content of the constitutional order: a nation dedicated to the proposition that "all men are created equal." If we want to know how to elaborate that proposition within a legal order of rights and responsibilities, we might turn to a philosopher—perhaps John Rawls or even Plato himself. Such inquiries describe the just content of any legal order. Rawls and Plato are the universal possessions of mankind. Socrates, however, does not owe an act of sacrifice to the idea of justice, which is why we can never quite make the arguments of the *Apology* and the *Crito* work. Sacrifice runs only to the actual state: one founded at a particular moment and in a particular place by the pledge of "our fathers." That state gives us our particular burden to ensure that it "shall not perish from the earth." Of course, no one need accept this burden, and my point is that it is neither a just nor an unjust demand. A person willing to sacrifice for the cause of justice wherever it arises appears oddly stateless. He is practicing politics as a saint, not a citizen. If we are honest about him, he appears as the least political of men. When entire communities purport to pursue such a practice, they are rightly suspected of neocolonialism.[35]

Politics begins not in the social contract but in the pledge that expresses a willingness to sacrifice the self for the particular community.[36] It begins with Abraham's response to God's demand for sacrifice with the single affirmation, "Here am I." The pledge establishes a kind of transparency between self and community—a literal coincidence of boundaries. The pledge is not simply an agreement of reciprocal defense. Nor is it merely the creation of a corporate agency. Reciprocal defense and the structure of the corporate agency are only possible after the political community has come into existence. The pledge is a performative utterance in the same way that every ritual brings forth the sacred. The pledge to sacrifice shows forth the self-evident truth that is the transcendent value realized in the coming into being of the sovereign community. In Arendt's terms, the pledge is the equivalent of birth; in religious terms, it is the equivalent of communion.[37]

The founding pledge of a democratic community steps into the place of the earlier oath of allegiance to the sovereign. As with the oath, it only makes sense in reference to a transcendent value of sovereignty. The sovereign does not gain its value from the pledge, as if it were the aggregation of the value of all these lives. That is to measure the immeasurable. Rather, the pledge is made from within the experience of the sacred value of sovereignty. The dynamic here is beyond the ordinary categories of active and passive. It is instead the dynamic of sacrifice: pledging a life, one is born again into a sacred life. The pledge puts one in a position to realize the grace of sovereignty, but without the pledge there is no showing forth of that grace. This is a very old point: God is as much in need of man's prayers as man is in need of God.[38]

The pledge, then, is the point of contact between sovereign and sacrifice. It is the acknowledgment of the sovereign power to claim a life: one pledges one's life. Whether one lives or dies is no longer the important point, for one has already given oneself to the sovereign. Symbolically, one has already given up one life for another. This is the political replication of Paul's assertion that the Christian has already died on the Cross with Jesus. To sacrifice is to act on the pledge; to pledge is to enter a sacrificial world. As long as that world exists, sovereignty remains present.

No individual can make a unique claim to sovereignty in the postrevolutionary world. The execution of the king, however, is hardly the death of the sovereign. The popular sovereign is potentially present in every body; it appears wherever sacrifice is accomplished. Similarly, without a king the personal oath of allegiance is displaced by the pledge, and the object of the pledge must be a symbol of sovereign existence. Famously, Americans "pledge allegiance to the flag."[39] The flag can call forth sacrifice, and, indeed, we know that soldiers will fight and die for the flag.[40] Upon their deaths, they are literally wrapped in the flag. To those outside the sacrificial community, this must look like idolatry. For this reason, certain religious groups refuse to perform the act of the pledge.

Not surprisingly, Americans fight endless battles over the appropriate character of the intersection of law, pledge, and flag. Pledge and flag exist in a world of sacrifice while the world of law is one of justice and well-being. Again not surprisingly, the locus of these battles is often the classroom, which must pass on a conception of citizenship that encompasses both law and sovereignty, well-being and sacrifice. We can never get this intersection exactly right, for it is subject to neither logic nor measure. Nevertheless, the revelatory moment of the sacred must found and refound a state of law: revolution must lead to constitution. The American Pledge of Allegiance connects flag to nation and nation to liberty and justice. Conversely, through the Constitution one sees the sovereign, or at least traces of sovereignty, in our ordinary lives.[41] Law, justice, and reason never fully displace sovereignty and sacrifice in our political life.

A political community has a transcendent meaning for its members. If it loses that meaning, then it will lose the capacity to demand sacrifice, even if it remains a just community. Such a community, we would say, lacks sovereignty or sovereign power. One can believe, for example, that an economic community represents a just distribution of goods and services, but that hardly means that one is willing to sacrifice the self for the maintenance of that community. No one sacrifices himself for the maintenance of the World Trade Organization, even if one truly believes in the justice of its project. No one pledges allegiance to the United Nations, much as we might appreciate its efforts in support of international justice. These institutions aspire to justice, but they are not sovereign communities. Justice as a moral norm simply does not create an obligation of sacrifice, although it surely creates obligations of redistribution. Redistribution, however, is not sacrifice no matter how much it takes from the wealthy.

To think we can displace political sacrifice by other forms of the intersubjective creation of political meaning is like thinking that we can displace belief in God yet hold onto the ethical practices of the religious community. Perhaps we can, but the meaning of the community is no longer the same. Even were the community to become more just, we would be in a different sort of world. The church did not come into existence to do good but to save souls. A religion without God is one without the possibility of sacred presence of a transcendent other. This may remain an ethical community to which individuals are attached by tradition or choice, but it does not exist in the same category as a practice of faith in the sacred. A polity without sacrifice may be a just community, but it is not the sovereign nation-state.

Justice does not, and cannot, explain the destructive power of the modern nation-state any more than it can explain Socrates' death. When the state becomes as deadly as the state of nature—or, in fact, far more deadly—we can no longer believe in the social contract as the foundation of political obligation. There was no appeal to the social contract in the trenches of World War I and none on the Eastern Front in World War II. Nuclear weapons would not be imaginable if the state were only the vehicle for the enforcement of a just legal regime seeking individual well-being. To understand the threat of such destruction, we need to distinguish pledge from contract and love from self-interest.

The individual's death for the state is not the short and nasty death of the state of nature, in which each person dies alone. Death for the state is sacrifice. It occurs in a symbolic dimension simply not available in a prepolitical state of nature. The state does not make life safer; it makes it meaningful. Today some argue that the military power of the state should be used in the pursuit of human rights: humanitarian intervention. This might very well contribute to the achievement of justice around the world. But one still must explain to the citizen asked to sacrifice why the injustice suffered by noncitizens is worth his life. I may object to the injustices of others, but I am not ordinarily required— morally, legally, or politically—to sacrifice my life to prevent that behavior. I do not throw myself on that hand grenade; I will not sacrifice my child for their god. Sacrifice, whether for family or state, is grounded in love, which is bound to a particular community.

Citizens will defend the state with their lives. This is not the conclusion of an argument but the phenomenon of the political as it has appeared in the West. In politics, as in religion, we do not seek to understand in order to believe but believe in order to understand. In neither case can we understand these practices without faith. Believing in our participation in a transtemporal sovereign, we understand the demand for sacrifice. We are no better at grounding this demand in the language of justice and law than was Plato.

The cultural phenomenon of the political is not a fact about human nature, as if every organized community is necessarily based on sacrifice. Nor am I making the normative claim that every society should be based on a willingness to sacrifice. Rather, I offer a reflection on the character of the Western experience of the political. Our politics is just that: ours. One can trace the genealogy of this cultural construction, observing the intertwined character of the political and the religious—the political-theological—and one can describe the architecture of the social imaginary of the political.[42] Standing within it, one can try to reform the practices and beliefs of the state. One can try to make them more just. But one cannot create gods where they do not already dwell, and one cannot defeat their presence by argument.

Of course, we must question whether this cultural formation will survive in the competition with other forms of contemporary life. What we cannot do, however, is make any sort of global judgment as to whether its demise would be good or bad, just as we cannot make a judgment of whether its past has been good or bad. Every actual construction of the social imagination is bad compared to one that we might imagine to be better, but that is just playing games with history. Would the West have been better off without the sacrificial imagination of the political? Why stop with politics? How about religion or capitalism? When we ask such questions, we imagine everything else staying the same but for the elimination of one set of practices and beliefs. This is like asking whether I would have been better off had I been born in a different era or a different country. At best, it is nonsense; at worst, it is a failure of intellectual courage masquerading as idealism. To those in thrall to the sovereign, the sacrificial demand simply is the way the world is. The force of sovereignty is not different, in this respect, from the force of gravity—or, more pointedly, from the fact of death. We can imagine a world without gravity, and one without death, but that is not our world.

Sacrifice and Revelation

Neither the quest for justice nor the calculation of costs and benefits will bring us to sacrifice. Only the sacred can do that. Revelation is the religious expression for the experience of a displacement of the profane by the extraordinary claim of meaning that is the sacred. An ethos of sacrifice rests on an experience of revelation. This religious language of revelation quickly merges with the language of love—love of God, of family, or of state. For the secular minded, it is easier to think of love than revelation, but both point to the same experience. The object of love reveals a domain of transcendent value that is not subordinate to any other interest, including life itself.[43] The action of love is sacrifice—to give up the self alone—through which one realizes a meaning revealed in the object of love.[44] This is a tradition that can easily slide from the hand grenade to the ticking time bomb, from sacrifice to torture. Did not Isaac experience a kind of torture as his father prepared the sacrifice? For love of the state, we not only die but we injure and kill.

This tradition of sacrifice is one into which our practice of citizenship squarely fits. It draws equally on an idea of revealed truth—"We hold these truths to be self-evident"—and on love of the nation. The sovereign is, as Lincoln explained, constituted by those who hold these truths to be self-evident. This "holding forth" is not merely belief in their truth. Belief that these are correct moral propositions is not bound by national borders. Liberal states are in general agreement about the fundamental principles of a constitutional order. Such agreement by itself, however, does not constitute a political community. Americans and Canadians share a common belief in liberal principles; they also live in close proximity to each other and freely interact in private life. They are not, however, members of the same political community because such a community arises only out of a holding forth in the pledge to sacrifice. Americans and Canadians do not pledge allegiance to the same sovereign.

None of this means that our lives are ordinarily filled with dreams of martyrdom, although that can emerge under certain circumstances. It does mean that such sacrifice appears at the edge of possibility; it is a not so suppressed memory of the future. We remember past sacrifices as future possibilities. We might be "conscripted" to sacrifice for the object of our love. In that case, we would not be unwilling conscripts, even though we might be undesirous of that role. We would show ourselves, we hope, capable of sacrifice—of course, not everyone and not all the time. But such is the national ethos of the political, and we will not understand the political situation in which we find ourselves without beginning here. The young dream of being heroes while their parents hope that the occasion does not arise. That dream contributes to the militaristic edge of our own republican tradition, which was very much alive in the imagination of the American founders, who did seek fame through action. They put the possibility of sacrificial service at the center of their romance of the political.[45] We go wrong, however, to focus on this romantic longing. The demand for sacrifice can expand to the entire citizenry, and it might not be romantic at all.

Liberalism, despite its claim to express a normative order derived from reason itself, is the "fighting faith" of particular communities. The liberalism that supports faith is never free floating, any more than Athenian democracy was without borders. We are attached to *our* liberalism, not to liberal systems wherever they appear. Our Constitution, Americans believe, is both the product of the new science of government and a "sacred" expression of the will of the popular sovereign. The former is universal; the latter is not. Our nation was "brought forth" by our "forefathers" not by John Locke.[46] We are the inheritors of their sacrificial acts. When American children learn that it is a political virtue to "defend to the death" the right of someone to proclaim an idea with which they deeply disagree, they are not thinking of a global market in free speech.[47] They are thinking of the character of the community to which they are attached through a political imagination that includes, at its border, the idea of their own sacrifice. Free speech as a legal ideal remains just that—an idea—until someone is willing to take up the burden of sacrifice to make it real. To take up that burden is to found, or to refound, a political community. When Jefferson writes, "We hold these truths to be self-evident," the politically important aspect of the proposition is the "we hold," not the propositional content that is the object of that act. As long as the "we" holds, the popular sovereign continues even as citizens debate what exactly is included in these self-evident truths.[48]

The state begins with a showing forth of the sovereign—the founding pledge. That showing forth is always self-evident to those in its grasp. The truth of revolution is self-evident not in the sense of taken for granted but in the sense of revealed. Self-evidence moves in the dimension of the sacred, not the rational. We may be convinced of the truth of many propositions, but they do not found a political community. Even communities with substantially similar constitutions do not, for that reason, become indistinguishable; they do not necessarily even become friends. The sacred is self-evident because there is no test of its truth apart from the character of the experience itself. It is fundamentally incommensurable with propositional claims in the same way that all religious truths are incommensurable with ordinary language. My god is never "like" your god. It is either wholly the same or wholly different.[49] One either falls within the experience of the sacred or one does not. The mutual experience of the self-evidence of the sacred leads to the reciprocal acknowledgment of the pledge.

We cannot explain how or why it is that an individual finds some group, person, or idea worthy of sacrifice. It is not the reasonableness of the idea that grounds its transcendent quality. Sacrifice never makes sense within the terms of our ordinary lives—that is the whole point. It is ground never consequence. There is no justification of love, no argument by which I can deduce what I love or should love. There is no calculation by which I can determine whether I am better off with love. Love, personal or political, can be full of pain and tragedy. Indeed, it is inevitably touched with pain. All that can be said is that this is where I find a claim so powerful that I take my stand and can do no other. Here is where I find myself, and without taking up this idea fully and completely I would not be who I am. Indeed, the risk is that I would not be anyone at all.

This link between revelation, love, and sacrifice explains why we are so quick to speak of "truth" in all of these contexts. This is not the truth of an empirical proposition but the "truth that sets you free." *Truth* here refers to the objective character of a transcendent value. These truths are always "self-evident." Truth—whether the truth of Christ or the truth of the popular sovereign—is realized in the giving up of the finite self. In politics, that giving up—sacrifice—takes the form of a willingness to kill and be killed. We must literally "make something of ourselves"; we must make of the body a signifier, transforming our identity from body to idea. The word must become flesh. We give ourselves over to an idea that is revealed to us as a truth that tells us who we are and must be. Failure to live—and die—in accordance with this truth is felt as if it were to accept the conditions of the slave, which are always the opposite of those of the citizen. The Jews literally lived as slaves until they were brought forth by the truth God revealed to Moses. They had to be that truth. The American revolutionaries continually accused king and Parliament of treating them as if they were slaves. Slavery figures in the revolutionary imagination as a failure to take up the burden of sacrifice. Dignity begins only with the willingness to give up the body. The slave, Hegel argued, chooses life over death. This is one of the oldest and most enduring legacies of the West: true life begins only with the acceptance of death. A person is a slave just as long as he fails to take up the cause of his own freedom by embracing sacrifice.[50]

Men of goodwill are continually attracted to the idea that they can create a new form of political order simply by setting forth their vision of a rational constitution. But the problem of politics has never been the absence of reason. Individuals are always present who actively imagine a perfect politics of reason in one form or another. The problem is that these ideas fail as politics because they are not the object of anyone's will. No one will take them up as a project for which they are willing to sacrifice. Until then, they are literally dreams: insubstantial imaginings. These ideas might be demonstrable, but they are not self-evident.

Ritual and Contest

Broadly speaking, Western sacred practices take two forms.[51] One form links the sacred to ritual; the other links the sacred to a sacrificial contest. At stake are competing forms of access to a transcendent meaning. The Catholic Church remains an example of the former: one is born again in the body of Christ only in and through the rituals of the sacrament. The foundation of the Church is a sacrifice that the faithful view not just as paradigmatic but as one in which they must participate. That participation is mediated through ritual. Absent the institutional structure of ritual, the host is only bread. Outside the rituals of the Church, the body remains firmly bound to the world of death that characterizes all that is material. Such ritualized access to the sacred stands in contrast to that immediate presence of the sacred celebrated in forms of charismatic Protestantism. The immediacy of the sacred presence, which is always felt as a contest with the ordinary state of fallen man, takes a particular agonistic shape in Western political culture. Here the heroic personality models the ethos of sacrifice as killing and being killed.[52]

The two forms can be hard to distinguish in any particular case. Nevertheless, certain broad characterizations are possible. Both share an aspiration for overcoming the limits of finitude. Ritual, however, denies the individual subjectivity from the beginning. We don't remember the names of those who participate in a ritual. The giving up of the self is a precondition of entering into the ritual process—confession before grace—whereas that giving up is the outcome of the agonistic contest. Ritual is an activity directed from without; it follows a script. Because it follows a script, it becomes the object of its own self-reflection. There is no ritual that does not generate a theology. Without an external script, the heroic contest has a uniqueness about it: it is bound to particular circumstances. The heroic sacrifice is a test in which failure is a possibility as well as a matter of personal responsibility. The speech of the sacrificial contest shares the immediacy of the practice; it is rhetoric—poetry, praise, or memorialization—not theory.

Ritual is a mediated form of sacrifice. Mediation allows not only the theorizing of reason but also the displacement of that destruction of the self, which is sacrifice. It also allows security: the faithful know when a ritual is complete, for it contains its own measure of success. The contest, on the other hand, is an unmediated form of sacrifice: the combatant kills and is killed. He realizes in his own body the presence of the sovereign in the act of sacred violence. The unmediated exchange of life and death in the contest actually makes problematic the combatant who fails to die.[53] Lacking assurance of ritual transformation, those who live may lack proof of their sacrificial identity. When others have died, they will ask themselves—and others will ask of them—the meaning of their survival. Did they give enough? In a sacrificial culture, life, not death, is problematic. We puzzle about the suicide bomber in Iraq, but he is no different in his agonistic character from the numberless American citizens who have made the "ultimate sacrifice" for the nation. Their death registers as the life of the sovereign.

According to René Girard, ritual develops in order to displace the cycle of violence—of killing and being killed—that arises out of the first act of killing. The ritual acts as a symbolic affirmation of sacrificial violence while containing its spread.[54] Girard's account, in my view, is too totalizing and mechanical; it is not sufficiently responsive to the meanings realized in and through the violence itself. Yet the distinction between the unmediated violence of the contest, on the one hand, and ritual, on the other, must be observed if we are to understand our own culture of political meaning. Girard is right to emphasize the way in which ritual closes down violence while the contest opens up violence. He does not, however, pay enough attention to the sacrificial character of the contest, for it, too, is a form of sustaining the presence of the sacred.

American political life appeals to both forms, the ritual and the contest. Generally, however, it keeps them separate.[55] One defines the ethos of the rule of law; the other, the ethos of popular sovereignty. We practice a form of unmediated sacrifice in the commitment to political violence, which can demand of each of us the heroic act of killing and being killed. The ordinary citizen who rises above himself to become the site of violent self-sacrifice is one of our most popular national narratives. The story we want to hear is that of heroic transformation moving the ordinary citizen—farmer, laborer, student—to a sacrificial performance. We see constant efforts to memorialize the individual actor in his sacrificial death. The heroic act of sacrifice is always unique and always beyond the law. As I have argued, law, even the law of the battlefield, can never quite demand individual sacrifice.

That law has elements of ritual is obvious—for example, the behavior of the judge and jury, the procedure of courtroom argument, and even the structure of the courtroom. Nevertheless, the significance of ritual is often overlooked in considering the ground of law. Instead, we see the legal order as an expression of reason. We imagine the end of law to be individual well-being and legal rules to be a means to that end.[56] As participants in a culture of law, we see law through the frame of its own self-understanding or what I have elsewhere called "auto-theory."[57] This view of law is not wrong; it is just incomplete as an account of our investment in law. We do locate our hopes for the ordinary benefits of political security in the rule of law. After all, part of the point of ritual—religious or political—is to relieve the pressure for sacrifice and thereby make it possible for individuals to go on with their ordinary lives.[58] Religion, too, promises individual well-being and the security of daily life. It does so by routinizing the sacred, which means ritualizing—that is, creating mediated forms of access to—the sacrificial. Law follows this same pattern.

The judge offers a paradigm of the function and meaning of the rule of law as ritual. He personifies the sacrificial conditions required of a system of ritual. This sacrificial demand is most evident in moments of transition, for example, in the American process of judicial confirmation.[59] The nominee must publicly disavow his previous opinions, interests, and connections. He must promise to bring none of his prior self to his future role as judge. He gives up his former self and puts on the judicial robe. Only when he has done so can he appear to speak as a representation of the sovereign voice. This is not just the creation of a legal priesthood; it is a paradigmatic performance of a common ritual of citizenship under the rule of law. The court offers this ideal of symbolic sacrifice in and through law when it seeks to avert the literal violence of political conflict—for example, it recently asked all those opposed to abortion to give up their personal views for the sake of the rule of law.[60]

Those who claim that there is no politics beyond law, and that the ground of law is reason, have failed to grasp the continuing role of sacrifice and the sacred in the modern state. Not even the rule of law rests on reason alone. The Constitution operates as a sacred text. It is not just a particularly successful effort to establish the rule of reason. It is grounded, on the one hand, in the act of sacrifice that begins with the Revolution and, on the other, in rituals of self-denial maintained by our legal institutions. Both grounds lead back to a vital idea of sovereignty as a source of the sacred. That our law has, for the most part, been successful at relieving this pressure by localizing the violence of the state—for example, in the penitentiary—and mediating sacrifice does not mean that it can absorb and mediate every form of sacrificial violence. We cannot set the limits in the abstract. The question of torture in response to terror is just the question of where the mediating function of law ends and the politics of sovereignty as unmediated sacrifice begins.

Traditionally, the political space beyond law was the domain of war. That is the space from which the contemporary phenomena of terror and torture emerge. The legal theorist's understanding is exhausted when he describes torture and terror as "illegal." This is true but trivial. It fails even to take up the nature of the political imagination that supports these practices. Theorists fear that any effort to take up a phenomenology of the political could have the effect of legitimating what they view as political pathology, which is understood as the pursuit of emotion in place of reason, of violence in place of well-being. On this understanding, religious sensibilities, including revelation and sacrifice, have no place in politics. This vision of the nature of political order fails as a description of modern political practices precisely because it has no idea whatsoever of sacrifice as the realization of the sovereign presence. In fact, liberal states—and particularly the American state—have been deeply committed to a sacrificial politics of sovereignty in its unmediated, agonal form.

A state that no longer thinks of itself as capable of demanding a life has passed out of the political ethos of modernity. The narrative of such a state can no longer invoke the myth of sacrifice or the experience of revelation. The politics of revolution and the dynamic of sovereignty give way to an idea of a global order of law as the rule of reason. Law is no longer a mediated form of sacred presence, pointing back from Constitution to Revolution, but a forward-looking, ever-expanding order of markets and human rights. This postmodern state, which no longer imagines a place for sacrifice, must conceive of itself as an instance of a global order because it cannot imagine its borders as marking a distinction between self and other that might have to be defended. It has given up the distinction of citizen and alien for a cosmopolitan idea of contractual partners. It no longer regards the border as a place of life and death because nothing is at stake internally that cannot be equally realized externally.[61] It no longer imagines its revolutionary past as anything but a developmental stage on the path to globalization. It thinks of its constitutional powers as an aspect of an international legal order. The state has become a function of the global, inverting the classical idea that international law is a product of state sovereignty.[62]

This is the dream of a rational politics that emerged from the severe trauma of the twentieth century's great wars. It is the equivalent of the dream of a religion within the limits of reason alone that emerged after the great religious wars of the Reformation. What is not clear is whether this is a dangerous or an idle dream. The danger is captured in the ticking time bomb hypothetical: the bomb goes off. Until the bomb goes off, we can dream of a world with political order but without politics. Once it goes off, we go to war, if not after the first, then after the second. We return to a politics of killing and being killed—a politics that the imagination never fully left behind.

The Rhythm of American Political Life

The difference between the social imaginaries of sovereignty and law is well illustrated in American history, where we find a regular, rhythmic movement between the two. The Declaration of Independence is a violent act—an act of war—that gains its power from the mutual pledge of sacrifice: to pledge one's life. The Declaration appeals to the language of revelation: "self-evident truths." There is no way to get from a politics that has fallen into a state of "slavery" to a new politics of truth without the demonstration of a willingness to sacrifice. While a large part of the Declaration is taken up with an account of the failed efforts to achieve reform through legal mechanisms, the Declaration supersedes those efforts. It marks an end and a beginning: an end to one legal order and the birth of a new sovereign. The link between self-evident revelation and sacrifice is literally acted out in the Revolution. Signing the Declaration puts one into an ethical space of killing and being killed. To sign is to transform one's own identity as well as to redefine who is a friend and who is an enemy. Those who make the pledge simultaneously become traitors and free men. They must succeed or they will die, and they will not succeed unless they are willing to die.

The Constitution is strikingly different. It contains neither an invocation of revealed truth nor a sacrificial pledge. Violence appears now only as a generalized need "to ensure domestic tranquility [and] to provide for the common defense." Apart from the rather opaque Second Amendment, no memory of the violent foundation of the state is expressed. Unlike the Declaration, the Constitution is not a performative act at all. It claims to speak in the name of the people, "We the people," but it does not purport to be an actual performance of revolutionary speech. Those who sign it do not put their lives at risk; there is no change in their identity by virtue of their signatures. Their signature is not a personal pledge but a representative act. They are the drafters of a proposal that may remain merely that, a proposal for a reformed system of governance. They do not, and cannot, claim actually to speak as the popular sovereign, for their proposal requires ratification. The Declaration is tested in battle, but it requires no further ratification. If the proposed constitution fails, however, another could take its place or the existing system—however defective—could remain. Neither the drafters nor anyone else has a life or death stake in the reform effort. Their ends are reformist, not revolutionary: "to form a more perfect Union." There is no new truth to be realized; rather, the self-evident truths of the Revolution are to be better embodied in an appropriate legal form. The real danger of such moments is not the failure of a reform proposal but that the effort might trigger a renewed revolutionary moment with a new definition of friends and enemies.[63]

The Constitution does pass from proposal to institutional reality. It becomes the law and, as such, takes for its foundation the sacred meaning of the Revolution. Today we can see the Constitution only as the product of the popular sovereign.[64] The Constitution sets forth in law the revolutionary achievement of a sovereign political presence. It institutionalizes, and thus mediates, a heroic achievement. Quickly, the sacrificial foundation of the constitutional order is tested. Washington marches off with an army to put down the Whiskey Rebellion. He discovers that those who object to the injustice of the law—a tax on whiskey production—are not willing to go to war against the state. In America, Socrates appears as the manufacturer of spirits. We are to be a commercial republic, not a nation of philosophers. But even with that the law remains a deadly business.

Nevertheless, enemies do exist. In a seeming replay of the Revolutionary War with Britain, a new war breaks out in 1812. Like many wars since, this one lacks adequate cause or clear reason. The issues are confusing; it makes little sense to take on the British Empire. The country barely has an army or a navy; it has a weak economy and few institutions of governance. The opening engagements are quite disastrous—in part, a consequence of relying on the leadership of aging Revolutionary War heroes. Nevertheless, the nation has a political ethos of sovereignty that it will defend in acts of sacrificial violence. What is symbolically intolerable is the British practice of impressment: seizing the body of an American citizen for service to the British sovereign. This is literally that form of humiliation—to be sacrificed for a foreign sovereign—that grounds the political psychology of warfare. Impressment is political slavery, which must be met with that sacrificial killing and being killed that is the condition of freedom and the ethos of sovereignty.[65]

More important than this lingering conflict with the old enemy, the British, however, is the revolutionary instability—the threat of secession—that continually hangs over the project of law in the nation's first decades.[66] Can law fully absorb the sacrificial character of politics? The American answer is no. Within three generations, the Constitutional order suffers its own revolutionary response in the form of southern secession. Once again declaration—now literally of secession, not independence—and pledge characterize political experience. The Civil War is a new exchange of killing and being killed, of heroic sacrifice of self and others. It puts on permanent display the agonistic, sacrificial truth at the foundation of American politics: that a nation with negligible external enemies will create for itself a frenzy of killing and being killed for the sovereign. We are still living within the shadow of those sacrifices.

The violence of American politics must be understood as a practice of sacrifice for the sake of maintaining the material reality of a transcendent idea, which is the revealed truth of sovereign existence. Thus, Lincoln returns to the language of pledge and sacrifice at Gettysburg. He again tells the nation of the revealed truth on which sacrifice rests in his Second Inaugural. In the end, he becomes the archetypal sacrificial figure in American politics.[67] No figure is more responsible for killing, and none makes a greater sacrifice. He personifies the ethos of the political as unmediated sacrifice. For just this reason, law professors continue to puzzle about the legality of his conduct of the war—as if law must be the measure of politics.[68]

History approximates an ideal of fiction in this narrative. This is the pulse of American history: from the order of law to the presence of sovereign violence. The ritual displacement of the self under law easily becomes the violent sacrificial act for the sovereign. This was the fundamental American narrative of the twentieth century, during which time the nation existed almost continuously under the threat of war. The narrative maintains the constitutional order by simultaneously linking it directly to the popular sovereign that revealed itself in the Revolution and to the regular reappearance of sacrificial acts of killing and being killed over the last two hundred years. This is again the narrative of American politics at the start of the new millennium.

Conclusion: Law, Sovereignty, and 9/11

The modern legal order often appears as a structure for the realization of rights and the production of goods. Arguably there is an increasing global convergence on the necessary conditions of a legal order that is adequate to meet these ends—for example, protection of property, specification of substantive rights, mechanisms for resolving contract disputes, protection of civil society institutions, a well-regulated police force, and governmental transparency and accountability. If these were the totality of the ends of politics, there would be no reason in theory why a single order of law could not grow to the limits of the globe. The modern project of international law has pursued this goal in a piecemeal fashion, for example, in the trade regime or the law of the sea. But, if the legal order is only a partial view of the larger political character of the state, this aspiration for global expansion will continually confront pressures from a politics beyond law. Traditionally, we called that politics "sovereignty," which is exactly why the pursuit of a global order of law has been so determined to cast sovereignty as an empty idea, an anachronism, or a pathology.[69]

Part of the strength of a legal order arises from its insistence on its own completeness, its claim that there is no problem that is not subject to legal resolution. It takes just a moment of reflection to realize that this is only completeness from a particular point of view.[70] The order of law is a truncated political space. In exceptional moments, the legal system itself reflects its own limits. Elsewhere, this is the moment of formal "derogation." The American Constitution lacks a doctrine of derogation apart from the possibility of suspension of habeas corpus. Nevertheless, we are no less familiar with the idea of the limits of law in the face of the political exception. Legal process does not extend to the decision to take up the politics of sovereignty, that is, of killing and being killed. The politics of revolution—the mutual pledge—as well as the politics of war—killing and being killed—remain outside of law.

To call an act criminal today is to deny it political significance.[71] We do not speak of a contest between the criminal and the police that is to be settled by the appeal to arms. There is nothing for the criminal to win because he stands for no idea.[72] At best, he can "escape punishment." Law enforcement, in that case, fails as a practical activity but not in its self-conception. The depoliticization of the criminal was, according to Foucault, directly linked to new forms of disciplinary power.[73] Regardless of whether he correctly identifies the genealogy of contemporary forms of power, he is undoubtedly correct to note that crime and punishment are no longer sites for political contestation in the West.

For this reason, the first response of legal institutions to violence—regardless of its motive—will be to describe it as criminal. The revolutionary will be called a "common criminal." Terrorism will be reduced to a series of criminal acts: murder, kidnapping, conspiracy, blackmail. If terror is a crime, then the response of the state is law enforcement, which means the application of force pursuant to legal norms. The police neither have, nor can they be granted, a license to act outside the law. The guards at Abu Ghraib may have thought themselves at war, but they were judged as if they were performing a law enforcement role. They were prison guards, not combatants. The capacity to measure all violence by law, to see it all as crime and law enforcement, is an expression of the strength of the legal order. Success would mean that the rhythm of political life had fundamentally altered, that we had reached a "steady state" of law.

The refusal of law to acknowledge violent political ambitions may be an effort to render them invisible. Timothy McVeigh was never given any political space whatsoever. He was considered a mass murderer, not a political actor. Similarly, to label terrorism criminal is to refuse to see it as an existential challenge; it is a refusal to regard it as a political act at all. But terrorism is such a powerful presence today precisely because it asserts an existential threat to the state. This is not a question of measuring the actual threat, which may or may not be serious, but of understanding the meaning the terrorist conveys. The terrorist who blows himself up attacking Israeli targets expresses the idea that Israel should not exist. He is not violating the law; he is denying sovereignty. The September 11 attacks targeted the symbols of the United States as the most powerful political entity in the world. At issue was not a difference of opinion but an expression of disregard for the existence of the state. To recognize this is already to move from law to war. Israel has engaged in a practice of extrajudicial killing—that is, targeted assassinations. So has the United States since 9/11. Both do so because they find themselves in a situation of "extrajudicial" dying: political deaths that are not murder but sacrifice. Sacrificing for the state creates the license to kill for the state. This is neither a legal nor a moral license. Rather, it is the familiar form of the sacrificial politics of sovereignty.

The 9/11 attack immediately posed the question of which narrative would frame our response: war or law, counterattack or criminal prosecution. The terrorists had already made clear the narrative within which they placed their action: they were at war. A suicide attack is always beyond law. Its metric is sacrifice made literal and complete; it is the unmediated violence of the contest. Ideally, there is no one left behind to prosecute. Terrorism invokes a kind of schizophrenic response:

the rhetoric of crime and the practice of war.[74] The modern state lives a "noble lie" that sovereign violence has been displaced by law. The myth of the social contract projects extrajudicial violence back into the prehistory of the state. The myth is "noble" because to some extent "saying it makes it so." Sometimes, however, the tension between the myth and the practice becomes an unavoidable problem. The American administration has found itself continually caught up in this contradiction since September 11.

The ticking time bomb hypothetical is difficult precisely because it invokes this schizophrenia: law or war? Those who argue vigorously against the ticking time bomb example are trying to preserve law as the sole framework within which we understand our political life. Nevertheless, to see the issue in these terms—law *or* war—misreads history and fails to understand the character of the political imagination. Law exists within a sovereign sphere created and maintained by sacrificial violence. The rule of law is not coextensive with the political. The belief that it could be is just another dream of men of goodwill. Efforts to subject the sacrificial ethos of killing and being killed to legal process express an essential optimism that the failures of reason are only aberrations well within the corrective powers of the law. But, while law may be a project of reason, politics has not been. Contemporary American politics shows no signs of moving decisively in that direction. Beyond law is the politics of sovereignty, where violent sacrifice is the measure of meaning, where the inequality between citizen and alien is the first principle, where historical memory has priority over legal reform, and where the rhetoric of self-evident truth displaces deliberative reason.

Law is a product of the will of the sovereign—"We the people"—but it does not exhaust that will. The action of sovereignty beyond law is violent sacrifice, which is the contest of killing and being killed. There is even something monstrous about the idea of juridifying killing and being killed for the sovereign. Such a project would look too much like the Nazis' Final Solution—administrative murder. Legal form and regularity are not a virtue attachable to every sovereign act. Eichmann's odd appeal to Kantian morality should have taught us that.[75]

The torture and self-sacrifice that are, respectively, at the heart of the ticking time bomb and hand grenade examples locate us in this domain of sovereignty beyond law. The law professors' arguments over the ticking time bomb are debates over the attitude law should adopt toward that extralegal space of sovereignty. Should law try to fill that space? Should it push right up to the border? Can law enter this space without appealing to the category of "plenary power," which does little more than denote a space beyond legal regulation. Law would give the impression that it controls the boundaries of the plenary, that it decides its own limits.[76] But when law goes silent in the ticking time bomb case, when it says you may not torture but you may have to torture, is it acknowledging or creating a space of political necessity? In the end, there is no distinction to be made.

Arguments over the ticking time bomb for the most part fail to understand the relationship between sovereignty and law in the modern nation-state. All agree that the point of the rule of law is to constrain the state's use of force against those subject to its power. Most worry that a failure strictly to maintain legal control over the deployment of violence will undermine the liberal state.[77] These are not idle worries. When criminality is addressed as an existential threat to the state, a regime of law gives way to authoritarianism. This was the path that various nations in Latin America followed in the 1970s and 1980s. A war on crime too easily casts the criminal as enemy. All of this might be true, but it does not eliminate the existential dimension of sovereignty.

The abuse of power should not blind us to the most evident characteristic of the last two hundred years of the politics of nation-states: the practice of sacrifice, of killing and being killed, for the sovereign. The ticking time bomb example takes us right up to the edge of this truth. Too often reactions to that truth are forms of denial: either the bombs fail to exist or law is fully adequate to the situation. But wars—our own and others—are constantly showing us that, regardless of whether the bombs are real, law cannot comprehend the course of violent sacrifice that carries forward the political project that is sovereignty.

Five

CROSSING THE BORDER
BETWEEN LAW AND SOVEREIGNTY

JUXTAPOSING THE TICKING TIME BOMB and the hand grenade hypotheticals poses the question of the relationship between torture and self-sacrifice. If I am willing to suffer terrible bodily injury and even die for the political community, should I be equally willing to do the same to others in order to protect the community? Ordinarily, suffering and acting do not stand in a relationship of reciprocal implication, morally or legally. I might, for example, be willing to give up a kidney for a friend or family member, but that does not mean I am willing to take one from an unwilling donor. Similarly, I might be willing to give up a meal to someone in need, but I am not willing to steal from another for the same purpose. Strikingly, even my willingness to give up something—a kidney or a meal—for someone does not give me a right—legal or moral—to demand one when I am in need. It does not even give me a right to demand reciprocity from my previous beneficiary, although under certain circumstances such "gifts" might create an expectation of response.[1]

Insofar as personal sacrifice enters into the modern legal regime, it looks like a unilateral gift. Stripped of a context of informal rules of exchange, sacrifice does not create rights or obligations. Before it can do so at law, it has to take on a quasi-contractual form—for example, in the doctrines of unjust enrichment, promissory estoppel, or implied contract. My willingness to sacrifice, accordingly, does not ordinarily give me rights against anyone else. Yet, in the context of political violence, our ordinary intuition of asymmetry between suffering and acting seems to miss the normative order of the exceptional situation. When we turn to the defense of the state, we find just the reciprocity that the legal order denies: sacrifice is inextricably linked to inflicting violent injury, being killed to killing.

Regularly, the state places its citizens in a position in which the willingness to sacrifice life stands in a reciprocal relationship to the license to kill. The ethos of the battlefield, including the combatant's immunity, rests on just this principle: a license to injure and kill is granted to those who suffer the risk of injury and death.[2] Approached from this perspective, the two examples of the ticking time bomb and the hand grenade are deeply interconnected: the willingness to throw oneself on the hand grenade creates a license to inflict injury and death. It is not just that the willingness to sacrifice creates a psychological willingness to injure in the form of revenge or preemptive action. Killing and being killed here work in the dimension of political culture, which is both normative and objective. It is a literal license to kill. Acting on this license is not just excused; it is demanded and celebrated. It is political duty, not personal interest.

Killing and being killed is a demand that only the state can make on its members. It is the "sovereign prerogative" to demand a life. To act on that demand is more than accepting a delegation of sovereign power. It is to participate in sovereignty; it is to be as an instance of the sovereign. A sacrificial politics is not one in which I get something in return for offering up my life. One hundred years ago, Hubert and Mauss argued that sacrifice is misconceived as an exchange with the gods. Rather, sacrifice is a means of consecrating, of participating in the sacred.[3] Short of that, sacrifice is either suicide or murder, which is exactly how it will appear to those not enthralled by the sovereign god of the sacrificial community.

The problem of the torturer is not that he injures for political reasons but that he has not crossed the border from law to sovereignty. The torturer acts as if he is at war, inflicting injury for the sake of a confession of defeat, but he does so within the borders of law. Accordingly, he remains outside of the sovereign ethos of violent reciprocity. Exactly for this reason, when perceptions of risk differ, there will be conflicting claims over whether an act of violence is torture or combat.

Torture is a form of riskless warfare, which is always ethically problematic.[4] The torturer injures without accepting the reciprocal burden of injury—a paradigm of illegality. Surely, however, it is not enough to view the torturer in isolation and ask whether he, at the moment of action, faces a sacrificial demand. The combatant whose role is to launch missiles or drop bombs may not be personally at risk. Similarly, the target need not be someone who is immediately threatening injury—for example, combatants may be attacked even while sleeping. In both directions, the risk runs to the group of combatants of which the actor or victim is a part and, through them, to the nation. The individual bears the sacrificial demand as a part of the sovereign. It is not any risk of injury or death but the life and death of the political entity that must appear to be at stake. This is the power of the ticking time bomb example. It asserts that the torturer is indeed at risk for the bomb is an attack on the sovereign. When we don't believe there is a bomb or we don't believe it constitutes a threat to the sovereign, then we see the threatened injury as the illegal act of torture.

The same dynamic of risk and no risk by which the torturer places himself inside and outside of the reciprocity of combat is visible with respect to terrorism. The suicide bomber literally sacrifices himself; he has adopted a form of warfare that allows him to display the reciprocity of killing and being killed characteristic of sacrificial violence. He may adopt this form of violence for purely tactical reasons, judging conventional forms of warfare to be futile given the asymmetry of resources. Nevertheless, his act of sacrifice places him in an entirely different category from the terrorist who causes injury but does not expose himself to reciprocal injury. For just this reason, there has never been universal condemnation of terror as a form of warfare, and the suicide bomber is a particular object of respect in much of the world. The terrorist as combatant in the wars of decolonization and liberation has been celebrated. He is condemned only when he crosses into the domain of riskless killing—for example, targeting soft, civilian targets and not exposing himself to the possibility of reciprocal violence.

The reciprocity of killing and being killed has nothing to do with agreement between the combatants. There is no meeting of the minds between particular combatants or between their respective states by which each grants the other a right to use deadly force. The decision to go to war usually results from a failure of agreement or a unilateral act of aggression.[5] The warrant for violence derives from the sovereign, not from the enemy either individually or collectively. That warrant, however, has nothing to do with a contractual relationship between sovereign and combatant. There is, for example, no distinction to be drawn between voluntary and compelled sacrifice. The conscript's death on the field of battle is no less a political sacrifice than that of the volunteer. The hand grenade example is not specific to combatants: the grenade can appear before anyone and at any time. This, for example, is the way in which United Flight 93, brought down by the passengers on 9/11, has been interpreted. Legal conscription is only a regularized form of a relationship that is always an implied possibility—a background condition—of popular sovereignty.

Western politics has expressed the same fundamental faith as Western religious practice: only by demonstrating a willingness to die does one participate in the sacred. This is the reciprocity of being sacrificed and sacrificing. If the aim of the political community were to exit the domain of death that is the Hobbesian state of nature, a sacrificial politics would be a logical contradiction. At the moment the state demands my life, Hobbes thought it exceeds the terms of the social contract with which the citizen must comply.[6] Experiencing a threat of death from the state—indeed, a threat of a short, nasty and brutish life—men are back in the Hobbesian state of nature. If so, they are free to flee the community and start over elsewhere—exactly the option that Socrates rejected. If the state is approached as a means to individual well-being, then neither sovereignty nor sacrifice will ever appear. We will be left with a theory of law that never reaches the experience of the political, which is just what liberal political theory has offered for three hundred years.[7]

A sacrificial politics is one in which the violent destruction of the self is the realization of the transcendent character of the sovereign. The infinite value of the sovereign displaces the finite value of the individual. That displacement is the violence that creates meaning: sacrifice. This is the violence at stake in both the ticking time bomb and the hand grenade examples—violence that is neither legal nor illegal but beyond law. Sanctified by sacrifice, the individual gains the sovereign power to take life.

Sacrifice as an act of creation through destruction is simply invisible to the law. Legal rights generally give the bearer either a right to exclude—for example, property or privacy—or a right to demand something—procedural or substantive—of the state or another person. The sovereign claim is wholly violative of the ordinary rights to life, property, procedure, and privacy that protect the person from state intrusion. The modern nation-state includes both of these moments: a symmetry of killing and being killed whenever sovereign existence is at issue and an asymmetry of rights and exclusions within the legal order. Negotiating between these two logics is a problem for both theory and practice. The problem, to use the terminology from the last chapter, is to negotiate back and forth between the pledge and the constitution, between the border and the interior of the state, between the ethos of sacrifice and that of law. This is a twofold problem of transgression and separation. When sacrificial violence occurs within the domain of law, we speak of torture and terror.

Transgressing the Border

The border is the point of contact between these two forms of the political imagination: the rule of law and the politics of sovereignty. It is simultaneously the point at which the existence of the sovereign is at issue and law has its origin. This makes the border an inherently dangerous place. Borders operate both temporally and spatially. The violence of the former is revolution; the violence of the latter is war. At both, the sign of the sovereign presence is sacrifice.

Time

Violence is inseparable from revolution because revolution only begins with the rejection of the possibility of reform through legal processes.[8] Revolution is change outside of law. The revolutionary goes beyond the civil disobedient even though the actions of both will be identified as criminal by existing legal institutions. The revolutionary, however, rejects the right of the government to label his behavior criminal and, accordingly, rejects its right to enforce that law. His fundamental challenge is not to particular laws but to the government's claim of the sovereign authority to use violence. The revolutionary always claims to speak in the sovereign voice—the voice of the people. He shows forth the sovereign character precisely in his willingness to sacrifice. A revolutionary unwilling to sacrifice himself is not imaginable as a serious political actor. We can, of course, imagine revolutionaries committed to nonviolence—they will sacrifice themselves but not injure or kill in return. This is the powerful presence of the Christian imagination, which shows us the priority of suffering in the construction of meaning.

The revolutionary founding of the state violates two fundamental moral commandments—the prohibition on worshipping new gods and the prohibition on murder. The sovereign appears as a new god, and for the sake of that god the citizen enters into a sacrificial space of killing and being killed. The violation of these norms takes us very close to the place of terror and torture in the politics of sovereignty. The appearance of the sovereign terrorizes. That appearance always conveys something of the mysterium tremendum. It condemns the existing order as fallen—or, in political terms, illegitimate—and threatens its destruction. Nothing, I imagine, is more horrific than living in the midst of the revolutionary birth of a new sovereign. War may be as terrifying as revolution, but terror has a special place in revolution because revolutionary violence extends across the entire populace. No one is excused from a revolution. The distinction of combatants from noncombatants can get no foothold.

The French label a moment in their revolutionary process "the Terror." That moment has been repeated in numerous revolutions ever since. Revolutionary violence can become an end in itself because no normalized institution, no ordinary course of living, appears adequate to embody this new, sacred force of sovereignty. Even the less violent American Revolution terrorized large elements of the population: little kindness or legal regularity was extended to loyalists or those suspected of being loyalists.[9] More recently, the birth of Israel was accompanied by the terror of Irgun and the practice of ethnic cleansing. These practices of terror were widespread in the process of decolonization. Not surprisingly, the leaders of the Cambodian and Iranian revolutions had spent their exiles in Paris. More recently still, the violence of the former Yugoslavia demonstrated the potential for revolutionary terror that remains in Europe itself.

If successful, this moment of terror is recorded as a moment of transcendent significance in the state's narrative. There is no memory of failure except in the record of the application of law to criminality. Soldiers, too, report this double experience of terror and the transcendent as a characteristic experience of the battlefield. Terrorized, they are nevertheless touched by the sacred—so much so that what may appear from the outside as the worst experience of a life becomes, from the inside, the organizing point of meaning for an entire life.[10] Terrorists are supported in their practices and beliefs by the same experience of sacred violence. That does not mark a moral equivalence among terrorists and revolutionaries any more than all religions have the same moral value even when they rest on a similar experience of the sacred. Just the opposite, moral evaluation should not be confused with the political-theological experience of the sacred. Sovereign violence never speaks a universal language of morality.

The sovereign is born in a sacrificial shedding of blood that marks a new appearance of the sacred. One knows that the popular sovereign is present not by counting the numbers in the crowds but by witnessing acts of sacrifice.[11] The power of the sovereign is that of taking possession of the body of the citizen, emptying it of any meaning that it may have previously represented, and claiming it entirely. That claim takes the twofold form of killing and being killed. Traditionally, the power of a god was displayed in its capacity to destroy. Sovereign violence perpetuates this elemental form of the sacred. Terrorist violence, no less than lawful forms of combat, is an insistence that others see the same presence of the sacred.

I don't offer any of this as a prescription for violence in the place of nonviolence. The point is not that violence is good but that we cannot disavow political violence—and the terror that accompanies it—without disavowing revolution. From the perspective of revolution, the choice between violence and nonviolence, even at a moment of great political possibilities, can come down to a matter of tactics. The velvet revolutions in Eastern Europe were largely tactical successes; the protests at Tiananmen and Beirut were not.[12]

The revolutionary emergence of popular sovereignty in the West was obviously marked by sacrificial violence. Even nonviolent revolutions, however, require a willingness to sacrifice. A revolutionary movement cannot succeed if at the threat of violence the people retreat from the public forum. This is illustrated not just by the recent velvet revolutions but also by the American civil rights movement. Sacrifice was a lingering demand on the American black community, in part, because the slaves had been freed largely through the sacrificial acts of others.[13] The Civil War, not a slave rebellion, ended slavery. The change of legal rights was not enough in itself, however, to change the perception of political meaning attached to the black person's body. Participation in the sovereign body could not be advanced short of the demonstration of a willingness to sacrifice, to bear in one's own body the violence of the state.[14] For the nation's black community, this change in symbolic perception began in earnest during World War II. It became a revolutionary program with the civil rights movement, which was characterized by suffering bodies in the streets. When southern states mobilized the coercive mechanisms of law enforcement against the protestors, they created a classic confrontation between law and sovereignty. Who stood for the nation became an open question: Bull Connor or Dr. Martin Luther King Jr.?[15]

Nonviolence, for King, did not mean an absence of violence. Rather, it meant sacrifice: creative destruction. In politics, sacrifice is always the foundation; dying always has an existential priority over killing. The point is lost if one views a political movement only as conveying a moral message. Of course, political actors believe in the morality of what they are doing. But those moral norms are embedded in a political experience of sacrifice. At issue is not merely the moral character of the nation's laws and practices. Rather, the soul of the nation is at stake. The achievement of the civil rights movement was to displace the image of the suffering black body from that of the lynch victim to that of the political martyr—for example, Medgar Evers and—most important—King himself.[16] These sacrifices are misread and belittled if stripped of their political claim to the sovereign presence. They are not only representations of injustice; they are a new showing forth of the sacred character of the sovereign. If it is seen only within the lens of a claim for justice under law, then the black community looks no different from a community of aliens that might also seek the equal protection of the law. Sacrificial suffering was about more than such legal treatment. It was about that intersection of being and meaning that is the politics of sovereignty.

The civil rights movement and the largely concurrent antiwar movement differed fundamentally in their achievement of the politics of sacrifice, even though the moral positions of the two were linked. The civil rights protesters are remembered as martyrs; not so the antiwar activists of the 1960s. One group is memorialized; the other is amnestied. There is no memorial for those Vietnam protesters who went to jail or those draftees who fled the country. Even if we agree with the moral claims behind their actions, they are not memorialized, just as there is no memorial for those who suffered the police violence in Chicago in the summer of 1968. Martin Luther King Jr.'s sojourn in a Birmingham jail, on the other hand, is recognized as a form of sacred suffering. The letter he wrote there is part of the canon of American political life. The suffering in Selma and Birmingham is memorialized in books, films, and monuments.

The participants in these "revolutionary" political movements often claim for themselves the virtues of the "true" Constitution in the same way that the American founders appealed originally to the "rights of Englishmen." But law, constitutional or otherwise, is not a hypothetical argument that can be made from the reading of a text. Rather, it is a practice linking interpretation to institutional forms of coercive power. A court's interpretation of the text is not authoritative because it is the "best" interpretation but because the mechanisms of state authority act on that interpretation and not on others.[17] Regardless of their legal claims, revolutionary actors stand against law; they stand instead in the tradition of "self-evident truths." We know this precisely because they are willing to sacrifice themselves in their opposition to the judgments of legal institutions. King bases his authority on a "dream" not a court order. His dream is just another way of speaking of "self-evident" truths in an age skeptical of natural law. These conflicts do not end when the court speaks; they end when the court speaks the "truth."

Revolution is direct action of the popular sovereign. Short of that, a political movement is one only for reform, in which case violence is not threatened and sacrifice is not demanded. Reformists seek to mobilize voters; they do not challenge the claim of the institutions of governance to represent the sovereign. Liberal states successfully transit from revolution to constitution, from the ethos of sovereign violence to the rule of law. That transition, however, is never complete, not just because the revolutionary reappearance of the sovereign remains a possibility but also because sovereign violence threatens as an imaginative possibility at the spatial border of the state.

There is nothing liberal about sacrificial violence. When the ends of politics move from advancing well-being to sacrifice, we have moved from law to sovereignty. Only the sovereign can claim a life; only for the sovereign are citizens willing to give their lives. One could abandon the World Trade Organization; one could even cause it to break down. But there is no conceptual space for a revolution against the WTO, for it makes no claim to sovereign authority. At the core of revolution is the existential claim of the sovereign to dwell in the state. When all possible change is seen from within the imaginative matrix of reform, when every issue becomes a suggestion for a legislative initiative or a matter of litigation, then sacrifice has no place and sovereignty is no longer an aspect of political experience.

Space

The popular sovereign makes an appearance that is the origin of history within a people's narrative. Equally, every sovereign is attached to a land. Traditionally, a sovereign god was always the god of a particular place. A universal god is as disturbing a thought as a universal, political sovereign. Christianity appears as a religion making a universal claim, but in order to make that claim the Christian must engage in self-sacrifice without sacrificing the other. He must be killed without killing. Absent that, claims to universality become just another form of imperialism—the victory of one faith over another. A universal politics of suffering without killing would not be a politics of sovereignty at all. To the ordinary political imagination, it looks like nothing more than slavery.

War, like revolution, puts at issue the same existential claim of sovereignty. It does so, however, in the spatial dimension. War begins with a transgression of the border. Its end is to push the enemy back across the border.[18] Not every war is literally fought at the border, but every war imagines itself as a "pushing back" of an enemy across a border. To-day we know that war can as easily take the form of the expulsion of peoples—ethnic cleansing—as the movement of borders. These are two expressions of the same phenomenon of securing a space of sovereignty.

There is an implicit threat of war as long as one can imagine a contest across a border. Even today, when advanced technology shapes the imagination, what is "star wars" but a technological fantasy of securing the borders? The dream of peace remains that of sealing the country from any form of cross-border invasion.[19] This is why the UN Charter models the "inherent right of self-defense" as the response to an armed attack across a border.[20] It is also why the fundamental principle of the postwar, international legal order turned out to be the immutability of borders: *uti possidetis juris*.[21] If the charter imagined a world without war, then it necessarily had to try to create a world in which borders would not be contested. In the first decades of the UN's existence, this meant trying to match borders to a communal imagination of political identity—the movement of decolonization. In recent decades, it meant to create a transnational sense of identity in which borders were merely administrative demarcations—the movement of globalization.

The European Union represents a largely successful shift in the political imagination of the border. Member states can no longer imagine, vis-à-vis each other, a threat across the border. The border ceases to be a space for sovereign action; it is merely administrative. The border between Canada and the United States has long had a similar status: it is not just demilitarized but depoliticized. Once imagination of the cross-border threat is gone, problems between states appear as policy issues to be negotiated in the same manner as domestic issues. For most of the world, however, including the United States in its other relations, this borderless world has never materialized. Indeed, the dangers from across the border became all the greater with technological advances in weapons delivery systems, as well as with the turn to terror as a form of warfare.[22] In the West, the fear of the terrorist transgression is, for the most part, a fear of alien penetration, while in the rest of the world it is often a fear of revolution.

The post–Cold War world presented a conceptual puzzle. On the one hand, it was to be an era of globalization in which borders would no longer function as barriers to the free flow of commerce, ideas, and people. An increasingly cosmopolitan identity would expand the horizon of concern beyond the localism of place. The global rule of law and the global market were the most important projects of social construction at the beginning of the new millennium. This idea of a global order that transcends borders was only imaginable, however, to the extent that states felt no existential threat. Absent such security, the lowering of the valence of borders simultaneously pointed to a global order of law and a threat to sovereignty.[23] This tension was substantially ignored until September 11, 2001. In the aftermath of the attack, however, there were immediate arguments that globalization was a threat to national security. The reaction has been a focus on the border—on fences, surveillance, and, of course, the cross-border movement of peoples. To many, that focus seems disproportionate to the actual threat from this source.[24] The real point is just the opposite: the hysteria over the border is not an indication of actual threat but of the imagined existential challenge to sovereignty. War, including a war on terrorism, requires defense of the borders and expulsion of the alien. This is exactly what we have seen over the last six years in the United States and increasingly in Europe as well—not to speak of Israel's commitment to the construction of an actual fence.[25]

The border provides a geographical representation of the possibility of the existential threat that is war. Because the border symbolizes sovereign danger, it is imagined as a violent place that never fits easily into the legal regime. This is true even during periods in which there is no explicit, direct threat. For example, the American law of the border has repeatedly affirmed the "plenary" power of Congress. *Plenary* is a technical term for identifying points at which political discretion effectively supersedes a judicially enforceable legal regime.[26] The ordinary rule of law doesn't apply in this place—so much so that the geography of the border is itself destabilized. At law, the border is not a geographical place: people who literally cross a geographical marker have not necessarily "entered" the space of the country.[27] They only enter the country when they pass from the regime of sovereignty to that of law. The function of the border is symbolic transit. That function may appear deep within the geography of the national space.[28] It may also appear outside that space entirely. There is, for example, a tradition of understanding flagged vessels as sovereign territory.[29]

The border unavoidably has this unstable nature, for there is no ideal of justice by which we can distinguish between citizen and non-citizen. This is a political distinction maintained by force and the threat of force. Aliens are those who can be excluded at the border; citizens are those who can freely cross. Because exclusion and penetration are at issue, the border is quite literally a space of life and death.

Wherever the violent act of exclusion occurs, we are at the border. There the citizen can be asked to sacrifice himself to maintain the sovereign while the alien quite literally puts his life at risk as he approaches. The violence of the border, its existence beyond the order of law, is nothing other than a recognition and replication of the killing and being killed that is at the foundation of the polity. The border is, in this sense, the archetypal space of sovereignty, just as revolution is the archetypal time of sovereignty. Even the peaceful border between the United States and Canada and the somewhat less peaceful border with Mexico are remnants of past violence.

The ticking time bomb example places us at an imagined border. Indeed, the power of the hypothetical arises from its paradigmatic representation of the problem of establishing the secure borders that are the condition of law. The presence of the bomb represents a breach of the border. The jurisdiction of law, represented by the no-torture principle, shrinks to the dimensions of the cell itself. The question is whether even those borders will be breached. We can defend law, but only in a rapidly diminishing space, as the threat of terror appears as if it could burst forth anywhere. Thus, the ticking time bomb is a kind of parable that asks the central question of modern politics: At what point does the domain of law give way to the violence of the border? When are we secure enough that violence can be pushed out of sight and we can live as if law and politics were coextensive? The hand grenade example answers this question: it shows us the violent transgression of the border of the cell itself and, with that, the end of law.

The juxtaposition of the two hypotheticals suggests a kind of political phenomenology: law gives way at the border, and citizens are at the border when they confront a demand for sacrificial violence. Whether an act is perceived as torture or warfare depends on this perception of the security of the border.[30] Accusations of torture often look unjust to the perpetrators precisely because they do not share the view that the space of custody has established secure borders within which there has been or can be a return to law. They believe that they are pursuing the sacrificial symmetry of warfare—killing and being killed. The dirty warriors of Argentina thought they deserved medals for winning the war on subversives, not prosecution for violating the law.[31] Torture is the continuation of warfare within the space of custody. Because terror breaches the borders in an indeterminate and amorphous fashion, a war on terror will always be mired in ambiguity: Is it torture or combat? Torture and terror both exist in this gray zone of transgression when sacrificial violence appears within the bordered space of law.

The Disappeared

Torture and terror are violent forms of the production of truth: the truth of political sovereignty. The task of political philosophy is not to condemn their lawlessness but to understand the social imaginary within which this political violence not only makes sense but appears necessary. That social imaginary is one in which the polity is an expression of the will of the sovereign, the community rests on an erotic bond—not a judgment of reason—and citizen participation in the sovereign is realized through sacrifice. The sovereign has its origin in the pledge, the action of the pledge is sacrifice, and the locus of sacrifice is the border. Sovereign and sacrifice form a linked pair: sacrifice is the transformation of the finite self into an expression of the infinite value of the sovereign, and sovereignty comes into existence only through the sacrificial destruction of the finite body.[32]

The subject, or bearer, of sovereignty in the West has moved from God to monarch to the people.[33] The point, however, is always the same. The sovereign is the source of meaning: it is not a means to any end apart from itself. It reveals itself in the act of sacrifice. Terror and torture are contemporary forms of killing and being killed in the political-theological space of sovereignty. We can try to cabin sacrificial violence by law. Indeed, that has been the project of modern international law.[34] It has not, however, had great success. In the twentieth century, we had more and more law, but violence always escaped the boundaries of law. The forms of violence may be changing in the twenty-first century, but the general pattern of more law and more violence looks to remain the same.

Today's war on terror is a confrontation between two political-theological constructions of meaning, only one of which is Western but both of which operate on the same ground of sacrificial violence. Once politics enters the domain of sacred violence, conflict takes the form of each side seeking to prove the other an idolater—that is, a worshiper of false gods, which means a worshiper of nothing at all. The body of the enemy must be read as a sacrifice for our god alone. In the classical tradition, defeat was the moment at which all the men were killed, the women and children sold into slavery, and the city razed. A people are literally destroyed to prove the emptiness of their faith. Today we call that practice genocide. The legal prohibition has hardly done away with the impulse; it has not even eliminated the practice.

A war on terror practices its own form of victory over idolatry: to disappear the enemy. The general theme is as old as Sophocles' *Antigone,* which begins with the dead body of Polynices lying outside the city's walls. The issue is whether that body will become the object of traditional religious ritual. To leave the body unattended outside the walls— the borders—is to leave it in an empty space where sovereign power expresses itself in death without memory. Polynices' body expresses nothing except the power of the city to exclude and thus make of him nothing at all. What his sister, Antigone, demands out of respect for family and religion would, were it to be granted, simultaneously create the possibility of political memory.

Similarly, in the contest of meaning over today's terrorist, the state would treat him as less than a common criminal. Criminals remain members of the community; they are extended recognition through law.[35] Like the observance of a religious ritual for Polynices, participation in the legal process implies recognition and respect. The terrorist, however, is to be denied even that much recognition. Best of all, from the sovereign point of view, would be to "disappear" him, to remove him from the human world of memory. This was no doubt the impetus behind the creation of extrajudicial prisons by the Americans after September 11. The state's end is to leave the terrorist perpetually in the space of sovereignty beyond the walls of law. For the United States, that space was to be Guantánamo.[36]

Just as Polynices is left to be eaten by animals, and so made invisible in death, the modern state would render the terrorist invisible. He is denied the visibility of the sacrificial act—that is what it means to be an "unlawful combatant." Invisible, he cannot appear as a martyr for his own political faith. The most basic privilege of the lawful combatant is to claim recognition for his sacrifice. Each side to a conflict between nations recognizes the reciprocal possibility of sacrifice. This, I have argued, is war modeled on the duel: it combines violence and recognition in the symmetry of risk.[37] A war on terror lacks this reciprocity. Each side seeks total defeat of the other's god by destroying the conditions of sacrifice. The terrorist may practice his own form of "disappearing"—for example, kidnapping. More deeply, the same symbolic exchange is at the heart of terror. By targeting civilians arbitrarily, the terrorist attempts to create the conditions of a meaningless death. It is a death without the ritual of sacrifice; death as if from nowhere. The plane disappears from the radar screen somewhere over the ocean.

The ambition of the terrorist is to demonstrate that there is no border behind which law can displace sovereignty. Rather, sovereign identity defines the state at every point. All are potential targets of violence wherever they are. Sovereign politics is all about life and death—sacrifice and being sacrificed. With that, the distinction between combatant and noncombatant disappears. The terrorist practices yet another form of that total war—a low-tech form—which characterized twentieth-century violence. Total war, whether by terrorists or armies, denies that there is any space apart from the exceptional space of the sovereign contest; it denies that law has succeeded revolution or secured national borders. The reciprocal response is to eject the terrorist and leave him in the legally unorganized space of sovereignty. The terrorist will die, as the trial court judge recently told Zacarias Moussaoui, "with a whimper."[38] That whimper is the missing voice of any symbolic force whatsoever. Like Polynices, he is denied the human.

Disappearance is the direct way of attempting to eliminate the possibility of a memory of sacrifice. We do not know whether the disappeared are alive or dead.[39] They are literally removed from the human world of order. To disappear someone is to deploy the personal psychology of hope—one hopes that the loved one is still alive—against the political psychology of faith. It requires faith to see through a murder to an act of sacrifice, to see the infinite informing the violated body. As long as one cannot know whether the disappeared lives, hope will struggle against faith. More than that, the perception of sacrifice is itself tactile. We need to come into contact with the sanctified body. Antigone wants to perform the rites of the dead on the body of Polynices. The state goes to great effort to obtain the return of the war dead; it buries them under the flag. The sacred is not an idea but a presence. The tomb of the unknown soldier is not just a memorial; it must contain the body of the fallen soldier.[40] The maimed veteran is a kind of living memorial that intrudes into our everyday life to remind us of the claim of the sovereign on the citizen's body.

When the mother demands to know her child's fate, she is, of course, also protesting against state injustice. Her demand as a mother, however, follows the sisterly demand of Antigone: it depoliticizes the contested body. She maintains one form of the human—familial love—against the denial of humanity by the state. Only so does she gain a certain immunity—tenuous as it is. It is tenuous because, as Sophocles expressed it, we cannot neatly separate the forms of our humanity. Creon may exclude Polynices for political reasons but the result is his own destruction through the effect of that exclusion on familial love. The state fears that the disappeared will be seen as the locus of a sovereign act of sacrifice. The mother responds that she wants her child, not revolution. But the multiple forms of meaning intersect in the same body, and there is no returning of the body to the family that does not potentially disrupt the state.[41]

The sacred, unlike justice, exists only as an experience. There is no abstract conception of the sacred against which we can measure particular instances. We cannot argue about what the sacred should be. When we no longer experience the sacred in a particular time or space, we don't say that once the gods were present but they are no longer. We think, instead, that there was never anything there but false belief—idolatry. There is, accordingly, no memory of the sacred that is not itself an experience of the sacred.[42] We are either enthralled or we are not. When we lose that faith, those who were holy warriors may come to be seen as terrorists and torturers. Acting on sovereign truth, they are judged by law. If they, too, lose that faith, they may come to the same conclusion about themselves.

If the sacred is inextricably tied to experience, then the need for presence is a need for the body. It is a need for the thing itself, not just the abstract memory. Even Christ must be experienced as a real presence after his death. It is not enough to have the memory. As a memory, he becomes only an example of how to lead a good life. An example is always understood by reference to an abstract principle. This attitude produces such works as Jefferson's redaction of the Bible, in which all claims of the sacred are removed, leaving only the ethical. Without the material reality—the presence—of the sacrificed body, a refounding of the sacred character of the political community is impossible. A community might be re-formed on the basis of a principle of justice; it would become an example of the abstract principle. But justice does not ground sacrifice. It might be a just community about which no one particularly cared, for it would make no claim on the body.

If power worked in only one dimension, a state that could disappear its enemies would have to be judged powerful. It would be acting out the first commandment, "Thou shalt have no other gods before me." But power works in multiple dimensions, including the order of law: "Thou shalt not kill." To disappear the enemy simultaneously speaks to sovereign strength and legal weakness. Such a state can never end the exception; it is in a constant war on terror. It is the politics of sovereignty once the border has been breached. This is a form of sacrificial violence that cannot be spoken within the borders of law. That state of exception can be maintained only as long as the perception of an enemy's threat to sovereignty remains vital.

In Argentina, for example, the popular revolt against the military junta occurs as a consequence of dead bodies that are recovered by their families. The Argentine soldiers who die in the unsuccessful Malvinas war appear as failed sacrifices. The government cannot make them sacrificial objects. Instead, the state is seen as the agent of their meaningless deaths at the hands of the British. They are killed but not sacrificed, victims not martyrs. The Malvinas war shows us a state that had the power to disappear victims but lacked the power to invest those who died with sacrificial meaning. Killing and dying for the state had fallen out of the symmetry that characterizes sacrificial violence. At that point, killing—or disappearing—became an extremely weak political force, bordering on murder. Without self-sacrifice, there is no license to kill. The soldier who kills but does not sacrifice is the torturer.

Some fear that the United States today is approaching a similar position. It has the power to maintain extrajudicial prisons in which it secretly disappears the enemy terrorist, but it may lack the power to sacrifice its own citizens. This is what is at stake in the deaths of more than four thousand Americans in Iraq: Are they experienced by the larger community as engaged in an act of sacrifice or are they the unfortunate victims of poor policy by a government that no longer speaks with the sovereign voice?

These political events trace the architecture of a social imaginary that spans death, sacrifice, sovereignty, and law. Of course, extrajudicial prisons and killings offend the idea of law. To disappear the enemy is to make him invisible to law. This is why the "disappeared" became such a symbol of the global human rights campaign. Sovereign violence cut free from law in all its forms looks like the formlessness of the disappeared, who may be alive or dead, who lack names, and who, if the state is successful, leave no trace of meaning. This is power as pure violence—the point at which destruction and creation exactly coincide. It is a modern form of the Terror.

The Argentine experience, however, reminds us that none of these descriptive claims refers to facts. Each of these propositions is contested, and not just by the generals, who may really believe that theirs, too, was a sacrificial politics of sovereignty.[43] The sovereign state cannot exist for long in an imperial mode in which violence is separated from faith. Either law will extend to these invisible prisons or sovereign faith will assert itself through the perception of a continuing existential threat. The privilege of writing the history of the state, including the theological history of the sovereign, belongs to the victors.[44] Victory, however, is only as stable as the faith on which it rests. There is no last word. Less than ten years after their convictions, the Argentine generals were pardoned. Ten years after that, we see a renewal of prosecutions.

Law and Sovereignty, Again

Modern law puts the rights-bearing individual at its center: it declares his rights against the state, as well as those rights he has against others, which the state will enforce. Doing so, the state promises the individual the personal security that Hobbes envisioned as the end for which the state comes into being. Individual rights and personal security, however, cannot provide the frame of reference for understanding the state at war. The fundamental feature of war is killing and being killed, the destruction of life and property, not security. It is as if the state that structures itself through law in order to secure individual well-being enters into a parody of itself in which all values, including life itself, are inverted. War always borders on the carnivalesque.

At stake in war is neither the life and death of the individual nor the distribution of goods but the existence of the sovereign as an imagined reality of transcendent value. The existence of the sovereign is not a state of being of individuals or institutions that can be objectively measured. The scale of an existential threat works entirely in the imagination, just as a threat to religious belief cannot be measured in actual numbers. The sovereign is threatened whenever the perception of threat arises. In retrospect, individuals and communities may come to believe their perception of the threat was wrong. They wonder what it was that moved them to sacrifice, just as an adult may wonder what it was that moved him so deeply when he was in love in his youth.

When the killing and being killed of war begins, we see that instead of the state offering a means to the end of individual well-being sovereignty shows itself as an end in itself. For this reason, there is nothing liberal about war.[45] Because liberalism is fundamentally a commitment to a politics of reason through law, its ambition will always be to extend the rule of law first to those conflicts that can lead to war and second to the conduct of warfare.[46] To think that war arises from substantive disagreements that can be resolved through law is like thinking that religious disputes over the locus of the sacred can be resolved in court. Today we do not even know how to frame our dispute with the terrorist. Nor do we have a Geneva to which we and our potential or actual enemies can retire in order to establish a set of legal rules for the conduct of a war on terror.

Nations can go to war even when they have no substantial disagreements over the content of their law. The long wars of Europe, beginning with the religious wars of the Reformation and going right through the Cold War, were more like family disputes than conflicts over fundamental values. That, of course, does not make them any less intense; civil wars often take this form. The American Revolution against the British may have been framed initially in terms of rights, but postrevolutionary Americans were quickly puzzled over what exactly had been the problem with British law.[47] Only over the course of its development did the American Civil War come to focus on a difference in fundamental values: slavery. Even here, in light of the continuation of racism and Jim Crow legislation after the war, there is reason to doubt that race was at the center of the sacrificial politics that was the war. Of course, not all wars are between brothers.[48] The point is neither similarity nor difference; rather, it is that war operates in a different dimension from the substantive concerns of a legal order and cannot be explained as if it were simply a failure of law. The modernist ideal of displacing war by legal institutions that would resolve the disputes between nations assumes that law and sovereign violence work in the same dimension of problem solving. If they do not, law won't solve the problem of political violence.

The killing and being killed of war occur on a symbolic field of sacrifice and sovereignty, which simply cannot appear within the ordinary order of law. We do not enjoin armies; we do not provide just compensation for the property and lives lost.[49] Today we may imagine enforcing such an injunction in the form of humanitarian intervention, but that is only war by another name.[50] Similarly, enforcing a regime of compensation is only to require reparations from the losing side of a war. There are attempts to bring law into war itself, but for this an entirely new legal regime must be created—one that puts death, not life, at its center. This law tells us who can be intentionally killed and who can suffer death as a result of collateral damage.[51] This is no longer law cast in the Hobbesian mode. It is the order of Hell, not that image of divine creation that is the Hobbesian Leviathan. If war were not so serious, this law would appear as comedy, specifying the permissible boundaries of death and injury.

The justification of a law of warfare is always to minimize the destructive consequences of war. But the turn to law for this end is always balanced by exactly the opposite turn: to push violence to an extreme in order to end the killing as quickly as possible.[52] The promise of an overwhelming threat of force is that it will not have to be used. We have no way of knowing which of these contrary moves is likely to be a more successful strategy.[53] We do know that, despite the international law-making effort of the twentieth century, it was the most violently destructive period of human history.

Entire populations can be destroyed within the parameters of humanitarian law. Moreover, humanitarian law will always give way—regardless of what might be said formally—at the moment of an extreme existential threat to the sovereign state.[54] When Winston Churchill spoke to the British nation before the threat of a German invasion, he said, "We shall defend our island, whatever the cost may be, we shall fight on the beaches . . ." He was not speaking of a fight limited to lawful combatants. Rather, he spoke to an entire nation—or even nations—engaged in sacrificial violence: "The British Empire and the French Republic . . . will defend to the death their native soil." Churchill captured the sovereign spirit of the modern nation-state in pointing to a campaign of popular resistance against an enemy that breaches the border: "[W]e shall fight in the fields and in the streets."[55] Ironically, he also anticipated the anticolonial wars of terror that Britain and France would face just a few years later.

The motivation for compliance with humanitarian law, when it is not the tactics of military reciprocity, is the professional soldier's regard for honor.[56] Different cultures locate honor in quite different practices—for example, the honor of the suicide bomber who takes up a religious conception of martyrdom. If there is no universal conception of honor, then there is no universal ground for humanitarian law. Even in the West, we know that, while honor has a place, it is not the dominant place when there is a perception of an existential threat to the sovereign. Honor, as well as tactical judgments of reciprocity, disappears in the face of that contemporary guarantor of sovereign existence: nuclear weapons. There is nothing limited and little that is honorable about the nuclear threat. The justification is purely existential.

Honor and reciprocity are values easily affirmed in the discourses of law. Where they give out, political speech becomes sacrificial rhetoric. The nation-state straddles this divide, but it cannot bring the two forms of its existence into contact. It cannot speak the language of law to appeal to sovereign sacrifice; it cannot explicitly disavow law for the sake of sovereignty. Each form of speech—including the institutions and practices that sustain it—must maintain an "acoustic separation" from the other.[57] We can hear only one at a time. The ticking time bomb example is a kind of test. Which form of discourse do we hear in the example? When the two forms are brought into contact, we literally lose our political balance. It is as if we don't know who we are. Can we really be torturers? Must we be?

Acoustic Separation

Metaphorically, the first citizen is Abraham and the last is Christ. All of the history of the nation occurs between the sacrifice of Isaac and the presence of Christ. This is a mythical rendition of a genuine ambiguity between difference and sameness in the political imagination. Abraham bears the burden of the sacred within the finite world; Christ bears the burden of finite man within the sacred world. Isaac would die for his god; Christ dies for man. The sacrifice of Isaac shows us the violent act of faith required to sustain a sovereign presence, which continues to work through acts of killing and being killed. Christ endures sacrifice without accepting the reciprocal license to kill. Breaking the reciprocity of killing and being killed, he is the last man.

The Western nation-state exists in a tension between the particularity of Abraham and the universality of Christ. There are many Abrahams but one Christ. Because of this tension, there is no politics without a guilty conscience. Our contemporary struggle with the ticking time bomb example reflects exactly this guilty conscience. Indeed, some argue that the struggle is to be resolved by accepting our guilt; follow Abraham but with the conscience of Christ.[58] What is not perceived, however, is that this guilt attaches to politics as a kind of metaphysical condition.

The claim to the universal can no longer take the form of an aspiration for a single religious faith. Still, we understand quite well the pull of the universal that stands against all particular claims of sovereign faith. Western moral theory has always taught the universality of justice. This idea is rooted equally in Athens and Jerusalem. It appeals simultaneously to the universal character of reason and to the idea that all men are created in the image of God. Today law has inherited this tradition of the universal. The modern state purports to base its law on standards of liberty, equality, and due process that are of universal application.

Because justice is universal, many imagine a seamless movement from a national rule of law to a global order of law. No state claims that its idea of justice is at variance with what it takes to be the "truth" of justice. We give institutional expression to the idea of universal justice when we measure a state's law against the international law of human rights.

Nevertheless, the state embodies the universal character of law within the borders of a very particular historical project. It understands itself as sovereign not by measuring itself against an abstract, universal standard but by standing within a particular history and at a particular place. Sovereignty literally creates a rent in the universal that is beyond repair. We kill and are killed for that particular god that is the sovereign. We stand with Abraham, not with Christ. We do so, however, fearing that our sacrifices may be a practice of idolatry. Our faith struggles against our knowledge of our own contingency.

The sacred erupts into political life in the same way that the sacred appears elsewhere—as if from nowhere. It cannot be explained as the consequence of a chain of causation that is either temporal or spatial.[59] It is just the other way around: the sacred creates the borders of time and space.[60] There is no polity without a homeland and no homeland without a founding narrative. This space is sanctified by the appearance of the sacred, which is preserved in memory by the national narrative. Political space, like national history, is created through the willingness to sacrifice. It reaches just as far as it has been or will be defended as a matter of life and death. Despite the universal aspiration of law, political communities exist in a world of polytheism. Each sovereign nation will defend its own continued existence against other claims to the sacred.

Judaism introduced the West to the puzzle of the relationship between universal law and a uniquely "chosen" community. The puzzle is replicated in every state that purports to order itself according to universal truths while simultaneously appearing to itself as a "chosen community." We are no better today at understanding the relationship between justice and the sacred, law and sovereignty, than were the Jews of the Old Testament. Revolutionaries may proclaim the "rights of man," but the state to which and for which they proclaim these rights comes into being by distinguishing itself from others. Indeed, it is the very act of declaring—"We hold these truths to be self-evident"—that distinguishes one state's history from all others. Revolutionaries often confuse the universality of their insight with the sovereign power they may temporarily embody. No one, however, has ever successfully led a world revolution. Jefferson, Lenin, and Mao all learned that actual power is located in the political life of the sovereign and that world revolution is a dream of law unleashed from the experience of the political.

The Universal Declaration of Human Rights did not found a single nation. It is relentlessly universal and therefore is not claimed as the founding truth of any particular community. This tension between the universal aspiration of law and the bordered character of sovereignty creates the familiar dualities of the state. Promising peace, it finds itself at war; promising an order of law that will preserve life and property, it demands the sacrifice of both; promising equality, it creates the fundamental inequality of citizen and alien. The legal order of the liberal state rests on notions of equal dignity, a right to life, due process, and equal opportunity to achieve material well-being. The liberal state at war, no less than other states, denies all of these claims. It, too, will kill and take; it will do all of this with no regard for ordinary legal process.

The sovereign state is structurally bound to this internal contradiction. The truth that it holds forth as self-evident has a universal aspiration ("all men are created equal") at precisely the same moment that it founds a particular community. Liberal states, no less than others, are caught in this contradiction. Insofar as they are liberal, they proclaim principles and values that they hold to be of universal significance. Insofar as they are states, they are bound to a very particular time and place. This tension produces the dual commitment to the rule of law and to political sovereignty. Both sides of the tension produce a vision of an absolute: the universal claim of justice and the sacrificial claim of sovereignty. When forced to confront this tension directly—for example, in the ticking time bomb example—we lose our way. We cannot decide on which side we stand: with Abraham or with Christ?

This conflict cannot be resolved. It can only be managed, first by practices of acoustic separation—we see and speak from only one perspective at a time—and second by rituals of stabilization—maintenance—when the two sides have come in contact. To disappear the enemy can be thought of as a dramatic form of acoustic separation. It is the practice of sovereign killing literally hidden from legal perception. Citizens "know and don't know" that sovereign power is being exercised beyond the law: they know it, but they need not confront it. Or at least they need not acknowledge it until the alleged enemy includes their child, friend, colleague, or comrade. Polynices may have been the enemy, but he was also a brother. When those lines cross, the sovereign claim will be judged from the perspective of law. What had appeared as an act of war will now be redescribed as "extrajudicial killing." The self-described warrior becomes the murderer.

A successful state knows how to maintain both law and sacrifice. It knows how to keep them acoustically separated and how to negotiate the line between the two. Most important, it knows who its enemies are. The perception of the enemy invokes the sacrificial imagination, which makes possible the double-sided violence of killing and being killed.[61] A government may have the legal power to declare war, but it has no similar declaratory power to create an enemy. Every act of identifying an enemy is fraught with risk, for if the populace fails to see that person or group as the enemy, it will see only murder, not sacrifice. True enemies can be sacrificed in a display of sovereign power, but it is certainly not the case that anyone who is sacrificed becomes the enemy.[62] The possibility of failure is built into the very idea of acoustic separation—that which cannot tolerate contact may, in fact, come into contact. When the victim is not the enemy, his death becomes murder and the agent of that death is a murderer.

The imaginative limits on sacrificial violence are very much at stake in the contemporary criticism of the U.S. intervention in Iraq. Critics argue that we are fighting the "wrong war" because Iraq is not the site of our enemies. Even if the ends at stake are just, the absence of an enemy means that there is no legitimate claim on Americans to sacrifice their lives. Nor is there a ground for Americans to be killing Iraqis. Without an enemy, there are only criminals subject to the processes of law and victims with claims for compensation from wrongdoers. The construction of Iraq as enemy was exactly what was at stake in the administration's efforts to portray Saddam Hussein's regime as an existential threat to the United States. That regime could appear as the enemy, but ordinary Iraqis were never imagined as anything but victims of the regime. The distinction left us wholly unprepared for the violence of Iraq today, which seems to come from everywhere but with no identifiable enemy. In the absence of the perception of an enemy, not sacrificial violence but law will provide the imaginative frame to govern our relationship with Iraqis. Not surprisingly, one legal claim after another has been brought against American combatants in Iraq. If they are not fighting an enemy, they risk being perceived as engaged in unlawful violence. Matters, of course, are entirely different with respect to members of Al Qaeda, against whom Americans have little inclination at all to apply the institutions of legal due process.[63] Here the perception of an existential threat calls forth sacrificial violence.

Knowing who its enemies are, the state knows when to appeal to sacrifice and when to deploy law. It can practice acoustic separation of the two rhetorical forms. The state knows all of this not as a set of propositions but as a combination of practices and beliefs that are already in place. The state constantly performs its own existence. The government does not control a community's political practices; rather, it is itself a product of the political imaginary that informs a set of practices. Of course, it contributes to the construction of that imagination, but so do civil society institutions, popular culture, families, global forces, and countless other sources.

Like other culture formations, the state practices a sort of bricolage. It is by no means committed to a principle of noncontradiction. The political imaginary includes a commitment to both law and sovereignty, rather like the simultaneous faiths in science and religion that many individuals hold today. The state lives within this contradictory world of law's rule and sovereign sacrifice—"lives" in just the double sense of drawing on and maintaining the imaginative conditions of both. It can abandon neither the language of law nor the rhetoric of sacrifice. It keeps each in its place by deploying the categories of citizen and enemy, of interior and border, of policing and war. Each of these sets of categories structures the political imagination from the inside. None can be measured against objective truths. Each element of a pair is understood only in the contrast with the other.

In hard cases, we don't know which set of categories to deploy. Acoustic separation can fail. One can always appeal to law to criticize the sacrificial practices of the state, just as one can appeal to those practices to criticize strict adherence to law. The ticking time bomb hypothetical pursues the former style of critique—but for law, we become torturers. The hand grenade example pursues the latter—too much law and we will all be blown up. Each form of critique represents a failure of the ordinary condition of acoustic separation. The competing practices have come into contact, at which point we learn what we have always known but could not speak: law and sacrifice cannot be reconciled.

Techniques of acoustic separation can be geographic—the battlefield is at the border—or temporal—revolution is in the past. They can be jurisprudential—doctrines of judicial self-limitation or substantive rules of plenary power—or rhetorical—Churchill's wartime appeal to sacrifice is not a judicial opinion. They are also institutional: the judiciary is not the military. There are moments, however, when contact is inevitable. The sacrificial violence cannot simply be left in the distant past or on the other side of the border. Thus, the towers of the World Trade Center fell on the most ordinary of days. More important, a constant threat of failure of acoustic separation is created by the returning soldier. The veteran presents a problem of managing contact rather than maintaining separation.

Rituals of Recovery: Memorialization

The ordinary means of managing the unavoidable crossing of the two narratives in the voice of the returning soldier is the memorial, which creates an exceptional domain within which past sacrifice can be celebrated without threatening to break into current space and time. This celebration works to cabin the threat that political violence poses to a regime of law. The memorial and its accompanying ritual bring forward a representation of violence, not the thing itself. Celebrating violent sacrifice, it disarms the veteran. We see this literally in the spiked cannon that appear as monuments of memorialization around the nation. Representing past sacrifice, the memorial simultaneously remembers and projects the violence to a different time and place. Its point is to transform the combatant into a memory of himself, separating past from present and here from there.

The primary space of memorialization in the United States is the Mall in Washington, DC. There we find juxtaposed the two narratives of the state. On the one hand, there are the memorials to sacrificial violence. On the other, there are the institutions of lawful governance, which are themselves linked to the Mall through the museums that pronounce a national project of advancing civilization. In one day, the visitor is to divide his time—usually his family's time, for this is an intergenerational project—among the Smithsonian, the Vietnam and Lincoln memorials, and the Capitol. We learn that we are a nation that sacrifices for the maintenance of a community dedicated to the project of enlightened self-government under law. We are particular in our sacrifices and universal in our law. We memorialize past violence within a space from which we can simultaneously see the rule of law. We turn from the sacrificial past to the narrative of the present as the stabilized order of law. Thus, the Mall gives geographic representation to the double narrative; it provides an ordered, bounded space for each, making possible an easy transition across these two domains. On the Mall, one cannot answer the question of which site best represents the nation. Rather, one absorbs them all, just as Congress, which presides on a hill overlooking this national bricolage, is to absorb them all, producing a law that is simultaneously an expression of the sovereign will and the progressive realization of reason.[64]

Sacrifice always has an ineffable quality. It is the act that follows the end of argument; it moves beyond that which argument can justify or law can demand.[65] The purpose of the memorial is to reclaim, and thus cabin, the violent, sacrificial act by giving it speech. That immediately makes the violence something other than itself: a representation, not an act of sacred presence. By converting the sacrificial act to a representation, the triumph of law is rendered secure from the violence of the sovereign. Has not the role of ritual and representation always been to convert the destructive character of the sacred presence into a memory of itself? Order, including law, depends on this triumph of representation over violence in the imagination of meaning.

If the memorial is the ordinary means of managing transition, the most dangerous form of breach of the acoustic separation in a democracy comes from the veteran as the "living dead." In the United States, this phenomenon was seen most recently in the Vietnam veteran as protester. He represented a twofold failure: first, he failed in the task of sacrifice, for he did not die; and, second, he failed to stay within the cabined space of the memorial. In a curious inversion, the problem of the speaking Vietnam veteran was often described as a failure on the part of state adequately to memorialize him. Instead of returning home to the political rhetoric of sacrifice, he returned to silence—a silence that he then filled with speech of his own. The veteran was not memorialized because the nation did not see his violence as sacrifice. Vietnam was, for many Americans, a "dirty war" that had to be disavowed. Not able to see himself as engaged in an act of sacrifice, the veteran saw his own experience through a legal/moral lens on killing and being killed. He was simultaneously murderer and victim. His speech expressed his guilt and victimization.[66]

Abraham returned from the mountain to say that through death is life: through the willing sacrifice of the sons, the nation will sustain itself as a sacred project. He returned with the knowledge that life is a gift from the sovereign. Only by means of a willing offer of that life does the subject realize a transcendent meaning, for the sovereign shows itself directly only at the moment of sacrifice. Every state has an existential need to sustain this belief in sovereignty and sacrifice. To sustain this myth is the fundamental task of the rhetoric of memorialization, which links recent sacrifices back through a chain of martyrs to the founding moment of sovereign revelation. The practice of memorialization secures the memory of the act as a sacrifice while preparing the imagination for the possibility of a sacrificial demand. It does all of this without disturbing the rule of law.

We can never be certain, however, that this is the narrative that the returning soldier will affirm. Multiple lessons can be learned at the front. Indeed, this is a space in which the state's power to control the imagination is exceptionally weak, for the combatant suffers pain in every dimension of his person. He is not just citizen, but son, lover, father, friend, religious believer, and moral agent. War may not teach a lesson of sovereignty and sacrifice. At the moment of sacrifice, Isaac could have turned on his father. If he did not see a saving god at that moment, then he might see only his own murder in the violent act. The message of the returning veteran may be that God failed to appear, that there was no experience of a sacred sovereign but only of murder and death that should be judged by law. At that point, he is speaking what cannot be said. One aim of memorialization is to preempt that speech with the language of sacrifice—whatever he may have thought of the violent act at the time.

What exactly is the lesson that the state cannot permit the returning soldier to speak? He may not speak of the failure of belief at the moment of death. He cannot say that he was there and saw only the destruction of the body, not the saving grace of the sovereign. He cannot say that his comrades died as victims, not martyrs. He cannot say that the enemy was a man who died just the same as his fellow citizens. The nation cannot tolerate this lesson of the universal. It can hear neither that there is no god nor that there is only one god of all men. It must hear the message of Abraham: the sovereign must accept the sacrifice, save the nation, and bring life to overcome death.

When what cannot be said is spoken, the "imaginative dissonance" can produce radical consequences. At one extreme is the possibility of revolution. The responsible government appears illegitimate and murderous. If killing and being killed is not sacrifice, it is murder. The government can now appear as the enemy to be met by the sovereign response of the nation. The failure of war can thus lead to civil war. Something like this happened in Russia with the collapse of the Eastern front in World War I. Conversely, the response may be to extend the rule of law: the problem is not the failure of sacrifice but the absence of law. This, too, can be fatal to an existing government. Now, however, the leadership goes to jail rather than before a revolutionary firing squad. We see both strategies at work in the management of the transition from authoritarian to democratic regimes in the 1980s and 1990s: the color revolutions, on the one hand, and the extension of the rule of law on the other.

A third possibility, and perhaps the most likely, is recovery of the rhetoric of memorialization. The Vietnam veteran is finally silenced when he is memorialized as himself a sacrificial patriot. He moves from victim/murderer to the citizen/soldier linked in the great chain of national martyrdom. He moves out of the streets and back into the cabined space of the memorial—quite literally onto the Mall. He is silenced by his own sainthood. The Vietnam veteran's accusation that the state is an instrument of torture and murder becomes a dim political memory that can no longer be spoken and of which we do not want to be reminded—as John Kerry recently discovered when he threatened once again to disrupt the narrative of citizen sacrifice with the cry of victimization.

At stake in these symbolic battles are not the dead but the meaning of history for the living. There is no moment of life that is more contested in its meaning than death. Even the person who affirms his faith, believing that he dies a martyr, may lose control and come to be seen as murdered—and vice versa when the person who experiences his death as murder is memorialized as a martyr. The sovereign promises life until the moment when it is seen as the instrument of death. This is the threat of failed memorialization: the veteran can report that it was not renewed life but only death that he saw.

The problem of the returning soldier is symbolic, not psychological. Of course, there will always be soldiers who find it difficult, if not impossible, to return from the violence of the front to the domestic order of law. They suffer post–traumatic stress disorder; they may need individual therapy. Their condition may be exacerbated by their perception that a "grateful" nation does not want to hear any message other than that of memorialization. They may feel silenced by the symbolic weight of the celebration of sacrifice and the closing of any other public space of discourse. That closing of the imagination, not the various psychological reactions to it, is the fundamental phenomenon.

All citizen-soldiers know a deeply disturbing truth: that in the face of death there is a certain homogeneity of fear, that all men can feel abandoned by their god—religious or political—on the battlefield. One does not need to be a combatant to know this to be true. Only with the structured performance of memorialization does death turn securely to sacrifice and fear to faith. These are meanings, after all, that must be secured for the survivors. War becomes a "force that gives us meaning," even if it was experienced as an overwhelming fear of nothingness.[67] The personal psychology of fear, however, is wholly compatible with the successful performance of memorialization, even though it inevitably leaves as victims those who cannot accomplish the transformation of the personal into the political. Like the collateral dead, they are the debris of war.

Managing Contact: The Scapegoat

Memorialization is one way of managing contact between law and sovereign violence. Scapegoating is another. The scapegoat bears the sins of the community, taking onto himself symbolically that which the community can neither do without nor acknowledge as its own. He is both polluted and sanctified. The sin must be cleansed. Memorialization refuses to see killing and being killed as anything other than sacrifice. Scapegoating sees the killing but pushes the killer out of sight. Where memorialization is not possible, scapegoating is necessary.[68]

We see just this relationship between memorialization and scapegoating in the case of the veteran. Celebration (memorialization) and prosecution (scapegoating) of the veteran have a way of turning into each other. We know that if pressed too hard, if we look too closely, that which we memorialize can easily show itself to be a subject for prosecution. The hero becomes the murderer. Conversely, the prosecuted veteran may feel the injustice of a failure to memorialize his deeds. This ambiguity is just what we should expect when acoustic separation fails. That there can be no social contract of well-being absent the pledge to engage in the violence of killing and being killed is a proposition that is both undeniable and inexpressible. The veteran bears this foundational sin of the political community. He is a site of the symbolic exchange that maintains the order of law within the sacred time and space of the sovereign.

The recently prosecuted guards at Abu Ghraib, for example, make visible elements of sacrificial violence usually hidden from view behind the rhetoric of memorialization. We sense that they were treated as scapegoats for what was a pervasive practice of abuse, if not torture, of those held in American and allied custody.[69] We do not necessarily conclude that they should not have been prosecuted, but we have to confront the relationship between law and the behavior of men at war. Abu Ghraib was a locus of degradation. At law, the issue is when degrading treatment passes a formal line and becomes a crime. The unspoken truth, and the reason the guards are scapegoats, is that all warfare is a practice of degradation. It is a practice entirely the opposite of law, which is founded on an ideal of individual dignity. Abu Ghraib was, from the perspective of law, a prison, but from the perspective of war it was just another site of violent conflict, that is, of sacrificial violence.

The method of combat is reciprocal physical injury, but its political psychology is humiliation and degradation. Degradation is too quickly described as treating someone as less than human. In fact, it is just the opposite. Not their humanness but their fundamental beliefs are the object of destruction. Degradation conveys the political meaning that the victim has placed his faith in the wrong god. Its end is the defeat of an imagination of sovereignty. It aims to "break the will of the enemy," but that will is always founded on faith. Combat, as a practice of degradation, is directed at faith, not reason. Indeed, it uses reason against faith.[70]

Degradation is a demonstration that that which one thought provided a transcendent meaning for life provides nothing at all. For the individual, it is degrading to be treated as if one's beliefs about the character and sources of meaning—the sacred—count for nothing. A parent is degraded when his beliefs about family are treated as nothing at all. It is degrading to learn that your children have no care for you. Even in the intimacy of love, an experience of degradation arises with rejection: to be told that one's love is empty, that it is nothing at all, is to experience that failure of faith that is degradation. In each of these examples there is an internal and external perspective. One does not experience degradation until one actually comes to a change of belief—that is, until one actually abandons faith. Until that point, what appears degrading from an external perspective is experienced internally as a sacrifice for faith. The martyr defeats degradation through sacrifice.

The victim is degraded whenever he experiences the emptying out of a symbolic world of meaning. Degradation is the experience of the collapse of that world, which leaves one literally alone. Combat works in the most elemental forms of degradation. It aims to reduce the body of the enemy to nothing but a field for the display of one's own sovereign power. This is the powerful connection between the physical destruction of combat and rape. Degradation works through the use of pain to destroy faith in that which provides meaning and identity. In this sense, degradation is the opposite of argument. Argument is a mutual effort to reach a common opinion with respect to truth. Each participant in an argument is open to persuasion by the other. There is nothing degrading about "changing one's mind" in response to argument—indeed, just the opposite. Faith, however, is beyond argument, which is why torture so often steps into the place of persuasion under extreme circumstances. Combat and torture are each experienced as a test of faith. To lose faith when tested is to experience degradation.

For the nation, nothing is more degrading than defeat. Defeat is the disappearance of the sacred from the world. To get to the concession of defeat one must pass through the possibility of martyrdom. This is the same dynamic that is at issue in torture: martyrdom is the alternative to confession. The degrading moment is not the injury itself but the failure to convert suffering to martyrdom. That is the moment of the failure of faith and, simultaneously, the experience of the body as nothing but an object of sacrifice for an alien god. Degradation lasts as long as the memory of the failure of the sacred. We know that such a memory can last a very long time—not just decades, as in the Middle East, but centuries as in the Balkans.

Injury becomes degradation when it is stripped of its sacrificial meaning. This is the degradation of defeat; it is a failure of self-sacrifice. This is also the goal of torture and, of course, of terror as well: to take control of the body of the other as a signifier. Torture, terror, and combat all work to deny the enemy/victim a space for sacrifice by showing in and through his body the total lack of power of his gods and the total presence of an alien power. This is the way in which the prisoners at Guantánamo are degraded. They are denied the possibility of self-sacrifice. Interestingly, the most potent form of protest to surface from this attempt to degrade has been suicide. This act was described by the American military commander as a continuation of combat by the enemy.[71] While much of the public was unsympathetic to this military response, it was exactly on point from the perspective of the underlying dynamic of combat: self-sacrifice competes with being sacrificed. Suicide is the act of taking possession of one's death.

In Abu Ghraib, we saw yet another variation on these themes. Again, the prisoners were degraded through the denial of a sacrificial space. There, too, they lost control of the meaning of their suffering. Instead of being forced to bear the image of the American sovereign, however, the power of the political was confused with a fantasy of the pornographic. These two forms of ecstatic power are deeply related.[72] Has there ever been a war in which the enemy was not represented in a pornographic image? The grotesque character of the pornographic displaces with comedy the tragic character of martyrdom. Ridicule stands with torture as a form of degradation. Again, the point is to destroy the symbolic space of sacrifice by seizing the entire domain of the possible representation of bodily suffering.

Warfare can be sustained only as long as there is a perception of an enemy. Without that perception, killing will be seen as murder and injury will not be seen as sacrifice. However, once there is a reciprocal perception of an enemy, once sovereign existence and the presence of the sacred is at stake, wars are won by eliminating the conditions under which sacrifice will continue. This means to destroy the faith in the alien sovereign. That act of destruction is exactly the experience of degradation. This is what combatants do. Without achieving this end, the destruction of war is no more meaningful than that of a natural disaster. It is only injury, to be repaired as quickly as possible. The Israelis learned this lesson in southern Lebanon in the summer of 2006. Success at arms affirms the twofold character of sacrifice: the victor engages in self-sacrifice, the loser is sacrificed. Degradation is the experience of being sacrificed. At the heart of humanitarian law is an image of warfare as reciprocal self-sacrifice. Torture and terror are beyond the Geneva Conventions because they work in the more fundamental political psychology of nonreciprocal killing and being killed: my sacrifice is your degradation.

The sense that the guards at Abu Ghraib are scapegoats arises from the perception that their behavior was continuous with that which combatants must do: degrade through the infliction of injury and death. It is far too narrow a view to think that only other combatants are the object of this activity, even if the direct injury is limited to them. The end, after all, is to defeat the enemy, not merely the enemy combatants. Often the enemy is an entire nation; always it is a community, only some members of which actually bear arms—or bombs. If Americans are fighting a war in Iraq, the enemy is still far from the experience of degradation that is the condition of defeat. One form of seeking to achieve that degradation was the destruction of Fallujah; another form was the practice of humiliation at Abu Ghraib. That one is celebrated and the other prosecuted should not blind us to their underlying unity in the domain of political psychology. Of course, it is entirely possible that neither worked: in both cases, the experience may have been one of martyrdom rather than degradation.[73]

By prosecuting the guards, the community displaces onto them the sins committed in our name. That sin is the complete inversion of the order of law in the name of the sovereign: not dignity but degradation, not well-being but injury, not reason but faith. Prosecution, like memorialization, recognizes and cabins what cannot be directly acknowledged. The process of prosecution cleanses, for those who are not prosecuted appear to themselves—and the rest of us—as innocent. We are innocent for we have given up the guilty. They are torturers; we are not. This division reestablishes the conditions of acoustic separation in which sovereignty and law are once again mutually reinforcing.

This process shows us in microcosm the larger dynamic that attaches to all veterans. They bear the violence of the state that cannot be acknowledged within the order of law. One form of silencing is the memorial; another is prosecution. The veteran is hero or criminal. Many, I suppose, secretly fear they are criminals; they cannot quite convince themselves that they are heroes. Others think they are heroes until they are exposed as criminals. They are, of course, both, which is just the status of the scapegoat: polluted and sacred. The veteran bears the burden of the state's sacrificial violence. All veterans, for this reason, have the right to be buried at Arlington National Cemetery, America's field of martyrs. Short of death, the veteran is to appear in public only in the ritualized practice of memorialization. If he should otherwise speak that which he knows, he risks prosecution at worst or therapy at best.

Politics beyond Law

The fundamental problem for the liberal nation-state is to maintain an acoustic separation between the double commitments that are constitutive of its own character: law and sovereignty. Whenever either commitment intrudes into the domain of the other, there is a crisis. This conflict provides a framework for understanding the confusion, for example, over the question of American participation in the International Criminal Court. The proposal is rejected as an inappropriate effort to juridify that which must remain outside of law: the sovereign action of killing and being killed. Many are genuinely puzzled as to how a nation committed to the rule of law can object to such an international court. The answer is that law represents only one half of a double commitment constitutive of our political life.[74] Another example of this same tension is the Bush administration's reluctance to subject the prison at Guantánamo to the ordinary rule of law. To it, Guantánamo is a space of sovereignty outside of law. To its opponents, this is an intrusion of the categories of sovereignty into what is perceived as the ordinary space of law. That space begins at the border and is represented symbolically in the idea of custody. Again, the problem arises because the acoustic separation of the order of law from that of sovereignty has been breached.

The liberal nation-state is truly committed to both of these dimensions of law and sovereignty. But the nature of that commitment is such that the two social imaginaries cannot easily be brought into actual contact. Whenever they do touch, there is a crisis, for neither is prepared to subordinate itself to the other. Those points of contact are negotiated daily at the border, celebrated at the memorial, and ritually purified with the scapegoat.

Law and sovereignty are bound to each other, but they cannot appear simultaneously. In ordinary times, we know how to maintain the line between law and sovereignty, between the criminal and the enemy. In extraordinary times, we lose our bearings. It is not clear in which direction the resolution will occur. That depends less on the structural characteristics of law and sovereignty than on the perception of threat. And that, we do not control. Before 9/11, many thought globalization meant that law would now rule everywhere. After 9/11, the ticking time bomb asks whether there is a politics beyond law.

The combatant is outside of the law without being in violation of the law. If there is any legal regime operative in fighting wars, it is not one insisted on by the courts as a matter of constitutional necessity or the rule of law. The legal regime of war is never at home in the courts, for it is a calculus of death, injury, and degradation.[75] The practice of sacrifice always eludes the ordering capacities of law. The combatant occupies the memorial, not the courts; the space of sovereignty, not that of law. If law is forced to gaze on this practice of violence, the combatant becomes the scapegoat. If law and sovereignty were exactly co-extensive, the scapegoat would disappear, but so would the memorial.

The ticking time bomb scenario puts in question just this line between sovereignty and law. The first mistake of legal theorists is to believe that there must be a legal answer to the problem, whether it is prohibition or judicial warrants. The second mistake is to think that the right answer can be found by turning to an analysis of the moral content of our law. Neither of these moves will give us access to the fundamental problem: the relationship between the sacrificial space of sovereignty and the jurisdictional reach of law.

CONCLUSION:

TORTURE, TERROR, AND SACRIFICE

BECAUSE SYMBOLIC SYSTEMS—including that of the political—are only partially self-conscious, there is no reason to expect a direct relationship between the forms of self-presentation and the forms of experience. We know this directly in our personal experience of ourselves and others. What we say about ourselves tells us—and others—something, but we would often be mistaken were we to take that expression as an accurate representation. The deeply insecure person may proclaim his attachment to others. The person who always feels guilty may express his innocence. One who is falling out of love may proclaim his or her love all the more. Deeply worried about death, I may throw myself into life. These tensions, in which one value is powered by the suppression of its opposite, are entirely familiar.

The same sorts of tensions are found in a community's self-understanding. A religion that proclaims love to be its first principle may be quick to turn to the sword. A polity committed to slavery may proclaim "all men are created equal" as its first principle. One divided by distinctions of inheritable wealth may maintain an ideology of individual merit. One that harbors deep racism may proclaim itself color-blind. If expressions of this sort were mere hypocrisy, then critical arguments based on such norms would have little effect. But slavery is indeed a problem for a society committed to equality, just as racial division is a problem for a society that believes it should be color-blind. These expressions of self-understanding can become points of leverage precisely because they capture some partial truth. The task of critical inquiry is not to hold the community or the individual to these express values but to bring to the surface that which is hidden behind them.

We meet just this problem when we examine political violence. The use of force in general, not just torture, is a problem for the liberal state, for there is nothing liberal about killing and being killed. Liberalism is a family of normative political theories all set in opposition to violence. This does not mean that liberal states cannot defend themselves or enforce their laws, but it does mean that reciprocal recognition, not sacrifice, must be the fundamental value—the ground norm—of political order.[1] Of course, no state ever went to war declaring anything but a peaceful intention: modern wars are always intended to "end war." Liberal states, including our own, will try to explain the use of force in terms of acknowledged values—for example, making the world safe for democracy. Peace, freedom, and democracy, however, are not the explanation for war.

To understand the use of force, including torture and terror, we have to turn to other elements of the imagination. We must begin with that most elemental of all forms of symbolic violence, sacrifice. The philosophically compelling question is not the elaboration of liberal principles nor the critique of illiberal practices but the elaboration of the phenomenology of modern political experience. How is a world of law and sovereignty, of well-being and sacrifice, constructed and maintained in the social imagination? For Americans at least, this is the world that spills forth as we analyze the ticking time bomb and the hand grenade hypotheticals. It is a world of acoustic separation and rituals of recovery, of memorials and scapegoats. It is a world in which terror is met by torture.

Torture and terror are reciprocal political phenomena. This has little to do with the effectiveness of torture as a countermeasure to terror, although that is the only argument with which liberalism can approach the problem. That attitude gives us the endless variations on the ticking time bomb problem.[2] No, to understand the turn to torture we need to understand the symbolic matrix of political violence: How exactly does violence work in the construction of political meaning? Like every other cultural form, the political must be approached as a network of meanings, images, and rituals within which practices and beliefs make sense to us. This is, in part, a psychological question—How does the individual imagine violence?—and, in part, an institutional question— How do various civil and political elements, including the military, place themselves in relationship to that imagination? These have been the central inquiries of this book.

Central to both torture and terror is the political psychology of degradation. Not wanting to confront the degradation that attaches to the use of force for political ends, the current debate over torture simply misses the most important issue. As it is framed, this debate will get nowhere. Scholars will proclaim the prohibition on torture to be a necessary principle—a *jus cogens* norm of international law, a matter of civilization itself, and an absolute moral rule—while our political practices will regularly apply torture. We will express surprise at the "excesses" of our security forces, yet we intuitively know that torture is virtually inevitable. So we will be sidetracked into debates about the point at which "rough treatment" becomes torture, about the necessity defense, or about the jurisdiction of the courts. These are strategies of avoidance by definition, exception, and exclusion. The few scholars who defend torture will appeal to the logic of material calculation—torture's contribution to the greater good—but they will be met with countercalculations. There will be disputes about short-term benefits and long-term costs. Of course, none of these calculations are based on anything more than rough intuitions that are often not widely shared. This debate will not change anyone's mind, for it never reaches the deepest issue.

In the end, we torture to degrade. Degradation, however, is not a small thing. Every use of violence for political ends relies on the psychological dynamics of degradation. If we would abandon degradation, we must abandon the use of force. We know what this world would look like, for Christ represents just such a break in the dynamic of degradation. He enacts the possibility of being sacrificed without sacrificing in turn, of being killed without killing in response. He thereby maintains control of the meaning of his own death: self-sacrifice, which is always the defeat of degradation. Just this asymmetry of dying without killing puts the fundamental tenant of Christianity beyond political experience in which being killed is always the license to kill. When Americans think of themselves as a "Christian" nation, they are not thinking of this image of Christ.

Contrary to what many people write and want to believe, our general disapproval of torture actually tells us very little about ourselves. Rather, our sensibilities over torture mask what is most important about our political culture: our willingness to kill and be killed. The torture debate is little more than a sideshow, a morally reassuring diversion from a confrontation with a profound truth about ourselves. We remain embedded in a culture of sacrificial violence.

At stake in the existence of the nation-state has been the presence of the sacred. The polity begins as a particular community with its own history only when the finite goings-on of individuals are touched by the sacred. Only then is the course of human life broken by a meaning that can endure; only then does history begin. This social imaginary comes to the West in the Old Testament narrative of the origins of the Jewish nation: the sovereign God reveals himself to Abraham.[3] For the individual, the presence of the sacred is expressed in the willingness to sacrifice. Thus, national history begins with the demand for an act of sacrifice. Everything that happened before the revelation to Abraham appears now as "preparation." The revelatory moment also gives us a way of reimagining space, for the promise of the Covenant is equally a promise of a bordered space within which this particular people can practice the rule of law. This is the paradigm within which the Western state has developed. It has a sacred origin and a sacred space. Sovereign survival is not one value but an ultimate value without which there can be no meaningful life. The means of survival is sacrifice not because killing and being killed are effective tools—although they might be at certain times and places—but because absent sacrifice there is no sacred presence of the sovereign. When sacrifice disappears from the political imagination, democracy becomes a voting rule and popular sovereignty an aggregation of individual preferences.

The political combines the imagination of revelation—the sacred appears in one place and to one people—and of transubstantiation—

the sacred displaces the finite life of the citizen. Together these give us the political community as a sacrificial community. A political community has a meaning that transcends the finite interests and needs of its members, who find in it the ground of the sacred in their own lives. Thus, God speaks to Abraham, and it is that revelatory moment that founds the nation of Israel. Israel is the community that is in-formed by this moment at which the sacred intersects the finite. The first burden of the polity is to continue in existence because only so does the sacred continue to have a presence in the world. That presence is constitutive of history. A political community is the organic form of the memory of the sacred, carrying that memory in the body of its citizens. To be a Jew is to maintain this history as a set of beliefs about the life and death of the self. To be an American is to listen to Lincoln speak the same lesson of sovereignty and sacrifice and to know it as one's own.

Of course, we write alternative histories today: histories of cultures, of subordinated groups or classes, of the practices of everyday life, or of international relations. In all of these, the polity has no special claim to be the privileged perspective on the past or the future. These histories make us aware of the way in which groups cross political borders, as well as of the multiple groups within those borders. In these histories, the polity disappears as an active subject—the sovereign—with the self-conscious task of creating and maintaining its own history. These are accounts of groups that are in time but not characterized by a self-conscious attitude toward time. Their histories are written from the outside. The unity of the group through time is the product of the historian's imagination.

The historian's account is judged on a scale of accuracy that has nothing to do with faith or the sacred, for there can be no third-person account of the sacred. Without the sacred, the practice of sacrifice can make no sense. No one sacrifices himself for a group that is not itself a historically self-referential actor. We cannot imagine sacrifice for the Atlantic community or that of the Pacific Rim. Neither can we imagine sacrifice for the group of domestic laborers or the group of single parents. Of course, any of these groups can enter into the political, but that entry begins with the production of a self-referential narrative that gives unity to the group by marking its creation and destiny as matters of ultimate concern to its members. Only then can the individual's sacrifice sustain the life of the group. Thus, the soldier dies but the sovereign lives. It lives just until the moment when it can no longer support the act of sacrifice. This is just another way of saying that sacrifice is the action of love, and there is no love of "statistically relevant" groups. Even those who would sacrifice themselves to a universal ideal of justice realize the sacrificial act within the very concrete circumstances of a political struggle pursued by a historically self-conscious community.

The intellectual pursuit of alternative histories tells us something about the contested place of the polity in the contemporary imagination. Or at least it tells us about the contemporary intellectual's imagination. I suspect that the historical narrative of the sovereign state continues to thrive as the subject of the popular imagination. This is true, at least, in the United States, where there is a never-ending thirst for new books, movies, and accounts of the national political history—the narrative of sacrifice—from the founding through the victory in the Cold War and now, of course, the war on terror.

Terror and torture are not simply failures of law—although they are that. Rather, they are products of the social imaginary of sovereignty. That imaginary has its roots in the long tradition of the sacred as it shows itself in the sacrificial act that destroys as it creates. Contemporary political violence is still a battle between love and evil; it still promises martyrdom to the faithful and degradation of the defeated. At issue is the coming into being and the maintenance of a transcendent source of meaning that promises life even as it threatens death. Terror and torture are contemporary forms of this experience of the sacred.

Thus, terror is not just a crime that is loosely or metaphorically spoken of as an act of war. Unlike the criminal, the terrorist works in the existential dimension of politics.[4] He intends his violent act to threaten the sovereign and not simply advance a set of personal interests. The terrorist performs his own sacrifice. Because he offers up himself in an act of self-sacrifice, he believes he has the right to kill his enemy.[5] Acting in this existential dimension, he will, in turn, be treated as an enemy. He will not be punished within the borders of the system of law. Instead, the state enters into a kind of competition of the sovereign power of killing and being killed. It wants not to punish but to kill the terrorist. The United States literally does not know what to do with the captured terrorist. A few may be tried but not with any expectation of release either at the end of a trial or the end of a judicial sentence. Those whom the state identifies as terrorists—regardless of what they actually did—are substantially disappeared; they are held in a limbo of space and time outside of the borders of the legal order.

Political violence seeks to undermine the capacity of the enemy to see his own death as a sacrifice for the sovereign to which he is pledged. He is to see himself as sacrificed but not martyred. At the point at which the enemy sees himself as pure victim, defeat occurs. The experience of moving from martyr to victim is degradation. Torture is a means of accomplishing this movement. When soldiers see themselves as pure victims, their experience, too, approximates that of torture. This is why the internal logic of combat is torture: to create such an asymmetry in force that the enemy has no capacity to injure but can only suffer injury.[6] It does not matter whether torture leads to death, for it has already succeeded when it negates the possibility of self-sacrifice. It succeeds when the victim confesses the truth of the alien sovereign. At this point of surrender, modern torture shows itself to be at one with its historical antecedents.

In the West, the sovereign has long been located in the state. If we approach the sovereign as the reification of an experience of the sacred through the action of sacrifice, then there is nothing necessary or essential in this political locus of sovereignty. Contemporary forms of terrorism often locate the sacred violence of sovereignty in a religious god. Earlier forms of terrorism, in the wars of decolonization, located the sovereign in a nationalist idea. The important point is that on both sides of the contemporary war on terror a political-theological project of creation through destruction is at stake. Islam may never have developed a political culture that separated the state from the practice of religious faith, but we deceive ourselves if we think that Western political practices operate in a secular world untouched by faith and the experience of the sacred. The sovereign is a kind of god, and the end of this war, just as in previous wars, is the destruction of the enemy's god. That god exists as long as believers engage in the sacrificial practices that are its historical presence. The sovereign dies when citizens are no longer willing to take up its presence in their own bodies.

Sacred violence shows us that death is both an end and a beginning. Our religions affirm that only through death is life, but our fear is that death is only emptiness. These are the elements at stake in the nation's wars. We must prove to ourselves that we receive life through death; we must so humiliate the enemy that he sees his own death as the degradation that comes with the death of his gods. To sacrifice the self is an act of love; to degrade is an act of evil. Love and evil intersect in the killing and being killed that is the practice of political violence. How could we end up anywhere else? Political violence is a conflict between love and evil not because the enemy is evil but because these are the forces at work in the soul of each of us.

There is no way to predict when or if the point of defeat will be reached. A community may choose self-sacrifice over defeat. The victors may find themselves standing over nothing but dead bodies. This is the myth of Masada. Alternatively, a community may protect its imagination of itself as sovereign even while suffering tactical defeat. It may think of itself as waiting for a renewal of its historical possibility. Something like this was true of the Baltic states during the years of Soviet occupation. The same possibilities exist for individuals. Some will give up the idea of self-sacrifice in the face of torture; others will not. They may hide their self-conception and wait for their time to come again. The Marranos of Spain sustained this position for centuries. Fear of the last possibility will propel a state fighting terror always to prefer to kill rather than defeat the individual terrorist. Defeat is simply too uncertain.

In all of these dimensions—persons, politics, religion—meaning enters the world through an experience of the sacred. There is no judging the truth of revelation, no measuring its normative value outside of the aura of the experience. Children seize us with their ultimate significance well before we ask whether our relationship to them is just or whether they will contribute to a better world. That does not make us indifferent to justice: we want our children to act justly. We love them, however, even as we forgive their injustices. The same is true of nations and gods. It is not a claim against faith that its god demands an unjust action. There is nothing just about the sacrifice of Isaac. There is nothing just about the way communities—political or familial—draw lines of inclusion and exclusion. To those outside of the experience, every claim of the sacred will look like a claim to worship false gods. Every such claim is likely to lead to unjust action against outsiders. Sacrifice will look like murder. There is no argument sounding in justice for the continued existence of any particular community. Indeed, we know that in the sweep of time communities come and go, just as religions grow and die. But this is never an argument from the inside. The aim of the political community is first and foremost its own continued existence—at stake is an entire world of meaning. When the community is no longer felt to bear a sacred meaning, the idea of the sovereign will simply disappear. At that point, we will be done with torture and terror except as a problem of individual pathology to be met with the twin institutions of therapy and criminal law.

The sovereign always has a double relationship with the community: promise and threat. It promises well-being, but it asserts the right to claim a life. This gives us the peculiar history of the political, which advances citizen well-being just up to the moment when it throws the state into the conflagration of war. This remains true today in a world confronting terror and nuclear threats. When it is no longer true, we will be in a position to celebrate—or to mourn—the passing of sovereignty and the emergence of a postmodern, cosmopolitan man. As with the death of God, were the sovereign to die neither man nor world would be the same. Whether we will get to such a point remains an open question, for the world-threatening character of the political is hardly over. The terrorist with weapons of mass destruction may very well put an end to our dream of a global community of human rights.

NOTES

Introduction

1. See J. Waldron, "Torture and Positive Law: Jurisprudence for the White House," 105 *Colum. L. Rev.* 1681 (2005).

2. Political theorists will see in the question a reference to Carl Schmitt's theory of the state of exception. Certainly elements of his idea of "the political" appear in the analysis I pursue. But where Schmitt focuses on the decision-maker—he who decides on the state of exception—I focus first on the character of the political imagination that makes possible the exception and second on sacrifice as the archetype of political behavior that is beyond law.

3. See C. Kutz, "The Lawyers Know Sin: Complicity in Torture," in *The Torture Debate in America* 241 (K. Greenberg, ed. 2006). ("One of . . . the victories for the Enlightened rule of law—a campaign fought by Voltaire and Beccaria—has been the erasure of torture from the menu of governmental policy choices.")

4. See M. Foucault, *Discipline and Punish: The Birth of the Prison* (A. Sheridan, trans. 1977).

5. See J. Langbein, *Torture and the Law of Proof: Europe and England in the Ancien Régime* (1977).

6. See, for example, N. Lewis, "Broad Use of Harsh Tactics Is Described at Cuba Base," *New York Times,* Oct. 17, 2004; and N. Lewis, "Red Cross Finds Detainee Abuse in Guantánamo," *New York Times,* Nov. 30, 2004 (discussing a report stating that interrogation techniques amounted to an "intentional system of cruel, unusual and degrading treatment and a form of torture"). But see D. Priest & J. Stephens, "Pentagon Approved Tougher Interrogations," *Washington Post,* May 9, 2004, A1 (describing approval of acts that have been ruled uncon-

stitutional within the United States but might not rise to the level of torture in international law). ("In April 2003, the Defense Department approved interrogation techniques . . . that permit reversing the normal sleep patterns of detainees and exposing them to heat, cold and 'sensory assault,' including loud music and bright lights.")

7. On Christian fundamentalists' relationship with the military, see C. Hedges, *American Fascists: The Christian Right and the War on America* (2006); and D. Segal & M. Segal, "America's Military Population," *Population Bulletin*, December 2004, at 25 (indicating that 68 percent of America's military personnel designate themselves as Christians).

8. See J. Whitman, *Harsh Justice: Criminal Punishment and the Widening Divide between America and Europe* 22–23 (2003) (on the "intoxication" of punishing); and D. Luban, "Liberalism, Torture, and the Ticking Bomb," 91 *Va. L. Rev.* 1425 (2005) (on the culture of torture).

9. See S. Cohen, *States of Denial: Knowing about Atrocities and Suffering* (2001).

10. They may, for example, be "private contractors" acting under unclear lines of authority. See J. Brinkley, "9/11 Set Army Contractor on Path to Abu Ghraib," *New York Times*, May 19, 2004, available at http://www.nytimes.com/2004/05/19/national/19CONT.html; and P. Chatterjee & A. Thompson, "Private Contractors and Torture at Abu Ghraib," *CorpWatch*, May 7, 2004, http://www.corpwatch.org/article.php?id=11285 (discussing a report by U.S. Army major general Antonio Taguba on the abuse of Iraqi prisoners). See also L. Dickinson, "Government for Hire: Privatizing Foreign Affairs and the Problem of Accountability under International Law," 47 *Wm. & Mary L. Rev.* 135 (2005–6).

11. See L. Fuller, *The Morality of Law* 33–39 (1964).

12. 18 U.S.C. §§ 2340–2340B.

13. See P. Aussaresses, *Special Services: Algeria, 1955–1957* (2001); B. James, "General's Confession of Torture Stuns France," *International Herald Tribune*, May 5, 2001, available at http://www.iht.com/articles/2001/05/05/france_ed3_.php; and J. Malamud-Goti, *Game without End: State Terror and the Politics of Justice* (1996).

14. The recent scandal over the care of veterans at Walter Reed Army Medical Center is an indication of the direction of future controversies.

15. This idea is central to Luban's recent critique (see Luban, supra note 8). The most powerful recent work connecting the liberal morality of the equal dignity of every individual to the rule of law is that of Ronald Dworkin, who sees this principle of dignity as the foundation of the legal order. See, for example, R. Dworkin, *A Matter of Principle* (1985).

16. Characteristic of this position of the hardheaded liberal is A. Dershowitz, *Why Terrorism Works: Understanding the Threat, Responding to the Challenge* (2002).

17. The U.S. Supreme Court has held that Americans are bound by Common Article 3 of the Geneva Conventions in dealing with the trial of detainees from the war on terror. *Hamdan v. Rumsfeld*, 126 S.Ct. 2749, 2796 (2006).

18. See S. Holmes, "Is Defiance of Law a Proof of Success? Magical Thinking in the War on Terror," in Greenberg, supra note 3, at 118.

19. Perhaps more accurately, this is a "crime against humanity," if it is "committed as part of a widespread or systematic attack directed against any civilian population." Rome Statute of the International Criminal Court art. 7, July 17, 1998, 2187 U.N.T.S. 90.

20. See C. von Clausewitz, *On War* 75 (M. Howard & P. Paret, eds. and trans. 1976) (on the ineffectiveness of humanitarian law) [1832].

21. This idea was already put forth by Kant as a general ground for observing what came to be called "international humanitarian law" or the law of combat. I. Kant, "To Perpetual Peace: A Philosophical Sketch," in *Perpetual Peace and Other Essays* 107, 109–10 (T. Humphrey, trans. 1983) [1795].

22. See P. Starr, *Freedom's Power: The True Force of Liberalism* (2007).

23. Franklin Roosevelt, for example, spoke of "four essential human freedoms," which included the negative freedoms of speech and belief alongside the positive freedom of economic well-being. Equally important, however, was "freedom from fear." President Franklin D. Roosevelt, The "Four Freedoms" Speech, Annual Message to Congress (Jan. 6, 1941), in *The Public Papers and Addresses of Franklin D. Roosevelt, 1940*, at 613–72 (1941).

24. For example, on August 23, 2006, the television network CNN reported that Osama bin Laden had received an imam's authorization to kill up to ten million Americans in a nuclear attack.

25. To acknowledge a situation of war is not by any means to concede that any particular act, including the intervention in Iraq, was an appropriate step in that war. Indeed, most of the critics of that intervention believe that the United States does stand in a relationship of war to the terrorists of Al Qaeda.

26. See B. Ackerman, *Before the Next Attack: Preserving Civil Liberties in an Age of Terrorism* (2006).

27. On the extension of the social contract beyond the domestic community, see J. Rawls, *The Law of Peoples* (1999).

28. I mean to suggest here a turn in the approach to the study of torture that resonates with Durkheim's turn in the study of religion. See E. Durkheim, *The Elementary Forms of Religious Life* (C. Cosman, trans. 2001) [1912].

29. P. Kahn, *Putting Liberalism in Its Place* chap. 6 (2005).

30. Susanne Langer captures this idea when she writes that the destruction of a symbolic system "is always felt as the most intolerable injury one man, or group of men, can do to another. . . . The very expression of an alien mythology, incompatible with one's own vision of 'fact' or 'truth,' works to the corruption of that vision." S. Langer, *Philosophy in a New Key* 290–91 (1960).

31. I have elaborated my approach to philosophy as an exploration of the "historical a priori" in P. Kahn, *The Cultural Study of Law* 35–36 (1999).

32. See J. Waldron, "What Would Hannah Arendt Say?" *New York Review of Books*, Mar. 15, 2007 (objecting to use of philosophical inquiry for political guidance).

33. See R. Girard, *Violence and the Sacred* 1 (P. Gregory, trans. 1977) [1972]

(on the double normative character of the sacrificial act as both sacred and criminal).

34. See E. Cassirer, *An Essay on Man: An Introduction to a Philosophy of Human Culture* (1944).

Introduction to Part I

1. Cf. B. Williams, *Moral Luck: Philosophical Papers, 1973–1980,* at 18 (1981).

2. A. Barak, "Foreword: A Judge on Judging—the Role of a Supreme Court in a Democracy," 116 *Harv. L. Rev.* 16, 148 (2002); HCJ 5100/94 *Pub. Comm. against Torture v. State of Israel,* [1999] IsrSC 53(1) 817 ¶ 39.

3. See W. Downey, "The Law of War and Military Necessity," 47 *Am J. Int'l L.* 251, 252–53 (1953).

4. On recent German efforts to claim a kind of symmetry, describing themselves as victims of the Allies, see J. Friedrich, *The Fire: The Bombing of Germany, 1940–1945* (A. Brown, trans. 2006) [2002].

5. See, for example, M. Walzer, *Just and Unjust Wars: A Moral Argument with Historical Illustrations* 255–68 (1977).

6. The state of Rhode Island, for example, still celebrates the victory over Japan as a public holiday.

7. Indeed, if we believe torture to be a reciprocal response to terror, not so long ago this pattern might have been recognized as the customary form of enforcement of limitations on the means of warfare. Customs of humanitarian practice in warfare, even after they were reduced to a positive legal form, were enforced by the threat and practice of reprisal. The use of reprisals in response to informal warfare was a practice associated with the Nazis. This association led to the postwar limitations on the practice of reprisal against civilians. See Geneva Convention Relative to the Protection of Civilian Persons in Time of War art. 33, Aug. 12, 1949, 75 U.N.T.S. 287. ("Reprisals against protected persons and their property are prohibited.")

8. See Convention against Torture and Other Cruel, Inhuman, or Degrading Treatment or Punishment art. 2(2), Dec. 10, 1984, 1465 U.N.T.S. 85. ("No exceptional circumstances whatsoever, whether a state of war or a threat of war, internal political instability or any other public emergency, may be invoked as a justification of torture.")

9. The Israeli Supreme Court opinion on torture—again written by Chief Justice Barak—while refusing to provide a legal rule under which torture may be used, nevertheless notes that a torturer may have available a "necessity defense" were a criminal charge to be brought against him. *Pub. Comm. against Torture v. Israel,* HCJ 5100/94.

10. While the official military code name of the initial American military thrust into Iraq in March 2003 was Operation Iraqi Freedom, it was widely referred to as "shock and awe" both by military personnel and by the press.

11. The British-based Iraq Body Count research group placed the number of reported Iraqi civilian deaths somewhere between 63,310 and 69,355 as of May 10, 2007. See Iraq Body Count database, available at http://www.iraq

bodycount.org/database. Since this number is limited to civilian deaths corroborated by at least two media reports, it is thought to be much lower than the true number of civilian deaths in Iraq. Estimates place the true number above 100,000 dead.

12. Estimates of the number of Lebanese civilians killed in the 2006 conflict range between a thousand and twelve hundred. See Amnesty International, "Israel/Lebanon: Deliberate Destruction or 'Collateral Damage'? Israeli Attacks on Civilian Infrastructure" (Aug. 23, 2006), http://web.amnesty.org/library/index/ENGMDE180072006.

Chapter One

1. J. Langbein, *Torture and the Law of Proof: Europe and England in the Ancien Régime* (1977). See also L. Hunt, *Inventing Human Rights* 76–77 (2007). ("In the sixteenth, seventeenth, and eighteenth centuries, many of Europe's finest legal minds devoted themselves to codifying and regularizing the uses of judicial torture in order to prevent abuses of it by overly zealous or sadistic judges.")

2. Langbein, supra note 1, at 3.

3. M. Foucault, *Discipline and Punish* 33 (A. Sheridan trans. 1977).

4. See H. Arendt, *On Violence* 44–56 (1970) (distinguishing power from violence).

5. See E. Scarry, *The Body in Pain: The Making and Unmaking of the World* 28–38 (1985).

6. See Foucault, supra note 3, at 236–39 (on conscience and reform).

7. Machiavelli's *The Prince* represents a desacralization of this practice of statecraft.

8. O. Gierke, *Political Theories of the Middle Age* 30 (F. Maitland, trans. 1913) [1900].

9. See R. Girard, *Violence and the Sacred* 17 (on the mimetic quality of violence).

10. See H. L. A. Hart, *The Concept of Law* 80–85 (1961).

11. "[B]y an act of 1585 the mere presence in England of a Jesuit or seminary priest constituted high treason." S. Greenblatt, "Shakespeare and the Exorcists," in *Shakespearean Negotiations* 94, 94 (1988).

12. See M. Walzer, *Introduction* to *Regicide and Revolution: Speeches at the Trial of Louis XVI* 1, 9 (M. Walzer, ed., M. Rothstein, trans. 1974).

13. See N. Feldman, *After Jihad: America and the Struggle for Islamic Democracy* (2003).

14. See R. Otto, *The Idea of the Holy* 12–19 (J. Harvey, trans. 1958) (on dread and awe before the mysterium tremendum).

15. Pierre Clastres describes a primitive form of the transformative powers of torture in the connection of pain, the sacred, and the transgenerational collective subject. That collective subject becomes the Western sovereign. See P. Clastres, "Of Torture in Primitive Societies," in *Society against the State: Essays in Political Anthropology* 177 (1987).

16. President Bush, for example, speaking of American plans in Iraq, said,

"The year ahead will demand more patience, sacrifice, and resolve . . . [for] times of testing reveal the character of a nation." President George W. Bush, President's Address to the Nation (Jan. 10, 2007), available at http://www .whitehouse.gov/news/releases/2007/01/20070110-7.html.

17. See S. Holmes, "Is Defiance of Law a Proof of Success? Magical Thinking in the War on Terror," in *The Torture Debate in America* 118, 120–22 (K. Greenberg, ed. 2006).

18. See P. Kahn, *Law and Love: The Trials of King Lear* 16 (2000).

19. See C. Taylor, *Modern Social Imaginaries* (2004).

20. For a contemporary example of the belief that consent is not central to the normative claim of faith, consider the case of Abdul Rahman, who was arrested and threatened with the death penalty in Afghanistan for converting from Islam to Christianity. See S. Munadi, "Afghan Case against Christian Convert Falters," *New York Times,* Mar. 23, 2006.

21. H. Hubert & M. Mauss, *Sacrifice: Its Nature and Its Functions* 28–32 (W. D. Halls, trans. 1981) [1898].

22. Augustine, for example, advocated the use of force against the Donatist heretics: "Does anyone doubt that it is preferable for people to be drawn to worship God by teaching rather than forced by fear of punishment or by pain? But because the one type of people are better, it does not mean that the others, who are not of that type, ought to be ignored. Experience has *enabled* us to prove, and continue to prove, that many people are benefitted by being compelled in the first place through fear or pain; so that subsequently they are able to be taught." Letter from Augustine to Boniface, no. 185 (c. 417) ¶ 21, in *Augustine: Political Writings* 186 (E. Atkins & R. Dodaro, eds. 2001). "Why shouldn't the Church, then, force her lost sons to return, when her lost sons have themselves compelled others to be lost? . . . Christ used force on Paul; the church imitates her Lord in using force on people in question" (¶ 23, at 188).

23. Consider the Spanish reading the Requiremento, in Spanish, to Native Americans.

24. See Foucault, supra note 3, at 57.

25. Hobbes still thinks it of little significance whether sovereignty arises from a freely given act of consent or from military defeat. See T. Hobbes, *Leviathan* 252 (C. Macpherson, ed. 1968) [1651].

26. See chapter 5 on memorialization.

27. See Foucault, supra note 3, at 62–65.

28. J. Whitman, *Harsh Justice: Criminal Punishment and the Widening Divide between America and Europe* (2003). See also L. Seidman, "Torture's Truth," 72 *U. Chi. L. Rev.* 881, 906 (2005) (arguing that torture works by proclaiming its victim to be nothing but the material body).

29. On the ritual of coronation, see F. Kern, *Kingship and Law in the Middle Ages* 33–38 (S. Chrimes, trans. 1939) [1914]; M. Fortes, "On Installation Ceremonies," 1967 *Proc. Royal Anthropological Inst. of Gr. Br. & Ir.* 5; C. Geertz, "Centers, Kings, and Charisma: Reflections on the Symbolics of Power," in *Culture and Its Creators* 150 (J. Ben-David & T. Clark, eds. 1977); M. Bloch, "Tombs and States," in *Mortality and Immortality: The Anthropology and Archaeology of Death* 137 (S. Humphreys & H. King, eds. 1981).

30. The testing of an oath of loyalty by torture is portrayed in the blinding of Gloucester in W. Shakespeare, *King Lear,* act 2, sc 7.

31. O. Holmes, "The Path of the Law," 10 *Harv. L. Rev.* 457, 469 (1897).

32. For this reason, limitations on military service—traditionally applied to women but now to homosexuals—will always appear as a denigration of equal citizenship.

33. See chapter 5.

34. That execution can be symbolic. The statue in New York of George III served this role. More recently, one saw the destruction of the statue of Sadam Hussein in Baghdad—an imitation of a revolutionary act perhaps? Compare "Saddam Statue Toppled in Central Baghdad," CNN.com, Apr. 9, 2003, available at http://www.cnn.com/2003/WORLD/meast/04/09/sprj.irq.statue/, to the painting by J. Oertel, *Pulling Down Statue of George III by the "Sons of Freedom" at the Bowling Green, City of New York, July 1776,* engraved by J. McRae, 1859, image reproduced at http://www.smithsoniansource.org/display/primarysource/viewdetails.aspx?PrimarySourceId=1077.

35. *Trop v. Dulles,* 356 U.S. 86, 102 (1958). ("The civilized nations of the world are in virtual unanimity that statelessness is not to be imposed as punishment for crime.") On the "inhumanity" of the stateless, see H. Arendt, *The Origins of Totalitarianism* 296–98 (1951).

36. The United States naturalization oath links foreign and domestic enemies, but today the latter category is essentially an empty set.

37. This is popularly represented, for example, in the film *The Dirty Dozen* (1967).

38. Contrast this story with the narrative of the rise of disciplinary power in Foucault and Agamben. G. Agamben, *Homo Sacer: Sovereign Power and Bare Life* (D. Heller-Roazen, trans. 1998).

39. Consider the execution of intellectuals in various modern revolutionary movements, for example, in Cambodia. Here, as in so much else, the practices of national socialism in Germany show us an extreme reflection of ourselves.

40. Agamben, supra note 38.

41. Oddly, George W. Bush manages to combine both forms of origin.

Chapter Two

1. Treason, *Columbia Encyclopedia* (6th ed. 2006). As long as laws are seen as an expression of the sovereign will, there is a tendency to see a violation of law as an act of betrayal—that is, as treason. See P. Kahn, *Out of Eden* 76 (2007).

2. Again, we hear in this word, a resonance of the religious—to surrender oneself to faith. See S. Weil, *Waiting for God* (E. Craufurd, trans. 1951); R. Wagner-Pacifici, *The Art of Surrender: Decomposing Sovereignty at Conflict's End* 36–37 (2005).

3. One should not overemphasize the claim that torture has been displaced by democratic combat. Torture fell out of place on the European battlefield, but Europeans—and Americans—have been quick to deploy torture when confronting the tactics of terror. This was true of the German response to resistance movements in occupied Europe and true as well of the French in Al-

giers, the British in the Middle East and Asia, and the Americans in Vietnam—and now, apparently, in Iraq.

4. See E. Kantorowicz, *The King's Two Bodies: A Study in Mediaeval Political Theology* (1957). See also works cited in supra note 29, chap. 1. Even today, the remaining ceremonial kings of Europe labor under an expectation of military service in their youth.

5. See C. Hedges, *War Is a Force That Gives Us Meaning* (2002).

6. See L. Hunt, *The Invention of Human Rights* (2007).

7. For this reason, the reform rhetoric of the twentieth century sounds surprisingly like that of two hundred years earlier, beginning, of course, with Thomas Paine's *The Rights of Man* (1791–92).

8. I explore degradation in chapter 5.

9. See, for example, H. Shue, "Torture," in *Torture: A Collection* 47, 51 (S. Levinson, ed. 2004). Consider also A. Dorfman, *Death and the Maiden* (1992).

10. The point here is similar to Arendt's analysis of the concentration camps, where the denial of recognition was so great that *torture* seems the wrong word to describe the destruction: it is administrative death. To care enough to torture is more recognition than was given in the camp or on the battlefield. See H. Arendt, *The Origins of Totalitarianism*, chap. 9 (1951).

11. Compare D. Sussman, "What's Wrong with Torture?" 33 *Phil. & Pub. Aff.* 1, 3 (2005); and D. Sussman, "Defining Torture," 37 *Case W. Res. J. Int'l L.* 225 (2006).

12. See C. von Clausewitz, *On War,* chap. 1, sec. 4. (M. Howard & P. Paret, eds. and trans. 1976).

13. During the Cold War, for example, whether the United States would actually use nuclear weapons—as it threatened—in defense of its European allies was often debated. See R. Dawson & R. Rosecrance, "Theory and Reality in the Anglo-American Alliance," 19 *World Pol.* 21 (1966) (on Britain and France and America's "credibility problem"). See also pages 24–25 (on Charles de Gaulle's doubts about America and France's nuclear ambitions); and G. Warner, "Review Article: The United States and the Western Alliance, 1958–63," 71 *Int'l Aff.* 801, 806 (1995). ("[Many European leaders] were beginning to have doubts, in the era of ICBMs, as to the dependability from their point of view of a purely U.S. controlled deterrent.")

14. Common Article 3 of the Geneva Conventions refers to "members of the armed forces who have laid down their arms." Geneva Convention Relative to the Treatment of Prisoners of War art. 3, Aug. 12, 1949, 75 U.N.T.S. 287.

15. See Uniform Code of Military Justice art. 99, which permits capital punishment against a member of the military "who casts away his arms or ammunition." 10 U.S.C. § 899 (2006).

16. See also the anonymous *A Woman in Berlin, Eight Weeks in the Conquered City: A Diary* (P. Boehm, trans. 2005) (describing a situation in which defeat encompasses torture—particularly rape—and martyrdom).

17. See *Mavrommatis Palestine Concessions,* 1924 P.C.I.J. (ser. A.) no. 2, at 12.

18. Accordingly, customary international law had to be understood as the "implied side [implicit consent] to the contractual theory that explains why

treaties are international law." M. Janis, *An Introduction to International Law* 43 (2003).

19. See P. Weil, "Towards Relative Normativity in International Law?" 77 *Am. J. Int'l L.* 413 (1983).

20. Grotius's work exemplifies this idea. See H. Grotius, *The Rights of War and Peace* (R. Tuck, ed. 2005) [1625].

21. This idea at the center of traditional international law becomes the foundation of Carl Schmitt's definition of the sovereign as he who decides on the exception. See C. Schmitt, *Political Theology: Four Chapters on the Concept of Sovereignty* 5 (G. Schwab, trans. 1985) [1922].

22. See UN Charter art. 2(4) ("All Members shall refrain in their international relations from the threat or use of force against the territorial integrity or political independence of any state"); and art. 51 ("Measures taken by Members in the exercise of this right of self-defence shall be immediately reported to the Security Council and shall not in any way affect the authority and responsibility of the Security Council . . . to take at any time such action as it deems necessary in order to maintain or restore international peace and security"). The Kellogg-Briand Pact of 1928 represented a wholly ineffectual attempt to use law to control international violence. See P. Kahn, "From Nuremberg to the Hague: The United States Position in *Nicaragua v. United States* and the Development of International Law," 12 *Yale J. Int'l L.* 1 (1987).

23. See, for example, A. Buchanan, *Justice, Legitimacy, and Self-Determination: Moral Foundations for International Law* (2004).

24. Typical of the new point of view is the following: "The State that claims sovereignty deserves respect only as long as it protects the basic rights of its subjects. It is from their rights that it derives its own." S. Hoffmann, "The Politics and Ethics of Military Intervention," 37 *Survival* 29, 35 (1995).

25. Of course, it is only a small step further to deny the power altogether and thus abolish capital punishment.

26. See A. Slaughter, *A New World Order* (2004); and R. Keohane, *After Hegemony: Cooperation and Discord in the World Political Economy* (1984).

27. See Jack Straw, "Secretary of State Statement in the House of Commons" (Mar. 2, 2000), in *The Pinochet Papers: The Case of Augusto Pinochet in Spain and Britain* 481, 482 (R. Brody & M. Ratner, eds. 2000) (explaining Great Britain's refusal to extradite Pinochet to Spain); and Legality of the Threat or Use of Nuclear Weapons, Advisory Opinion, 1996 I.C.J. 226, (July 8).

28. Reducing the role and range of this veto power—the requirement of unanimity—was a central goal of the proposed EU Constitution, which failed in French and Dutch referenda. See D. Chaibi, "The Foreign Policy Thread in the European Labyrinth," 19 *Conn. J. Int'l L.* 359, 387–89 (2004) (describing provisions in the draft constitution limiting the need for unanimity); and E. Sciolino, "European Leaders Give Up on Ratifying Charter by 2006," *New York Times,* June 17, 2005.

29. J. Assmann, *Moses the Egyptian: The Memory of Egypt in Western Monotheism* (1997).

30. See UN Charter art. 51 (protecting "inherent right of individual or collective self-defense if an armed attack occurs").

31. Convention against Torture and Other Cruel, Inhuman, or Degrading Treatment or Punishment art. 2(2), Dec. 10, 1984, 1465 U.N.T.S. 85.

32. For a review of the development of the concept, see C. Chinkin, "The Challenge of Soft Law: Development and Change in International Law," 38 *Int'l & Comp. L.Q.* 850 (1989).

33. See M. Howard, *War and the Liberal Conscience* 100–101 (1978).

34. See, for example, H. Kelsen, "Will the Judgment in the Nuremberg Trial Constitute a Precedent in International Law?" 1 *Int'l L.Q.* 153 (1947).

35. This is the ordinary form of argument justifying Security Council action under Chapter VII. See, for example, S.C. Res. 940, preamble, U.N. Doc. S/RES/940 (July 31, 1994) (justifying the international military mission to Haiti under Chapter VII powers in part because "the situation in Haiti continues to constitute a threat to peace and security in the region"); and A. Dowty & G. Loescher, "Refugee Flows as Grounds for International Action," 21 *Int'l Security* 43 (1996) (on the use of refugee flows into neighboring countries as a justification for force under Chapter VII of the UN Charter).

36. The United States had a parallel fear of the effect of international human rights on its regime of racial subordination, leading to the controversy over the proposed Bricker Amendment. The British had similar worries about the maintenance of their colonies. See M. Mazower, "The Strange Triumph of Human Rights, 1933–1950," 47 *Hist. J.* 379 (2004).

37. International Covenant on Civil and Political Rights, Dec. 16, 1966, 999 U.N.T.S. 171; International Covenant on Economic, Social, and Cultural Rights, Dec. 16, 1966, 993 U.N.T.S. 3.

38. The trial of Adolph Eichmann in Israel in 1961 was before a domestic not an international court. When the Nicaraguans took the United States to the ICJ, the United States simply walked away. See *Nicaragua v. United States,* 1984 I.C.J. Rep. 169.

39. See UN Charter art. 13(1)(a) (directing the General Assembly to encourage "the progressive development of international law").

40. Examples include China, Cuba, Zimbabwe, Russia, Pakistan, Saudi Arabia, Algeria, and Syria.

41. See O. Hathaway, "Do Human Rights Treaties Make a Difference?" 111 *Yale L.J.* 1935 (2002).

42. M. Doyle, "Kant, Liberal Legacies, and Foreign Affairs," 12 *Phil. & Pub. Aff.* 205 (1983); B. Russett, *Grasping the Democratic Peace: Principles for a Post–Cold War World* (1993).

43. Convention against Torture and Other Cruel, Inhuman, or Degrading Treatment or Punishment art. 1(1). The Convention does recognize the possibility of a "state of war" in Article 2(2) but only to affirm that it may not be invoked as a justification for torture. The only way, formally, to reconcile the definition and the recognition of war is through the concept of "lawful sanctions" at the conclusion of the definition. I suspect there was a vague idea that any legitimate use of force had to be a "lawful sanction"—including the use of force against a nation.

44. Compare this with the ICCPR, which at least acknowledges forced

military service as an exception to the prohibition on "forced or compulsory labor." International Covenant on Civil and Political Rights art. 8(3)(c)(ii).

45. Carl Schmitt famously linked sovereignty to the power to decide on the exception. See Schmitt, supra note 21, at 5.

46. Again, the model here is the EU. See, for example, J. Weiler, "The Transformation of Europe," 100 *Yale L.J.* 2403 (1991).

47. The International Criminal Court has a kind of supplemental jurisdiction: cases within its jurisdiction become admissible only when the relevant state "is unwilling or unable genuinely to carry out the investigation or prosecution." Rome Statute of the International Criminal Court art. 17(1)(a), July 17, 1998, 2187 U.N.T.S. 90.

48. Since the Geneva Conventions of 1949, its most basic norms, expressed in Common Article 3, have also extended to conflicts "not of an international character."

49. See M. Ignatieff, "The Warrior's Honor," in *The Warrior's Honor: Ethnic War and the Modern Conscience* 109 (1998).

50. See M. Koskenniemi, *The Gentle Civilizer of Nations: The Rise and Fall of International Law 1870–1960* (2002).

51. The Third Geneva Convention stipulates that the norms of treatment of prisoners of war shall be in large part governed by rank. See, for example, Geneva Convention Relative to the Treatment of Prisoners of War art. 39 ("Prisoners of war, with the exception of officers, must salute and show to all officers of the Detaining Power the external marks of respect provided for by the regulations applying in their own forces. Officer prisoners of war are bound to salute only officers of a higher rank of the Detaining Power; they must, however, salute the camp commander regardless of his rank."); and art. 43 ("Upon the outbreak of hostilities, the Parties to the conflict shall communicate to one another the titles and ranks of all the persons mentioned in Article 4 of the present Convention [prisoners of war], in order to ensure equality of treatment between prisoners of equivalent rank").

52. The Third Geneva Convention affords "prisoner of war" status to those captured who are not members of a "regular army" so long as they "fulfil the following conditions: (a) That of being commanded by a person responsible for his subordinates; (b) That of having a fixed distinctive sign recognizable at a distance; (c) That of carrying arms openly; (d) That of conducting their operations in accordance with the laws and customs of war." Geneva Convention Relative to the Treatment of Prisoners of War art. 4(2)(a)–(d).

53. Of course, the transition is hardly complete: slavery reappeared in the German war effort, just as it reappeared in Stalin's Soviet Union. A world of slavery will always include torture.

54. See R. Brooks, "The Politics of the Geneva Conventions: Avoiding Formalist Traps," 46 *Va. J. Int'l L.* 197, 197 (2005). ("[T]he Geneva Conventions were 'out of date' from the moment they entered into force; they laid out rules for a world more orderly than the world they had inherited, and hoped that by doing so, they would encourage life to imitate art.")

55. See, for example, F. Fanon, *The Wretched of the Earth* (C. Farrington, trans. 1963); and Kahn, supra note 1, chap. 4.

56. I owe this phrasing to Robert Post.

57. See J. Conroy, *Unspeakable Acts, Ordinary People: The Dynamics of Torture* (2000); and C. Browning, *Ordinary Men: Reserve Police Battalion 101 and the Final Solution in Poland* (1992).

58. See A. Slaughter, "A Liberal Theory of International Law," 94 *Am. Soc'y Int'l L. Proc.* 240 (2000).

59. See J. Waldron, "Torture and Positive Law: Jurisprudence for the White House," 105 *Colum. L. Rev.* 1681 (2005).

Chapter Three

1. David Luban calls this "the liberal ideology of torture." D. Luban, "Liberalism, Torture, and the Ticking Bomb," 91 *Va. L. Rev.* 1425, 1439 (2005). See also the essays by M. Walzer and J. Elshtain in *Torture: A Collection* (S. Levinson, ed. 2004).

2. Bernard Williams's consideration of the limits of utilitarianism begins with just such an example. See B. Williams, "A Critique of Utilitarianism," in J. Smart & B. Williams, *Utilitarianism: For and Against* 98–99 (1973) (on Jim and the Indians).

3. On utilitarianism as a form of consequentialism, see B. Williams, supra note 2, at 79–81.

4. See I. Kant, "On a Supposed Right to Lie Because of Philanthropic Concerns," in *Groundings for the Metaphysics of Morals* 63 (J. Ellington, trans. 1993) [1799].

5. See Luban, supra note 1.

6. See R. Brandt, *Ethical Theory: The Problems of Normative and Critical Ethics* (1959).

7. See G. Calabresi, *The Costs of Accidents: A Legal and Economic Analysis* (1970); and J. Murphy & J. Hampton, *Forgiveness and Mercy* (1988).

8. See the discussion of the asymmetrical logic of combat in chapter 2.

9. There has, for example, been an endless controversy over the appropriateness of a suppression of evidence remedy in cases of warrantless entry or voluntary confession obtained outside the *Miranda* requirements.

10. *Hamdi v. Rumsfeld,* 542 U.S. 507, 533–34 (2004) ("We . . . hold that a citizen-detainee seeking to challenge his classification as an enemy combatant must receive notice of the factual basis for his classification, and a fair opportunity to rebut the Government's factual assertions before a neutral decision-maker. . . . These essential constitutional promises may not be eroded. At the same time, the exigencies of the circumstances may demand that, aside from these core elements, enemy-combatant proceedings may be tailored to alleviate their uncommon potential to burden the Executive at a time of ongoing military conflict.") (internal quotations and citations omitted). See also T. Golden, "For Guantanamo Review Boards, Limits Abound," *New York Times,* Dec. 31, 2006 (detailing advocates' due process concerns about the operational rules of Combatant Status Review Tribunals).

11. Even human rights conventions include possibilities for derogation—though not from the torture prohibition—in situations of national emergency. See, for example, European Convention for the Protection of Human Rights and Fundamental Freedoms art. 15, Nov. 4, 1950, 213 U.N.T.S. 222.

12. The Supreme Court has, since 9/11, pursued a practice of judicial minimalism in considering issues arising out of the detention of alleged terrorists. It has taken a handful of cases and generally affirmed a right to legal process, but it has in each instance given narrow answers to particular questions. See *Hamdan v. Rumsfeld*, 126 S.Ct. 2749 (2006); *Rasul v. Bush*, 542 U.S. 446 (2004); and *Hamdi v. Rumsfeld*, 542 U.S. 507 (2004).

13. See M. Walzer, *Just and Unjust Wars: A Moral Argument with Historical Illustrations* 251–54 (1977).

14. See E. Posner, & A. Vermeule, "Should Coercive Interrogation Be Legal?" 104 *Mich. L. Rev.* 671 (2006).

15. *NLRB v. Jones & Laughlin Steel*, 301 U.S. 1, 41 (1937).

16. See, for example, F. Cohen, "Transcendental Nonsense and the Functional Approach," 35 *Colum. L. Rev.* 809 (1935); and O. Fiss, *History of the Supreme Court of the United States: Troubled Beginnings of the Modern State, 1888–1910*, at 1–8 (1993).

17. See P. Singer, *Animal Liberation: A New Ethics for Our Treatment of Animals* (1975); and *Animal Rights: Current Debates and New Directions* (C. Sunstein & M. Nussbaum, eds. 2004).

18. That community identity is at stake in the regimes that are to enforce the no-torture rule was recently illustrated in American practice. The no-torture principle may speak universally, but the legal structure of protection is divided along the line of citizenship. Citizens were quickly taken out of the prison on Guantánamo. Outside of Guantánamo, they had access to the ordinary courts. The British House of Lords rejected a dual-legal scheme in *A (FC) v. Sec'y of State for the Home Dep't*, [2004] UKHL 56 (holding that such a double structure violates the European Convention on Human Rights).

19. The torturer who breaks free of the community and becomes an independent entrepreneur of torture techniques becomes a powerful symbol of evil. He crosses the line between torture and terror. Consider the image in Latin America of the U.S. School of the Americas, which operated in the Canal Zone from 1963 to 1984.

20. See V. Held, *The Ethics of Care: Personal, Political, and Global* (2006).

21. See P. Kahn, *Law and Love* 145–48 (2000).

22. See P. Kahn, *Putting Liberalism in Its Place* 233–41 (2005).

23. See *id.* at 163.

24. For an effort to link rhetoric and moral argument, see E. Garver, *For the Sake of Argument: Practical Reasoning, Character, and the Ethics of Belief* (2004).

25. See A. Margalit, *The Ethics of Memory* 74–83 (2002).

26. For a history of the Doomsday Clock's movement, see *The Bulletin Online*, available at http://thebulletin.org/minutes-to-midnight/timeline.html.

27. Of course, individuals did try to make calculations of utility, but that always invoked a kind of horror. See, for example, H. Kahn, *Thinking about the Unthinkable* (1962).

28. See P. Kahn, "Nuclear Weapons and the Rule of Law," 31 *N.Y.U. J. Int'l L. & Pol.* 349 (1999).

29. See D. Luban, supra note 1, at 1442. ("The ticking-bomb scenario cheats . . . by stipulating that the bomb is there . . . and that officials know it and know they have the man who planted it. Those conditions will seldom be met.")

30. See R. Brooks, "Ticking Time Bombs and Catastrophes," 8 *Green Bag 2d* 311 (2005).

31. HCJ 5100/94 *Public Committee against Torture v. State of Israel*, [1999] IsrSC 53(1) 817.

32. See Rome Statute of the International Criminal Court art. 33(1)(c), July 17, 1998, 2187 U.N.T.S. 90 (on "manifestly unlawful" orders).

33. See G. Fletcher, *Rethinking Criminal Law*, chap. 10 (1978).

34. See chapter 5.

35. See J. White, C. Lane, & J. Tate, "Homicide Charges Rare in Iraq War," *Washington Post*, Aug. 28, 2006.

36. Oren Gross suggests that extraordinary measures of national defense should remain outside the legal order. O. Gross, "Chaos and Rules: Should Responses to Violent Crises Always Be Constitutional?" 112 *Yale L.J.* 1011 (2003). Retroactively, they might be approved by the state or they might simply be left in a kind of normative limbo—neither approved nor disapproved. The exact opposite position is offered by Bruce Ackerman in his work on the national emergency constitution: a legal regulatory scheme for the politics of emergencies. See B. Ackerman, *Before the Next Attack: Preserving Civil Liberties in an Age of Terrorism* (2006).

37. A. Dershowitz, *Why Terrorism Works: Understanding the Threat, Responding to the Challenge* 158–63 (2002); A. Dershowitz, "Want to Torture? Get a Warrant," *San Francisco Chronicle*, Jan. 22, 2002.

38. A. Dershowitz, "Is There a Torturous Road to Justice?" *Los Angeles Times*, November 8, 2001.

39. See R. Cover, "Violence and the Word," 95 *Yale L.J.* 1601, 1626–27 (1986); and A. Sarat, *When the State Kills* 187–208 (2002).

40. H. Arendt, *Eichmann in Jerusalem: A Report on the Banality of Evil* (1963).

41. Again, the similarity to Eichmann's sense of the Kantian morality of law is striking. See *id.* at 132–34.

42. See R. Cover, *Justice Accused: Antislavery and the Judicial Process* (1975).

43. *Planned Parenthood v. Casey*, 505 U.S. 833, 861 (1992).

44. *Id.* at 867–69.

45. See A. Sarat, "Violence, Representation, and Responsibility in Capital Trials: The View from the Jury," 70 *Ind. L.J.* 1103 (1995).

46. See, for example, J. Waldron, "Torture and Positive Law: Jurisprudence for the White House," 105 *Colum. L. Rev.* 1681, 1713–17 (2005); O. Gross, "Are Torture Warrants Warranted? Pragmatic Absolutism and Official Disobedience," 88 *Minn. L. Rev.* 1481 (2004); and S. Kreimer, "Too Close to the Rack and Screw: Constitutional Constraints on Torture in the War on Terror," 6 *U. Pa. J. Const. L.* 278 (2003).

47. See C. Marvin & D. Ingle, *Blood Sacrifice and the Nation: Totem Rituals and the American Flag* (1999).

48. In February 2005, Rep. Jane Harman (D-CA) announced her intention to introduce draft legislation allowing the president to authorize the use of "highly coercive interrogation" practices. See Amnesty International, Response to the Proposed "Interrogation Procedures Act," (Feb. 16, 2005), available at http://web.amnesty.org/library/Index/ENGAMR510392005. By the time Representative Harman introduced the bill in October 2005, this provision had been omitted. See Interrogation Procedures Act, H.R. 3985, 109th Cong. (2005).

49. See C. Schmitt, *Political Theology: Four Chapters on the Concept of Sovereignty* 5–7 (G. Schwab, trans. 1995) [1922].

50. This question dominated, for example, the hearings on Judge Samuel Alito's nomination to the Supreme Court. See *Hearing on the Nomination of Judge Samuel Alito to the U.S. Supreme Court before the S. Comm. on the Judiciary*, 109th Cong. (Jan. 10, 2006) (statements of senators Russell D. Feingold and Patrick Leahy).

51. See W. Benjamin, "Theses on the Philosophy of History," in *Illuminations: Essays and Reflections* 256 (H. Arendt, ed.; H. Zohn, trans. 1969).

Chapter Four

1. Bundesverfassungsgericht [Federal Constitutional Court], Feb. 15, 2006, 1 BvR 357/05 (F.R.G.) (invalidating a provision of the Aviation Security Act, which authorized the armed forces to shoot down civilian aircraft if hijacked). But see the proposal of the German interior minister, Wolfgang Schäuble, to amend the German Constitution in response to the decision. "Germany Plans to Change Constitution to Allow Hijacked Aircraft to Be Shot Down: Report," *Airline Industry Information*, Aug. 18, 2006.

2. See Restatement (Second) of Torts: Duty to Act for Protection of Others § 314 (1965).

3. One clear example is the Secret Service detail around the president. This generates a kind of mystique around them, and they are certainly operating in a zone beyond what law can compel. No one is conscripted into such a position.

4. See I. Clendinnen, *Aztecs: An Interpretation* 2 (1991). For a parallel discussion of the victors claiming the sacrificed body of the enemy as an instantiation of their—the victors'—beliefs, see E. Scarry, *The Body in Pain: The Making and Unmaking of the World* 116–17 (1985).

5. See chapter 3.

6. See S. Freud, *Totem and Taboo* 141–43 (J. Strachey, trans. 1950).

7. Consider, for example, the Stockholm syndrome.

8. See discussion of borders in chapter 5, see also H. Arendt, *Origins of Totalitarianism* 292 (1951).

9. See R. Girard, *The Scapegoat* (Y. Freccero, trans. 1986).

10. See P. Levi, *The Drowned and the Saved* 36 (R. Rosenthal, trans. 1988).

11. See Freud, supra note 6; and W. Benjamin, "Theses on the Philosophy of History," in *Illuminations* (H. Zohn, trans. 1968).

12. Shakespeare, *King Lear*, act 2, scene 4.

13. Sometimes the plot adds the ironic twist of having the threat to familial love come from the corrupt institutions of law, as in the films *A Time to Kill* (Warner Brothers 1996), *Above the Law* (Warner Brothers 1988), and *John Q* (New Line Productions 2002).

14. Ian McEwan's novel of this name is enmeshed in just these themes. A stranger appears as if from nowhere. He is the alien who wants to cross the border that defines the lovers' community; he wants to be a part, but there is no point of entry. Rejected, he threatens the beloved. The institutions of law fail to protect; sacrifice for the sake of love is demanded and performed. I. McEwan, *Enduring Love* (2004).

15. See R. Cover, "Foreword: Nomos and Narrative," 97 *Harv. L. Rev.* 4 (1983).

16. This is perhaps the most common theme of the popular genre of films that evoke the American myth of sacrifice: see, for example, *The Patriot* (Columbia Pictures 2000), *Armageddon* (Touchstone Pictures 1998), and *Saving Private Ryan* (Amblin Entertainment 1998).

17. W. H. Auden, "September 1, 1939," reprinted in *Another Time* (1940).

18. See Freud, supra note 6, at 64–69; consider also Richard Wagner's opera *Tristan and Isolde.*

19. Of course, I am not making any claims here for the particular form of the modern nuclear family.

20. See, for example, L. Bosniak, "Multiple Nationality and the Postnational Transformation of Citizenship," in *Rights and Duties of Dual Nationals: Evolution and Prospects* (D. Martin & K. Hailbronner, eds. 2002); and *Citizenship Today: Global Perspectives and Practices* (T. Aleinikoff & D. Klusmeyer, eds. 2001). Compare the Hague Convention on Certain Questions Relating to the Conflict of Nationality Laws, Apr. 12, 1930, 179 L.N.T.S. 39, the preamble of which states that "every person should have a nationality and should have one nationality only."

21. See, for example, P. Spiro, "Dual Nationality and the Meaning of Citizenship," 46 *Emory L.J.* 1411, 1416 (1997).

22. Arendt points out that even the foreigners fighting in the Spanish Civil War tended to understand their sacrificial politics in terms of their unique national situations. See Arendt, supra note 8, at 280.

23. There is nothing comparable to the international jihadist movement.

24. See P. Singer, *Corporate Warriors: The Rise of the Privatized Military Industry* (2003).

25. See D. Rieff, *A Bed for the Night: Humanitarianism in Crisis* 250–65 (2002) (on the difficulties that arise for aid workers when soldiers share in these tasks).

26. See, for example, M. Mutua, "Savages, Victims, and Saviors: The Metaphor of Human Rights," 42 *Harv. Int'l L.J.* 201 (2001).

27. Ultimately, for the sake of his friends, he allows them to propose a trivial fine that they would pay on his behalf—probably Plato's attempt to justify his own failure to save his teacher.

28. This is often referred to as the "persuade or obey" doctrine. See, for ex-

ample, C. Reeve, *Socrates in the Apology: An Essay on Plato's Apology of Socrates* 117–20 (1989).

29. I. Kant, "To Perpetual Peace: A Philosophical Sketch," in *Perpetual Peace and Other Essays* 112–13 (T. Humphrey, trans. 1983) [1795]; M. Doyle, "Kant, Liberal Legacies, and Foreign Affairs," 12 *Phil. & Pub. Aff.* 205 (1983); B. Russett, *Grasping the Democratic Peace: Principles for a Post–Cold War World* (1993).

30. T. Hobbes, *Leviathan* pt. 2, chap. 21, ¶¶ 11–16 (C. B. Macpherson, ed. 1968) [1651].

31. See G. Bataille, *The Accursed Share: An Essay on General Economy*, vol. 1: *Consumption* (R. Hurley, trans. 1988).

32. See P. Kahn, *Out of Eden: Adam and Eve and the Problem of Evil*, chap. 5 (2007).

33. Aristotle *Nicomachean Ethics* 6.1134a25–b17.

34. On memorialization, see chapter 5. On rhetoric as the language of sovereignty, see P. Kahn, *Putting Liberalism in Its Place* 244–55 (2005).

35. See, for example, J. S. Mill, "A Few Words on Non-Intervention," in *Essays on Equality, Law, and Education* (J. Robson, ed. 1984) [1859].

36. If one were interested in the historical origins of the political community, I imagine it began with the willingness to sacrifice to defend the family. We can speak of the arrival of a political state when the community of sacrifice extends beyond those whom one knows intimately. See B. Anderson, *Imagined Communities: Reflections on the Origin and Spread of Nationalism* (1991). The connection from beginning to end is the erotic bond: politics steps into the place held by the erotic life of the family as the community of meaningful sacrifice. Compare the father's right to demand the death of his child: this is a legal configuration of the familial right to sacrifice the child. See G. Agamben, *Homo Sacer: Sovereign Power and Bare Life* (1998); and J. Bodin, *Six Books on the Commonwealth* 11–13 (M. J. Tooley, trans. 1967) [1576].

37. Whether birth—natality—is the better image than communion is the question that divides Arendt's secularism from Schmitt's political theology. See H. Arendt, *On Revolution* (1963).

38. See H. Frankfurt, "On God's Creation," in *Necessity, Volition, and Love* 117 (1999).

39. Arguably the remaining monarchs of Europe are just such symbols of national sovereignty, that is, they have become the objects of a pledge rather than an oath.

40. See C. Marvin & D. Ingle, *Blood Sacrifice and the Nation: Totem Rituals and the American Flag* (1999).

41. See Kahn, supra note 34, at 257–58.

42. This was the ambition of my two-volume political theology of modernity. See Kahn, supra note 34; and Kahn, supra note 32.

43. On this view, self-love is a puzzling concept. But see H. Frankfurt, *The Reasons of Love* 71–100 (2004).

44. See P. Kahn, *Law and Love: The Trials of King Lear* 145–48 (2000).

45. See, for example, D. Adair, *Fame and Founding Fathers: Essays* (1974); and R. Chernow, *Alexander Hamilton* (2004). The formal legacy of this imagina-

tion of sacrifice is the Second Amendment, which sits awkwardly with our own liberalism. See S. Levinson, "The Embarrassing Second Amendment," 99 *Yale L.J.* 637 (1989). An armed citizenry is not just prepared to kill but also to die for the state. Indeed, because it is prepared to die, it is prepared to kill.

46. See A. Lincoln, "The Perpetuation of Our Political Institutions," Address before the Young Men's Lyceum of Springfield, Illinois (Jan. 27, 1838), in *Abraham Lincoln: His Speeches and Writings* 76–85 (R. Basler, ed. 1946) (on reverence for law and for a new religion based on that reverence).

47. This may well have been Voltaire's thought, for he spoke from a position of political exile.

48. Though a nation of immigrants, the United States is marked by a consistent worry over who can bear the burden of the "we." *Dred Scott* declared that no black could be a part of that "we." *Dred Scott v. Sanford*, 60 U.S. 393 (1857). Fifty years later the worry was over Asians. Today the worry is directed at Latinos. See S. Huntington, *Who Are We? The Challenges to America's National Identity* (2004). The gendered character of that "we" has been the subject of scholarship for more than a generation. See, for example, R. Siegel, "She the People: The Nineteenth Amendment, Sex Equality, Federalism, and the Family," 115 *Harv. L. Rev.* 947 (2002).

49. See J. Assmann, *Moses the Egyptian: The Memory of Egypt in Western Monotheism* 44–47 (1997).

50. G. Hegel, *Phenomenology of the Spirit* 234–40 (J. B. Baille, trans. 1967) (on the master/slave dialectic). Nietzsche's charge that the Christian morality of individual well-being was the triumph of a "slave morality" arises directly out of this point.

51. See generally K. Armstrong, *The Great Transformation: The Beginning of Our Religious Traditions* (2006).

52. Consider the imagery of the hymn "Onward, Christian Soldiers, Marching as to War."

53. See chapter 5.

54. R. Girard, *Violence and the Sacred* (P. Gregory, trans. 1977).

55. See chapter 5 on acoustic separation.

56. Capital punishment, in this view, can appear as a kind of internal contradiction of the purpose of a legal order. Indeed, there is something lawless about the modern practice of capital punishment. Its practice is shot through with the arbitrariness of selection for death, and it cannot be practiced without invoking counterpractices of mercy.

57. See P. Kahn, *The Cultural Study of Law: Reconstructing Legal Scholarship* 86–89 (1999) (on "auto-theory").

58. See Girard, supra note 54, at 18.

59. See P. Kahn, "Legal Performance and the Imagination of Sovereignty," 31 *E-Misferica* (2006), available at http://www.hemisphericinstitute.org/journal/home.php?issue=april%202006&language=English.

60. See *Planned Parenthood v. Casey*, 505 U.S. 833, 869 (1992). ("A decision to overrule *Roe's* essential holding under the existing circumstances would address error, if error there was, at the cost of both profound and unnecessary damage to the Court's legitimacy, and to the Nation's commitment to the rule

of law. It is therefore imperative to adhere to the essence of *Roe's* original decision, and we do so today.") But consider also *Dred Scott* as a failure of legal ritual, discussed in P. Kahn, *Legitimacy and History: Self-Government in American Constitutional Theory* 46–53 (1992).

61. On borders, see chapter 5.

62. See, for example, the report of the UN High-Level Panel on Threats, Challenges, and Change, which concluded, "Whatever perceptions may have prevailed when the Westphalian system first gave rise to the nation of State sovereignty, today it clearly carries with it the obligation of a State to protect the welfare of its own peoples and meet its obligations to the wider international community." UN High-Level Panel on Threats, Challenges, and Change, *A More Secure World: Our Shared Responsibility*, pt. 1, sec. II.C, ¶ 29, U.N. Doc. A/59/565 (Dec. 2, 2004), available at http://www.un.org/secureworld/re port2.pdf. See also A. von Bogdandy, "Constitutionalism in International Law: Comment on a Proposal from Germany," 47 *Harv. Int'l L.J.* 223 (2006).

63. In American history, that danger of revolutionary renewal may have been more prominent in the election of 1800, which Jefferson labeled the "Second American Revolution."

64. But see C. Beard, *An Economic Interpretation of the Constitution of the United States* (1935).

65. See M. Mason, "The Battle of the Slaveholding Liberators: Great Britain, the United States, and Slavery in the Early Nineteenth Century," 59 *Wm. & Mary Q.* 1, 6 (2002) (in the lead-up to the War of 1812, "The rhetoric of slavery pervaded American attacks on [British] impressment. . . . Prowar Americans employed the language of slavery in part because its force matched their outrage at the seizure of their fellow citizens. Forced labor on the high seas presented a natural parallel to the Atlantic slave trade. . . . President James Madison echoed such expressions, writing of Britain's entire maritime policy that 'such an outrage on all decency was never before heard of even on the shores of Africa'"). Earlier, in dealing with Barbary pirates, Jefferson had confronted the slavery issue—and committed force in response. See A. Whipple, *To the Shores of Tripoli: The Birth of the U.S. Navy and Marines* (1991).

66. The Hartford Convention during the War of 1812 and the earlier plot of Aaron Burr to lead a seccession of western states are two examples. On the Hartford Convention, see J. Banner, *To the Hartford Convention: The Federalists and the Origins of Party Politics in Massachusetts, 1789–1815* (1969); on Burr's plan to break off the Southwest from the United States, see D. Loth, *Chief Justice: John Marshall and the Growth of the Republic* 218–19 (1949).

67. In the South, of course, for a long time Lincoln remained the archetypal figure of aggressor: political sacrifice is always killing as well as being killed.

68. Compare, for example, M. Paulsen, "The Merryman Power and the Dilemma of Autonomous Executive Branch Interpretation," 15 *Cardozo L. Rev.* 81, 98–99 (1993); and A. Amar, "Architexture," 77 *Ind. L.J.* 671, 697–98 (2002).

69. See, for example, S. Strange, "The Declining Authority of States," in *The Global Transformations Reader: An Introduction to the Globalization Debate* 149

(D. Held & A. McGrew, eds. 2003) ("Where states were once the masters of markets, now it is the markets which, on many crucial issues, are the masters over the governments of states. And the declining authority of states is reflected in a growing diffusion of authority to other institutions and associations, and to local and regional bodies, and in a growing asymmetry between the larger states with structural power and weaker ones without it."); S. Krasner, "Compromising Westphalia," 20 *Int'l Security* 115 (1996); S. Krasner, *Sovereignty: Organized Hypocrisy* (1999); Y. Soysal, *Limits of Citizenship* (1994); and J. Camilleri & J. Falk, *End of Sovereignty? The Politics of a Shrinking and Fragmenting World* (1992).

70. What I have elsewhere called "political action" exists right alongside the rule of law. See P. Kahn, *The Reign of Law: Marbury v. Madison and the Construction of America* 27–34 (1997).

71. Compare J. Whitman, *Harsh Justice: Criminal Justice and the Widening Divide between America and Europe* 179 (2003) (on the European tradition of distinguishing those who were " 'really' criminals" from political prisoners).

72. For this reason, liberal theorists such as Kant argue that the person who violates his moral duty is living a contradiction: he must affirm the very rule that he violates. Modern theorists speak instead of a free-rider problem.

73. See M. Foucault, *Discipline and Punish: The Birth of the Prison* (A. Sheridan, trans. 1977).

74. See D. Luban, "The War on Terrorism and the End of Human Rights," 22 *Phil. & Pub. Pol'y Q.* 9 (summer 2002); N. Feldman, "Choices of Law, Choices of War," 25 *Harv. J.L. & Pub. Pol'y* 457 (2002).

75. See H. Arendt, *Eichmann in Jerusalem: Report on the Banality of Evil* 120–22 (1963). The harsh reaction to Dershowitz's proposal of torture warrants is yet another example. See chapter 3.

76. See Kahn, supra note 70, at 156–60.

77. For an interesting exception, see O. Gross, "Chaos and Rules: Should Responses to Violent Crises Always Be Constitutional?" 112 *Yale L.J.* 1011 (2003).

Chapter Five

1. There can be quasi-legal regimes of gift. See M. Mauss, *The Gift: The Form and Reason for Exchange in Archaic Societies* (W. D. Halls, trans. 1990) [1923–24].

2. See P. Kahn, "The Paradox of Riskless Warfare," 22 *Phil. & Pub. Pol'y Q.* 2 (summer 2002).

3. See H. Hubert & M. Mauss, *Sacrifice: Its Nature and Functions* 44 (W. D. Halls, trans. 1964) [1899]. ("The victim is the intermediary through which the communication [with the sacred] is established. Thanks to it, all the participants which come together in sacrifice are united in it.").

4. See Kahn, supra note 2.

5. Even states that agree to comply with humanitarian law are not thereby agreeing to a mutual exchange of deadly force: compliance with *jus in bello* has no bearing on *jus ad bellum*. Modern international law has simultaneously pro-

hibited the use of force under the UN Charter and regulated the forms of warfare under the Geneva Conventions.

6. See T. Hobbes, *Leviathan*, pt. 2, chap. 21, ¶¶ 11–16 (C. B. Macpherson, ed. 1968) [1651] ("[C]ovenants not to defend a man's own body are void. Therefore . . . a man that is commanded as a soldier to fight against the enemy, though his sovereign has right enough to punish his refusal with death, may nevertheless in many cases refuse without injustice."); and M. Walzer, *Obligations: Essays on Disobedience, War, and Citizenship* 82–88 (1970).

7. See generally P. Kahn, *Putting Liberalism in Its Place* (2005).

8. As politics has become more democratic around the world in the twentieth and twenty-first centuries, the incidence of violent civil war has dramatically increased. See N. Ferguson, "The Next War of the World," 85 *Foreign Aff.* 61 (Sept.–Oct. 2006).

9. See C. Moore, *The Loyalists: Revolution, Exile, Settlement* (1984); and C. van Tyne, *The Loyalists in the American Revolution* (1959).

10. See J. G. Gray, *The Warriors: Reflections on Men in Battle* 28 (1970) (describing war years for soldiers as "the one great lyric passage in their lives") (quoting Dixon Wecter).

11. The Cedar Revolution in Lebanon provides a recent example of such a struggle over the meaning of a political death—that of Rafik Hariri. For many Lebanese, Hariri died a martyr. If he was not sacrificed for the revolution, then his murder expressed only Syrian power.

12. Here one needs to compare the dissolution of Czechoslovakia to that of Yugoslavia. The former was an example of a desacralized politics of the sort that has been advancing within the European Union project. Even in the 1990s, however, the choice of nonviolence was not always tactically possible. In particular, the long wars over the breakup of the former Yugoslavia remind us just how violent the struggle for a historical and geographical presence can be.

13. Slave rebellions occurred, but, because they were unsuccessful, they were not memorialized—remembered—in the national narrative.

14. *Demonstration* is deliberately ambiguous with respect to whether its meaning lies with the actor or the spectator. A demonstration must be perceived, which means that the sacrificial act of the black person had to occur under conditions within which it could be perceived as such. The need for a common ground of perception sets the practical limits of any nonviolent campaign for political recognition.

15. This clash is at issue in *Walker v. Birmingham*, 388 U.S. 307 (1967), in which the Supreme Court upheld a contempt citation against King for failing to comply with legal procedures in disobeying a state court's temporary restraining order.

16. That sacrificial victim as an instantiation of the sovereign can now move back and forth across the color line—consider the murders of civil rights activists Andrew Goodman, James Chaney, and Michael Schwerner.

17. See R. Cover, "Foreword: Nomos and Narrative," 97 *Harv. L. Rev.* 4 (1983); and P. Kahn, "Interpretation and Authority in State Constitutionalism," 106 *Harv. L. Rev* 1147 (1993).

18. The category "civil war" is, therefore, always difficult to maintain unless it rests on a spatial division—expressed in classic international law in the concept of "belligerency." What appears to one side as a civil war appears to the other as the revolutionary appearance of the popular sovereign. For example, the British lost their civil war with the American colonies while the Americans won their revolution. The American Civil War had the same conceptual shape with an opposite outcome. The North won its civil war, while the South lost its revolutionary claim to speak in the name of the popular sovereign.

19. Accompanying this "dream" is often a parallel fear of the presence of a "fifth column," that is, a worry about an unseen presence.

20. UN Charter art. 51. ("Nothing in the present Charter shall impair the inherent right of individual or collective self-defense if an armed attack occurs.")

21. See Frontier Dispute Case (*Burkina Faso v. Mali*), 1986 *I.C.J. Reports* 554 (Dec. 22) (holding that *uti possidetis juris* is a "general principle, which is logically connected with the phenomenon of the obtaining of independence, wherever it occurs"). See also W. M. Reisman, "Protecting Indigenous Rights in International Adjudication," 89 *Am. J. Int'l L.* 350, 360–61 (1995); and Resolution on the Inviolability of Frontiers, OAU Doc. AGH/Res. 16(I) (1964), quoted in Reisman at 361 (all the member states of the Organization of African Unity "solemnly . . . pledge themselves to respect the frontiers existing on their achievement of national independence").

22. See, for example, the International Court of Justice's judgment in the Nicaragua case, identifying American support for the Contras as a transborder violation even if it was not an "armed attack." Military and Paramilitary Activities (*Nicaragua v. United States*), 1986 *I.C.J. Reports* 14. See also T. Franck, "Who Killed Article 2(4)? or Changing Norms Governing the Use of Force by States," 64 *Am. J. Int'l L.* 809 (1970).

23. The United States, in particular, lived in the ambiguity, supporting international law for others while constantly worrying that an effective, institutionalized international law would undermine its own sovereignty. See *American Exceptionalism and Human Rights* (M. Ignatieff, ed. 2005).

24. By virtue of its disproportion, the reaction raises questions of racism. Race can easily become a marker of difference at the border.

25. The United States has also authorized construction of a fence in response to what is perceived as a challenge to sovereign identity from illegal immigration through Mexico. Secure Fence Act of 2006, Pub. L. No. 109–367, 120 Stat. 2638 (codified at 8 U.S.C. § 1101 [2006]).

26. See *United States v. Flores-Montano*, 541 U.S. 149, 152–53 (2004) ("The Government's interest in preventing the entry of unwanted persons and effects is at its zenith at the international border. Time and again, we have stated that searches made at the border, pursuant to the longstanding right of the sovereign to protect itself by stopping and examining persons and property crossing into this country, are reasonable simply by virtue of the fact that they occur at the border. Congress, since the beginning of our Government, has granted the Executive plenary authority to conduct routine searches and seizures at the

border, without probable cause or a warrant") (internal quotations and citations omitted).

27. U.S. immigration law has traditionally distinguished between "deportation," the expulsion of an alien already present in the country, and "exclusion," the refusal to admit an alien into the country. Despite the apparent simplicity of the distinction, a legal presence has never been coterminous with an actual presence: aliens who are physically located within U.S. territory have often been "excluded" not "deported." Congress unified the terminology with the passage of the Illegal Immigrant Reform and Immigrant Responsibility Act of 1996 (IIRIRA), but many of the functional distinctions remain. The delinking of a physical and legal presence leads to serious consequences for individual aliens, some of whom have lived in the United States for years but, for purposes of their removal proceedings, are treated as though they have not yet crossed the border. See, for example, 8 U.S.C. § 1101(a)(13)(B) (on parolees); and *Leng v. Barber*, 357 U.S. 185, 187–89 (1958) (distinguishing between legal and physical entry).

28. Consider, for example, the altered operation of the Fourth Amendment at the international border, allowing for "border searches" without a warrant or probable cause. See supra at note 26; and *United States v. Ramsey*, 431 U.S. 606, 619 (1977). Notably, the "border search" rule applies not only at the physical border but also at certain locations within the interior of the United States such as some checkpoints along roads leading from the border, which are considered to be the border's "functional equivalents." See *United States v. Martinez-Fuerte*, 428 U.S. 543 (1976); and *United States v. Hill*, 939 F.2d 934, 936 (11th Cir. 1991).

29. See the United Nations Convention on the Law of the Sea art. 92(1), Dec. 10, 1982, 1833 U.N.T.S. 397. ("Ships shall sail under the flag of one State only and, save in exceptional cases expressly provided for in international treaties or in this Convention, shall be subject to its exclusive jurisdiction on the high seas.") The same logic extends by analogy to aircraft. See 18 U.S.C. § 7 (extending U.S. jurisdiction to U.S. maritime vessels, aircraft, and other vehicles).

30. Traditionally, prisoners could be shot when they could not be taken safely behind a secure border. See, for example, U.S. Army General Order No. 100, Instructions for the Government of Armies of the United States in the Field [the "Lieber Code"] art. 60, Apr. 24, 1863, available at http://www.yale .edu/lawweb/avalon/lieber.htm. ("A commander is permitted to direct his troops to give no quarter, in great straits, when his own salvation makes it impossible to cumber himself with prisoners.")

31. See L. Rohter, "Death Squad Fears Again Haunt Argentina," *New York Times*, Oct. 8, 2006, § 1, at 6 (describing the Argentine Association of the Victims of Terrorism as the counterpart of the Torture Victim Association); and M. Osiel, *Mass Atrocity, Ordinary Evil, and Hannah Arendt: Criminal Consciousness in Argentina's Dirty War* (2001).

32. The full elaboration of this perspective is the project of my two-volume *Political Theology of Modernity*. See Kahn, supra note 7; and P. Kahn, *Out of Eden: Adam and Eve and the Problem of Evil* (2007).

33. Kofi Annan, the former secretary general of the United Nations, went further, suggesting that sovereignty has moved to the individual. K. Annan, "Two Concepts of Sovereignty," *Economist,* Sept. 18, 1999, available at http://www.un.org/News/ossg/sg/stories/kaecon.html. ("State sovereignty, in its most basic sense, is being redefined—not least by the forces of globalisation and international co-operation. States are now widely understood to be instruments at the service of their peoples, and not vice versa. At the same time individual sovereignty—by which I mean the fundamental freedom of each individual, enshrined in the charter of the U.N. and subsequent international treaties—has been enhanced by a renewed and spreading consciousness of individual rights.") But compare the Constitution Restoration Act, S. 520, 109th Cong., 1st sess. (Mar. 3, 2005) (proposing to protect from judicial review any official acknowledgment of "God as the sovereign source of law, liberty or government").

34. See chapter 2.

35. See H. Arendt, *Origins of Totalitarianism* 292 (1951) (the stateless would gain legal recognition, and thus be better off, were they to commit a crime).

36. The president's asserted power to label a citizen as an "enemy combatant" and detain him on that ground indefinitely was rejected in *Hamdi v. Rumsfeld,* 542 U.S. 507 (2004). In *Hamdan v. Rumsfeld,* 126 S.Ct. 2749 (2006), the Supreme Court ruled that under current law the president lacks such a power even with respect to noncitizens. Congress then responded by giving the president much of the authority to proceed as he had proposed. Military Commissions Act of 2006, Pub. L. No. 109–366, 120 Stat. 2600 (Oct. 17, 2006).

37. See chapter 2.

38. "Judge Hits Back in Moussaoui Spat," *BBC News Online,* May 4, 2006, available at http://news.bbc.co.uk/2/hi/americas/4972/84.stm.

39. This ambiguity ironically created an opening for law in Latin America. If disappearance is outside of law, then a statute of limitations cannot begin to run. See Inter-American Convention on the Forced Disappearance of Persons art. VII, June 9, 1994, 33 I.L.M. 1529 (entered into force March 28, 1996) ("Criminal prosecution for the forced disappearance of persons . . . shall not be subject to statutes of limitations.").

40. Because of technical advances in identifying remains, we are approaching a point where there may no longer be an "unknown soldier." The remains of the unknown Vietnam veteran were removed from the tomb at Arlington National Cemetery after they were identified in 1998.

41. Even truth and reconciliation commissions, when they name the disappeared, must negotiate a line between justice and memorialization. The former sees victims; the latter sees martyrs. These are not necessarily the same, as the failure of posttransition prosecutions around the world reminds us.

42. Sacred productions may, of course, continue to be appreciated as art, but while the aesthetic and the sacred may intersect in the same object they are not the same experience.

43. See J. Malamud-Goti, *Game without End: State Terror and the Politics of Justice* (1996).

44. See W. Benjamin, "Theses on the Philosophy of History," in *Illumina-*

tions 255 (H. Zohn, trans. 1968). ("Only that historian will have the gift of fanning the spark of hope in the past who is firmly convinced that *even the dead* will not be safe from the enemy if he wins.")

45. See M. Howard, *War and the Liberal Conscience* (1986).

46. See chapter 2.

47. On the American rule of law's continuity with British law, see P. Kahn, *The Reign of Law* 150–53 (1997).

48. See M. Ignatieff, "The Narcissism of Minor Difference," in *The Warrior's Honor: Ethnic War and the Modern Conscience* 34–71 (1998).

49. On December 12, 2006, the Israeli Supreme Court invalidated a ban on any lawsuit brought by Palestinians for damages for harm inflicted by the Israeli Defense Forces. The decision, however, specifically excluded damages resulting from "acts of war." See H.C. 8276/05 *Adalah v. Minister of Defense* [2006] IsrSC; see also S. Erlanger, "Israeli Court Rules Army Can Be Held Liable," *New York Times*, Dec. 12, 2006.

50. Schmitt already makes this point. C. Schmitt, *The Concept of the Political* 54 (G. Schwab, trans. 1996).

51. See N. Berman, "Privileging Combat? Contemporary Conflict and the Legal Construction of War," 43 *Colum. J. Transnat'l L.* 1 (2004).

52. For example, U.S. Civil War General William T. Sherman is quoted as saying, "War is cruelty . . . the crueler it is, the sooner it will be over." H. Hathaway & A. Jones, *How the North Won* 548 (1983). Others have echoed this statement. See "Note, Discrimination in the Laws of Information Warfare," 37 *Colum. J. Transnat'l L.* 939, 958 n.73 (1999) (referring to similar statements from Harold Selesky); "Colonial America," in *The Laws of War: Constraints on Warfare in the Western World* 61 (M. Howard et al., eds. 1994) (reporting that the British strategy in Ireland evinced a belief that a "short war was . . . better for the Irish . . . because the terror sown by cruelty to a few would break resistance sooner . . . than would . . . a campaign of attrition"); and U.S. Army General Order No. 100, Instructions for the Government of Armies of the United States in the Field [the "Lieber Code"] art. 29, Apr. 24, 1863, available at http://www.yale.edu/lawweb/avalon/lieber.htm ("The more vigorously wars are pursued, the better it is for humanity. Sharp wars are brief.").

53. The "Powell Doctrine" is a contemporary variant on this idea of deploying an overwhelming force. See C. Powell, "U.S. Forces: Challenges Ahead," 71 *Foreign Aff.* 32, 40 (winter 1992–93). ("Decisive means and results are always to be preferred . . . . [War] is the scourge of God. We should be very careful how we use it. When we do use it, we should not be equivocal: we should win and win decisively. If our objective is something short of winning—as in our air strikes into Libya in 1986—we should see our objective clearly, then achieve it swiftly and efficiently.")

54. See chapter 2.

55. W. Churchill, Speech on Dunkirk before the House of Commons (June 4, 1940), in 6 *Winston S. Churchill: His Complete Speeches, 1897–1963*, at 6231 (R. James, ed. 1974).

56. See generally Ignatieff, supra note 48; see also chapter 2.

57. I borrow the term from Meir Dan-Cohen. See M. Dan-Cohen, "Deci-

sion Rules and Conduct Rules: On Acoustic Separation in Criminal Law," 97 *Harv. L. Rev.* 625 (1984).

58. See O. Gross, "Chaos and Rules: Should Responses to Violent Crises Always Be Constitutional?" 112 *Yale L.J.* 1011 (2003).

59. Arendt, for this reason, speaks of the political as miraculous. See H. Arendt, "Introduction into Politics," in *The Promise of Politics* 111–14 (2005).

60. See the discussion of borders earlier in this chapter.

61. Of course, it is also the case that the existence of the sacrificial imagination makes possible the perception of an enemy.

62. See M. Foucault, *Discipline and Punish: The Birth of the Prison* 59–65 (A. Sheridan, trans. 1977) (on the risk that the audience might judge the execution unjust and rebel against the executioner).

63. See the Military Commissions Act of 2006, supra note 36.

64. See P. Kahn, "Reason and Will in the Origins of American Constitutionalism," 98 *Yale L.J.* 449 (1989).

65. The speechless quality of sacrifice leads us to describe the sacred violence of others as "nihilism." Of course, that is only to say we don't live in the symbolic universe within which that violence gains its meaning.

66. This must have been the experience of the many European soldiers/victims of World War I.

67. See C. Hedges, *War Is a Force That Gives Us Meaning* (2002).

68. See R. Girard, *Violence and the Sacred* (P. Gregory, trans. 1972).

69. There have been, for example, allegations of British troops engaging in similar behavior in Iraq. See "UK Troops in Iraqi Torture Probe," *BBC News Online,* May 1, 2004, available at http://news.bbc.co.uk/2/hi/uk_news/politics/3675215.stm (reporting on the *Daily Mirror*'s publication of photos apparently depicting British soldiers torturing an Iraqi prisoner). But see also "Doubt Cast on Iraq Torture Photos," *BBC News Online,* May 2, 2004, available at http://news.bbc.co.uk/2/hi/uk_news/3677311.stm (reporting doubts about the photos' authenticity). The internal conflict in Iraq demonstrates a pervasive turn to torture. See Human Rights Watch, "The New Iraq? Torture and Ill-Treatment of Detainees in Iraqi Custody" (Jan. 2005), available at http://hrw.org/reports/2005/iraq0105/index.htm (documenting widespread abuse of prisoners by Iraqi police and security forces since late 2003).

70. To deny the rational requires more than torture. It requires the Nazi world of the Final Solution in which reason itself can no longer function as a guide. See P. Levi, *Survival in Auschwitz: The Nazi Assault on Humanity* (S. Woolf, trans. 1996).

71. "The Deaths at Gitmo," *New York Times,* June 12, 2006, at 16 (quoting the camp commander Rear Adm. Harry Harris Jr.: " 'I believe this was not an act of desperation, but an act of asymmetrical warfare waged against us,' he said. The inmates, he said, 'have no regard for life, neither ours nor their own.' ").

72. See Kahn, supra note 7, at 208–18 (on politics and pornography).

73. Degradation as the condition of defeat of an enemy state was traditionally also pursued in the violence peripheral to combat itself: rape, looting, and slavery.

74. See P. Kahn, "Why the United States Is So Opposed," in *Crimes of War*

Project: The International Criminal Court—an End to Impunity? (2003), available at http://www.crimesofwar.org/print/icc/icc-kahn-print.html.

75. For an expression of the opposite point of view, compare Israeli chief justice Barak's opinion in the targeted killings case in which the court extended elements of due process even as it held that extrajudicial killings of members of terrorist groups are not "inherently illegal." HCJ 769/02 Pub. Comm. Against Torture in Isr. v. Israel (Dec. 14, 2006).

Conclusion

1. See M. Howard, *War and the Liberal Conscience* 3 (1978). ("[T]he liberal tradition . . . regards war as an unnecessary aberration from normal international intercourse and believes that in a rational, orderly world wars would not exist.")

2. See D. Luban, "Liberalism, Torture, and the Ticking Bomb," 91 *Va. L. Rev.* 1425 (2005).

3. Undoubtedly the structure of the myth precedes its recording in the Old Testament.

4. Of course, a criminal can become an existential threat to the sovereign, at which point he would cross into the category of enemy. We see a metaphorical suggestion of this movement when the government declares war on drugs or organized crime. In each case, there is a sense that the state itself is in danger of being overwhelmed by the criminal activity.

5. See chapter 4 on the combatant's license to kill.

6. See chapter 2.

INDEX

Text design by Jillian Downey
Typesetting by Delmastype, Ann Arbor, Michigan
Text font: ITC New Baskerville
Display font: Trade Gothic Condensed No. 18

"British printer John Baskerville of Birmingham created the types that
bear his name in about 1752. George Jones designed this version of
Baskerville for Linotype-Hell in 1930, and the International Typeface
Corporation licensed it in 1982."

—courtesy adobe.com

The first cuts of Trade Gothic were designed by Jackson Burke in 1948,
and he continued to work on further weights and styles until 1960.

—courtesy myfonts.com